The Recognitions of Clement

Written by: Clement of Alexandria

Edited & Revised by: Douglas F Hatten

© 2007 Douglas F. Hatten

ISBN: 978-0-6151-8002-1

Introduction

The "Recognitions of Clement" is a captivating text dating back to the early Christian church. It has been referenced in the writings of early church fathers like Origen and Eusebius. The narrative is addressed to James the Just, the Bishop of Jerusalem, and is recorded by one Clement, a Greek, who chronicles a series of discourses by the apostle Peter, which he is witness to while accompanying Peter in his travels.

Clement begins his account by detailing his own religious search before hearing of Christ, and his anxieties concerning the welfare of his soul. While in Rome, Clement hears the preaching of Barnabas who testifies of the miracles and teachings of Jesus. Clement, being moved by the words of Barnabas, defends him from a mob and ends up following after him to Palestine where he meets up with Peter. A large portion of the text is devoted to an intriguing disputation between Peter and Simon the Sorcerer before an audience of onlookers. Peter invites Clement to accompany him in his travels from city to city, creating an opportunity for Clement to be instructed more perfectly concerning the faith.

Though the Clementine literature was in use at a much earlier date, it was reintroduced to the world around 360 AD, being revised and abridged in *Homilies*, and again in *Recognitions*, and translated into Latin. At the time they were reintroduced, Clement's writings served as a useful weapon against the resurrection of polytheism, mythology, sorcery, and idolatry.

The authorship, date of origin, and doctrinal character of this writing have been the subject of debate since the 19th Century, but the importance attached to it by theologians has compelled men of divers belief to examine the subject. After all their investigations, differing opinions continue to prevail regarding these books.

I personally became aware of the Recognitions of Clement nearly a decade ago while browsing the Internet. It has since had a very profound effect upon me. For years I sought to discover where I might obtain a published copy of this work for my own library, but could not find one available anywhere. Worse, there were very few places on the Internet where an electronic copy of it could be found, and those copies were often fraught with numerous errors due to inaccuracies in the scanning software. I feared that the text was in danger of being lost to the general public, should those websites cease to exist. With the advent of inexpensive self-publishing sites, such as Lulu.com, I have, with great delight, taken it upon myself to publish this work, not only for my own personal use, but in hopes that it may be a blessing to others.

I am not a scholar. I hold no doctorate, and I am not an expert in the Clementine literature, or its history. What I am is someone who has greatly benefited from this work and developed a very deep affection for it. With that said, I would like to write just a few words regarding the legal status and rights of this document, and explain the changes I have made to the text.

The original text is public domain, and it remains that way with the printing of this book. The last known published copy of this text in the English language, as best as I have been able to determine, was in the mid 19th Century in a book by Philip Schaff that, along with the Clementine literature, included works by other early Church Fathers. It is from this publication that I derived the original text.

The changes I have made are relatively minor. The English translation of Clement's work made use of some words that are rarely used in our modern vocabulary anymore. Some of those words would send even well educated persons scrambling to locate their dictionary. In these cases, and by no other method than to simply do what seemed right to me, I have, whenever a suitable and more common word could be found to replace it, substituted the more obscure terminology with the more common one. Wherever I have done this, I have placed a footnote that can be found at the bottom of the page for quick reference, informing you as to what the original word was.

In other cases, where no one perfectly suitable word could be found to replace it, I have placed instead a footnote at the bottom of the page denoting the word's definition for your convenience. In cases where I have either replaced a particular word, or noted its definition, I did not place any additional notes on any reoccurrence of that same word in the text, but simply made the same identical word replacement, or I have made the assumption that you now understand the definition of the word from its earlier notation. As I say, this method was not a scientific or scholarly one. But in all cases, I put forth considerable effort to remain true to the original intent of the text.

I have also footnoted encyclopedic information for some of the nations, peoples, or terminology used in the text, wherever I felt it would be beneficial. I did not provide this service where I either felt the terms or names were common enough, or in cases where I could find no reference for the name or place, in which case I leave it to you to investigate the mystery.

Any suggestions, corrections, or comments are welcome. You can contact me at: hopeofzion@hotmail.com

Sincerely,

Douglas F Hatten

"There is scarcely a single writing which is of so great importance for the history of Christianity in its first stage, and which has already given such brilliant disclosures at the hands of the most renowned critics in regard to the earliest history of the Christian Church, as the writings ascribed to the Roman Clement, the Recognitions and Homilies."

Excerpt from "Die Clementinischen Rekognitionen und Homilien, nach ihrem Ursprung und Inhalt dargestellt" by von Dr. Adolf Hilgenfeld, Jena, page 1, published in 1848.

Rufinus, (Presbyter of Aquileia); his preface to Clement's Book of Recognitions, to Bishop Gaudentius.

To thee, indeed, O Gaudentius, thou choice glory of our doctors, belongs such vigor of mind, yea, such grace of the Spirit, that whatever you say even in the course of your daily preaching, whatever you deliver in the church, ought to be preserved in books, and handed down to posterity for their instruction. But we, whom slenderness of wit renders less ready, and now old age renders slow and inactive, though after many delays, yet at length present to you the work which once the virgin Sylvia of venerable memory enjoined upon us, that we should render Clement into our language, and you afterwards by hereditary right demanded of us; and thus we contribute to the use and profit of our people, no small spoil, as I think, taken from the libraries of the Greeks, so that we may feed with foreign nourishment those whom we cannot with our own. For foreign things usually seem both more pleasant, and sometimes also more profitable. In short, almost everything is foreign that brings healing to our bodies, that opposes diseases, and neutralizes poisons. For Judaea sends us Lacryma balsami, Crete Coma dictamni, Arabia her flower of spices, India reaps her crop of spikenard; which, although they reach us in a somewhat more broken condition than when they leave their native fields, yet retain entire the sweetness of their odor and their healing virtue. Receive therefore, my soul, Clement returning to you; receive him now in a Roman dress. And wonder not if haply the florid countenance of eloquence appear less in him than usual. It matters not, provided the sense tastes the same. Therefore we transport foreign merchandise into our country with much labor. And I know not with how grateful countenances my countrymen welcome me, bringing to them the rich spoils of Greece, and unlocking hidden treasures of wisdom with the key of our language. But may God grant your prayers, that no unlucky eye nor any livid aspect may meet us, lest, by an extreme kind of prodigy, while those from whom he is taken do not envy, yet those upon whom he is bestowed should repine. Truly it is right to point out the plan of our translation to you, who have read these works also in Greek, lest haply in some parts you may think the order of translation not kept. I suppose you are aware that there are two editions in Greek of this work of Clement,--the 'Anagnwseis, that is, Recognitions; and that there are two collections of books, differing in some points, but in many containing the same narrative. In short, the last part of this work, in which is the relation concerning the transformation of Simon, is contained in one of the collections, but is not at all in the other. There are also in both collections some dissertations concerning the Unbegotten God and the Begotten, and on some other subjects, which, to say nothing more, are beyond our comprehension. These, therefore, as being beyond our powers, I have chosen to reserve for others, rather than to produce in an imperfect state. But in the rest, we have given our endeavor, so far as we could, not to vary either from the sentiments or even from the language and modes of expression; and this, although it renders the style of the narrative less ornate, yet it makes it more faithful. The epistle in which the same Clement, writing to James the Lord's brother, informs him of the death of Peter, and that he had left him his successor in his chair and teaching, and in which also the whole subject of church order is treated, I have not prefixed to this work, both because it is of later date, and because I have already translated and published it. But I do not think it out of place to explain here what in that letter will perhaps seem to some to be inconsistent. For some ask, Since Linus and Cletus were bishops in the city of Rome before this Clement, how could Clement himself, writing to James, say that the chair of teaching was handed over to him by Peter? Now of this we have heard this explanation, that Linus and Cletus were indeed bishops in the city of Rome before Clement, but during the lifetime of Peter: that is, that they undertook the care of the episcopate, and that he fulfilled the office of apostleship; as is found also to have been the case at Caesarea, where, when he himself was present, he yet had Zacchaeus, ordained by himself, as bishop. And in this way both statements will appear to be true, both that these bishops are reckoned before Clement, and yet that Clement received the teacher's seat on the death of Peter. But now let us see how Clement, writing to James the Lord's brother, begins his narrative.

Book I.

Chapter I.-Clement's Early History; Doubts.

I Clement, who was born in the city of Rome, was from my earliest age a lover of chastity; while the bent of my mind held me bound as with chains of anxiety and sorrow. For a thought that was in me-whence originating, I cannot tell-constantly led me to think of my condition of mortality, and to discuss such questions as these: Whether there be for me any life after death, or whether I am to be wholly annihilated: whether I did not exist before I was born, and whether there shall be no remembrance of this life after death, and so the boundlessness of time shall consign all things to oblivion and silence; so that not only we shall cease to be, but there shall be no remembrance that we have ever been. This also I revolved in my mind: when the world was made, or what was before it was made, or whether it has existed from eternity. For it seemed certain, that if it had been made, it must be doomed to dissolution; and if it be dissolved, what is to be afterwards?-unless, perhaps, all things shall be buried in oblivion and silence, or something shall be, which the mind of man cannot now conceive.

Chapter II.-His Distress.

While I was continually revolving in my mind these and such like questions, suggested I know not how, I was pining away wonderfully through excess of grief; and, what was worse, if at any time I thought to cast aside such cares, as being of little use, the waves of anxiety rose all the higher upon me. For I had in me that most excellent companion, who would not suffer me to rest-the desire of immortality: for, as the subsequent issue showed, and the grace of Almighty God directed, this bent of mind led me to the quest of truth, and the acknowledgment of the true light; and hence it came to pass, that ere long I pitied those whom formerly in my ignorance I believed to be happy.

Chapter III.-His Dissatisfaction with the Schools of the Philosophers.

Having therefore such a bent of mind from my earliest years, the desire of learning something led me to frequent the schools of the philosophers. There I saw that naught else was done, save that doctrines were asserted and contradicted[1] without end, contests were waged, and the arts of syllogisms[2] and the subtleties of conclusions were discussed. If at any time the doctrine of the immortality of the soul prevailed, I was thankful; if at any time it was challenged[3], I went away sorrowful. Still, neither doctrine had the power of truth over my heart. This only I understood, that opinions and definitions of things were accounted true or false, not in accordance with their nature and the truth of the arguments, but in proportion to the talents of those who supported them. And I was all the more tortured in the bottom of my heart, because I was neither able to lay hold of any of those things which were spoken as firmly established, nor was I able to lay aside the desire of inquiry; but the more I endeavored to neglect and despise them, so much the more eagerly, as I have said, did a desire of this sort, creeping in upon me secretly as with a kind of pleasure, take possession of my heart and mind.

Chapter IV.-His Increasing Disquiet.

Being therefore straitened in the discovery of things, I said to myself, Why do we labor in vain, since the end of things is manifest? For if after death I shall be no more, my present torture is useless; but if there is to be for me a life after death, let us keep for that life the excitements that

---

[1] Original word used in the text was **controverted.**
[2] A form of deductive reasoning consisting of a major premise, a minor premise, and a conclusion. *Reference: The American Heritage® Dictionary of the English Language, Fourth Edition.*
[3] Original word used in the text was: **impugned**.

belong to it, lest perhaps some sadder things befall me than those which I now suffer, unless I shall have lived piously and soberly; and, according to the opinions of some of the philosophers, I be consigned to the stream of dark-rolling Phlegethon, or to Tartarus, like Sisyphus and Tityus, and to eternal punishment in the infernal regions, like Ixion and Tantalus. And again I would answer to myself: But these things are fables; or if it be so, since the matter is in doubt, it is better to live piously. But again I would ponder with myself, How should I restrain myself from the lust of sin, while uncertain as to the reward of righteousness?-and all the more when I have no certainty what righteousness is, or what is pleasing to God; and when I cannot ascertain whether the soul be immortal, and be such that it has anything to hope for; nor do I know what the future is certainly to be. Yet still I cannot rest from thoughts of this sort.

Chapter V.-His Design to Test the Immortality of the Soul.

What, then, shall I do? This shall I do. I shall proceed to Egypt, and there I shall cultivate the friendship of the hierophants or prophets, who preside at the shrines. Then I shall win over a magician by money, and entreat him, by what they call the necromantic art, to bring me a soul from the infernal regions, as if I were desirous of consulting it about some business. But this shall be my consultation, whether the soul be immortal. Now, the proof that the soul is immortal will be put past doubt, not from what it says, or from what I hear, but from what I see: for seeing it with my eyes, I shall ever after hold the surest conviction of its immortality; and no fallacy of words or uncertainty of hearing shall ever be able to disturb the persuasion produced by sight. However, I related this project to a certain philosopher with whom I was intimate, who counseled me not to venture upon it; "for," said he, "if the soul should not obey the call of the magician, you henceforth will live more hopelessly, as thinking that there is nothing after death, and also as having tried things unlawful. If, however, you seem to see anything, what religion or what piety can arise to you from things unlawful and implores? For they say that transactions of this sort are hateful to the Divinity, and that God sets Himself in opposition to those who trouble souls after their release from the body." When I heard this, I was indeed staggered in my purpose; yet I could not in any way either lay aside my longing, or cast off the distressing thought.

Chapter VI.-Hears of Christ.

Not to make a long story of it, whilst I was tossed upon these billows of my thought, a certain report, which took its rise in the regions of the East in the reign of Tiberius Caesar, gradually reached us; and gaining strength as it passed through every place, like some good message sent from God, it was filling the whole world, and suffered not the divine will to be concealed in silence. For it was spread over all places, announcing that there was a certain person in Judea, who, beginning in the springtime, was preaching the kingdom of God to the Jews, and saying that those should receive it who should observe the ordinances of His commandments and His doctrine. And that His speech might be believed to be worthy of credit, and full of the Divinity, He was said to perform many mighty works, and wonderful signs and prodigies by His mere word; so that, as one having power from God, He made the deaf to hear, and the blind to see, and the lame to stand erect, and expelled every infirmity and all demons from men; yea, that He even raised dead persons who were brought to Him; that He cured lepers also, looking at them from a distance; and that there was absolutely nothing which seemed impossible to Him. These and such like things were confirmed in process of time, not now by frequent rumors, but by the plain statements of persons coming from those quarters; and day by day the truth of the matter was further disclosed.

Chapter VII.-Arrival of Barnabas at Rome.

At length meetings began to be held in various places in the city, and this subject to be discussed in conversation, and to be a matter of wonder who this might be who had appeared, and what message He had brought from God to men; until, about the same year, a certain man, standing in a most crowded place in the city, made proclamation to the people, saying: "Hear me, O ye citizens of Rome. The Son of God is now in the regions of Judea, promising eternal life to everyone who will hear Him, but upon condition that he shall regulate his actions according to the will of Him by whom He hath been sent, even of God the Father. Wherefore turn ye from evil things to good, from things temporal to things eternal. Acknowledge that there is one God, ruler of heaven and earth, in whose righteous sight ye unrighteous inhabit His world. But if ye be converted, and act according to His will, then, coming to the world to come, and being made immortal, ye shall enjoy His unspeakable blessings and rewards." Now, the man who spoke these things to the people was from the regions of the East, by nation a Hebrew, by name Barnabas, who said that he himself was one of His disciples, and that he was sent for this end, that he should declare these things to those who would hear them. When I heard these things, I began, with the rest of the multitude, to follow him, and to hear what he had to say. Truly I perceived that there was nothing of dialectic[1] hoax[2] in the man, but that he expounded with simplicity, and without any craft of speech, such things as he had heard from the Son of God, or had seen. For he did not confirm his assertions by the force of arguments, but produced, from the people who stood round about him, many witnesses of the sayings and marvels which he related.

---

[1] A **dialectic** is a form of reasoning or argumentation that focuses on resolving contradictions. *Dictionary.com Unabridged (v 1.1)*.

[2] The original word used in the text was **Artifice.** *Dictionary.com Unabridged (v 1.1)*.

Chapter VIII.-His Preaching.

Now, inasmuch as the people began to assent willingly to the things which were sincerely spoken, and to embrace his simple discourse, those who thought themselves learned or philosophic began to laugh at the man, and to flout[1] him, and to throw out for him the grappling-hooks of syllogisms, like strong arms. But he, unterrified, regarding their subtleties as mere ravings, did not even judge them worthy of an answer, but boldly pursued the subject which he had set before him. At length, some one having proposed this question to him as he was speaking, Why a gnat has been so formed, that though it is a small creature, and has six feet, yet it has got wings in addition; whereas an elephant, though it is an immense animal, and has no wings, yet has only four feet; he, paying no attention to the question, went on with his discourse, which had been interrupted by the unseasonable challenge, only adding this admonition at every interruption: "We have it in charge to declare to you the words and the wondrous works of Him who hath sent us, and to confirm the truth of what we speak, not by artfully devised arguments, but by witnesses produced from amongst yourselves. For I recognize many standing in the midst of you whom I remember to have heard along with us the things which we have heard, and to have seen what we have seen. But be it in your option to receive or to spurn the tidings which we bring to you. For we cannot keep back what we know to be for your advantage, because, if we be silent, woe is to us; but to you, if you receive not what we speak, destruction. I could indeed very easily answer your foolish challenges, if you asked for the sake of learning truth,-I mean as to the difference of a gnat and an elephant; but now it were absurd to speak to you of these creatures, when the very Creator and Framer of all things is unknown by you."

---

[1] To treat with disdain, scorn, or contempt. *Source: Dictionary.com Unabridged (v 1.1).*

Chapter IX.-Clement's Interposition on Behalf of Barnabas.

When he had thus spoken, all, as with one consent, with rude voice raised a shout of derision, to put him to shame, and to silence him, crying out that he was a barbarian and a madman. When I saw matters going on in this way, being filled, I know not whence, with a certain zeal, and inflamed with religious enthusiasm, I could not keep silence, but cried out with all boldness, "Most righteously does Almighty God hide His will from you, whom He foresaw to be unworthy of the knowledge of Himself, as is manifest to those who are really wise, from what you are now doing. For when you see that preachers of the will of God have come amongst you, because their speech makes no show of knowledge of the grammatical art, but in simple and unpolished language they set before you the divine commands, so that all who hear may be able to follow and to understand the things that are spoken, you deride the ministers and messengers of your salvation, not knowing that it is the condemnation of you who think yourselves skilful and eloquent, that rustic and barbarous men have the knowledge of the truth; whereas, when it has come to you, it is not even received as a guest, while, if your intemperance and lust did not oppose, it ought to have been a citizen and a native. Thus you are convicted of not being friends of truth and philosophers, but followers of boasting and vain speakers. Ye think that truth dwells not in simple, but in ingenious and subtle words, and produce countless thousands of words which are not to be rated at the worth of one word. What, then, do ye think will become of you, all ye crowd of Greeks, if there is to be, as he says, a judgment of God? But now give over laughing at this man to your own destruction, and let any one of you who pleases answer me; for, indeed, by your barking you annoy the ears even of those who desire to be saved, and by your clamor you turn aside to the fall of infidelity the minds that are prepared for faith. What pardon can there be for you who deride and do violence to the messenger of the truth when he offers to you the knowledge of God? whereas, even if he brought you nothing of truth, yet, even for the kindness of his intentions towards you, you ought to receive with gratitude and welcome."

Chapter X.-Intercourse with Barnabas.

While I was urging these and similar arguments, a great excitement was stirred up amongst the bystanders, some being moved with pity as towards a stranger, and approving my speech as in accordance with that feeling; others, petulant and stolid[1], rousing the anger of their undisciplined minds as much against me as against Barnabas. But as the day was declining to evening, I laid hold of Barnabas by the right hand, and led him away, although reluctantly, to my house; and there I made him remain, lest perchance any one of the rude rabble should lay hands upon him. While we were thus placed in contact for a few days, I gladly heard him discoursing the word of truth; yet he hastened his departure, saying that he must by all means celebrate at Judea a festal day of his religion which was approaching, and that there he should remain in future with his countrymen and his brethren, evidently indicating that he was horrified at the wrong that had been done to him.

Chapter XI.-Departure of Barnabas.

At length I said to him, "Only expound to me the doctrine of that man who you say has appeared, and I will arrange your sayings in my language, and will preach the kingdom and righteousness of Almighty God; and after that, if you wish it, I shall even sail along with you, for I am extremely desirous to see Judea, and perhaps I shall remain with you always." To this he answered, "If indeed you wish to see our country, and to learn those things which you desire, set sail with me even now; or, if there be anything that detains you now, I shall leave with you directions to my dwelling, so that when you please to come you may easily find me;

---

[1] Not easily stirred or moved mentally; unemotional; impassive. *Dictionary.com Unabridged (v 1.1)*.

for tomorrow I shall set out on my journey." When I saw him determined, I went down with him to the harbor, and carefully took from him the directions which he gave me to find his dwelling. I told him that, but for the necessity of getting some money which was due to me, I should not at all delay, but that I should speedily follow him. Having told him this, I commended him to the kindness of those who had charge of the ship, and returned sad; for I was possessed of the memory of the intercourse which I had had with an excellent guest and a choice friend.

Chapter XII.-Clement's Arrival at Caesarea, and Introduction to Peter.

Having then stopped for a few days, and having in some measure finished the business of collecting what was owed to me (for I neglected many things through my desire of hastening, that I might not be hindered from my purpose), I set sail direct for Judea, and after fifteen days landed at Caesarea Stratonis, which is the largest city in Palestine. When I had landed, and was seeking for an inn, I learned from the conversation of the people, that one Peter, a most approved disciple of Him who appeared in Judea, and showed many signs and miracles divinely performed among men, was going to hold a discussion of words and questions the next day with one Simon, a Samaritan. Having heard this, I asked to be shown his lodging; and having found it, and standing before the door, I informed the doorkeeper who I was, and whence I came; and, behold, Barnabas coming out, as soon as he saw me rushed into my arms, weeping for joy, and, seizing me by the hand, led me in to Peter. Having pointed him out to me at a distance. "This," said he, "is Peter, of whom I spoke, to you as the greatest in the wisdom of God, and to whom also I have spoken constantly of you. Enter, therefore, as one well known to him. For he is well acquainted with all the good that is in thee, and has carefully made himself aware of your religious purpose, whence also he is greatly desirous to see you. Therefore I present you to him to-day as a great gift." At the same time, presenting me, he said, "This, O Peter, is Clement."

Chapter XIII.-His Cordial Reception by Peter.

But Peter most kindly, when he heard my name, immediately ran to me and kissed me. Then, having made me sit down, he said, "Thou didst well to receive as thy guest Barnabas, preacher of the truth, nothing fearing the rage of the insane people. Thou shalt be blessed. For as you have deemed an ambassador of the truth worthy of all honor, so the truth herself shall receive thee a wanderer and a stranger, and shall enroll thee a citizen of her own city; and then there shall be great joy to thee, because, imparting a small favor, thou shalt be written heir of eternal blessings. Now, therefore, do not trouble yourself to explain your mind to me; for Barnabas has with faithful speech informed me of all things about you and your dispositions, almost daily and without ceasing, recalling the memory of your good qualities And to point out to you shortly, as to a friend already of one mind with us, what is your best course; if there is nothing to hinder you, come along with us, and hear the word of the truth, which we are going to speak in every place until we come even to the city of Rome; and now, if you wish anything, speak."

Chapter XIV.-His Account of Himself.

Having detailed to him what purpose I had conceived from the beginning, and how I had been distracted with vain inquiries, and all those things which at first I intimated to thee, my lord James, so that I need not repeat the same things now, I willingly agreed to travel with him; "for that," said I, "is just what I was most eagerly desirous of. But first I should wish the scheme of truth to be expounded by thee, that I may know whether the soul is mortal or immortal; and if immortal, whether it shall be brought into judgment for those things which it does here. Further, I desire to know what that righteousness is, which is pleasing to God; then, further, whether the world was created, and why it was created, and whether it is to be dissolved, and whether it is to be renovated and made better, or whether after this there shall be no world at all; and, not to mention everything, I should wish to be told what is the case with respect to these and such like things." To this Peter answered, "I shall briefly impart to you the knowledge of these things, O Clement: therefore listen."

Chapter XV.-Peter's First Instruction: Causes of Ignorance.

"The will and counsel of God has for many reasons been concealed from men; first, indeed, through bad instruction, wicked associations, evil habits, unprofitable conversation, and un-righteous presumptions. On account of all these, I say, first error, then contempt, then infidelity and malice, covetousness also, and vain boasting, and other such like evils, have filled the whole house of this world, like some enormous smoke, and preventing those who dwell in it from seeing its Founder aright, and from perceiving what things are pleasing to Him. What, then, is fitting for those who are within, excepting with a cry brought forth from their inmost hearts to invoke His aid, who alone is not shut up in the smoke-filled house, that He would approach and open the door of the house, so that the smoke may be dissipated which is within, and the light of the sun which shines without may be admitted."

Chapter XVI.-Instruction Continued: the True Prophet.

"He, therefore, whose aid is needed for the house filled with the darkness of ignorance and the smoke of vices, is He, we say, who is called the true Prophet, who alone can enlighten the souls of men, so that with their eyes they may plainly see the way of safety. For otherwise it is impossible to get knowledge of divine and eternal things, unless one learns of that true Prophet; because, as you yourself stated a little ago, the belief of things, and the opinions of causes, are estimated in proportion to the talents of their advocates: hence, also, one and the same cause is now thought just, now unjust; and what now seemed true, anon becomes false on the assertion of another. For this reason, the credit of religion and piety demanded the presence of the true Prophet, that He Himself might tell us respecting each particular, how the truth stands, and might teach us how we are to believe concerning each. And therefore, before all else, the credentials of the prophet himself must be examined with all care; and when you have once ascertained that he is a prophet, it behooves you thenceforth to believe him in everything, and not further to discuss the particulars which he teaches, but to hold the things which he speaks as certain and sacred; which things, although they seem to be received by faith, yet are believed on the ground of the probation previously instituted. For when once at the outset the truth of the prophet is established on examination, the rest is to be heard and held on the ground of the faith by which it is already established that he is a teacher of truth. And as it is certain that all things which pertain to divine knowledge ought to be held according to the rule of truth, so it is beyond doubt that from none but Himself alone can it be known what is true."

Chapter XVII.-Peter Requests Him to Be His Attendant.

Having thus spoken, he set forth to me so openly and so clearly who that Prophet was, and how He might be found, that I seethed[1] to have before my eyes, and to handle with my hand, the proofs which he produced concerning the prophetic truth; and I was struck with intense astonishment, how no one sees, though placed before his eyes, those things which all are seeking for. Whence, by his command, reducing into order what he had spoken to me, I compiled a book concerning the true Prophet, and sent it to you from Caesarea by his command. For he said that he had received a command from you to send you every year an account of his sayings and doings. Meantime, at the beginning of his discourse which he delivered to me the first day, when he had instructed me very fully concerning the true Prophet, and very many things besides, he added also this: "See,"

---

[1] To surge or foam as if boiling. To be in a state of agitation or excitement. *Dictionary.com Unabridged (v 1.1)*.

said he, "for the future, and be present at the discussions which whenever any necessity arises, I shall hold with those who contradict; against whom, when I dispute, even if I shall seem to be worsted, I shall not be afraid of your being led to doubt of those things which I have stated to you; because, even if I shall seem to be beaten, yet those things shall not therefore seem to be uncertain which the true Prophet has delivered to us. Yet I hope that we shall not be overcome in disputations either, if only our hearers are reasonable, and friends of truth, who can discern the force and bearing of words, and recognize what discourse comes from the sophistical art, not containing truth, but an image of truth; and what that is, which, uttered simply and without craft, depends for all its power not on show and ornament, but on truth and reason."

Chapter XVIII.-His Profiting by Peter's Instruction.

To this I answered: "I give thanks to God Almighty, because I have been instructed as I wished and desired. At all events, you may depend upon me so far, that I can never come to doubt of those things which I have learned of you; so that even if you yourself should at any time wish to transfer my faith from the true Prophet, you should not be able, because I have drunk in with all my heart what you have spoken. And that you may not think that I am promising you a great thing when I say that I cannot be moved away from this faith, it is with me a certainty, that whoever has received this account of the true Prophet, can never afterwards so much as doubt of its truth. And therefore I am confident with respect to this heaven-taught doctrine, in which all the art of malice is overborne. For in opposition to *this* prophecy neither any art can stand, nor the subtleties of sophisms[1] and syllogism; but every one who hears of the true Prophet must of necessity long immediately for the truth itself, nor will he afterwards, under pretext of seeking the truth, endure diverse errors. Wherefore, O my lord Peter, be not further anxious about

---

[1] A plausible sounding but deceptive argument based on a fallacy. *Dictionary.com Unabridged (v 1.1)*.

me, as if I were one who does not know what he has received, and how great a gift has been conferred on him. Be assured that you have conferred a favor on one who knows and understands its value: nor can I be easily deceived on that account, because I seem to have gotten quickly what I long desired; for it may be that one who desires gets quickly, while another does not even slowly attain the things which he desires."

Chapter XIX.-Peter's Satisfaction.

Then Peter, when he heard me speak thus, said: "I give thanks to my God, both for your salvation and for my own peace; for I am greatly delighted to see that you have understood what is the greatness of the prophetic virtue, and because, as you say, not even I myself, if I should wish it (which God forbid!), should be able to turn you away to another faith. Now henceforth begin to be with us, and to-morrow be present at our discussions, for I am to have a contest with Simon the magician." When he had thus spoken, he retired to take food along with his friends; but he ordered me to eat by myself; and after the meal, when he had sung praise to God and given thanks, he rendered to me an account of this proceeding, and added, "May the Lord grant to thee to be made like to us in all things, that, receiving baptism, thou mayest be able to meet with us at the same table." Having thus spoken, he ordered me to go to rest, for by this time both fatigue and the time of the day called to sleep.

Chapter XX.-Postponement of Discussion with Simon Magus.

Early next morning Zacchaeus came in to us, and after salutation, said to Peter: "Simon puts off the discussion till the eleventh day of the present month, which is seven days hence, for he says that then he will have more leisure for the contest. But to me it seems that his putting off is also advantageous to us, so that more may come together, who may be either hearers or judges of our disputation.

However, if it seem proper to you, let us occupy the interval in discussing among ourselves the things which, we suppose, may come into the controversy; so that each of us, knowing what things are to be proposed, and what answers are to be given, may consider with himself if they are all right, or if an adversary shall be able to find anything to object, or to set aside the things which we bring against him. But if the things which are to be spoken by us are manifestly impregnable on every side, we shall have confidence in entering upon the examination. And indeed, this is my opinion, that first of all it ought to be inquired what is the origin of all things, or what is the immediate thing which may be called the cause of all things which are: then, with respect to all things that exist, whether they have been made, and by whom, through whom, and for whom; whether they have received their subsistence from one, or from two, or from many; and whether they have been taken and fashioned from none *previously* subsisting, or from some: then, whether there is any virtue in the highest things, or in the lower; whether there is anything which is better than all, or anything that is inferior to all; whether there are any motions, or none; whether those things which are seen were always, and shall be always; whether they have come into existence without a creator, and shall pass away without a destroyer. If, I say, the discussion begin with these things, I think that the things which shall be inquired into, being discussed with diligent examination, will be easily ascertained. And when these are ascertained, the knowledge of those that follow will be easily found. I have stated my opinion; be pleased to intimate what you think of the matter. "

Chapter XXI.-Advantage of the Delay.

To this Peter answered: "Tell Simon in the meantime to do as he pleases, and to rest assured that, Divine Providence granting, he shall always find us ready." Then Zacchaeus went out to intimate to Simon what he had been told. But Peter, looking at us, and perceiving that I was saddened by the putting off of the contest, said: "He who believes that the world is administered by the providence of the Most High God. ought not, O Clement, my friend, to take it amiss, in whatever way particular things happen, being assured that the righteousness of God guides to a favorable and fitting issue even those things which seem superfluous or contrary in any business, and especially towards those who worship Him more intimately; and therefore he who is assured of these things, as I have said, if anything occur contrary to his expectation, he knows how to drive away grief from his mind on that account, holding it unquestionable in his better judgment, that, by the government of the good God, even what seems contrary may be turned to good. Wherefore, O Clement, even now let not this delay of the magician Simon sadden you: for I believe that it has been done by the providence of God, for your advantage; that I may be able, in this interval of seven days, to expound to you the method of our faith without any distraction, and the order continuously, according to the tradition of the true Prophet, who alone knows the past as it was, the present as it is, and the future as it shall be: which things were indeed plainly spoken *by Him*, but are not plainly written; so much so, that when they are read, they cannot be understood without an expounder, on account of the sin which has grown up with men, as I said before. Therefore I shall explain all things to you, that in those things which are written you may clearly perceive what is the mind of the Lawgiver."

Chapter XXII.-Repetition of Instructions.

When he had said this, he began to expound to me point by point of those chapters of the law which seemed to be in question, from the beginning of the creation even to that point of time at which I came to him at Caesarea, telling me that the delay of Simon had contributed to my learning all things in order. "At other times." said he, "we shall discourse more fully on individual points of which we have now spoken shortly, according as the occasion of our conversation shall bring them before us; so that, according to my promise, you may gain a full and perfect knowledge of all. Since, then, by this delay we have to-day on our hands, I wish to repeat to you again what has been spoken, that it may be the better recalled to your memory." Then he began in this way to refresh my recollection of what he had said: "Do you remember, O friend Clement, the account I gave you of the eternal age, that knows no end? "Then said I, "Never, O Peter, shall I retain anything, if I can lose or forget that."

Chapter XXIII.-Repetition Continued.

Then Peter, having heard my answer with pleasure, said: "I congratulate you because you have answered thus, not because you speak of these things easily, but because you profess that you remember them; for the most sublime truths are best honored by means of silence. Yet, for the credit of those things which you remember concerning things not to be spoken, tell me what you retain of those things which we spoke of in the second place, which can easily be spoken out, that, perceiving your tenacity of memory, I may the more readily point out to you, and freely open, the things of which I wish to speak." Then I, when I perceived that he rejoiced in the good memory of his hearers, said: "Not only am I mindful of your definition, but also of that preface which was prefixed to the definition; and of almost all things that you have expounded, I retain the sense complete, though not all the words; because the things that you have spoken have been made, as it were, native to my soul, and inborn. For you have held out a most sweet cup to me in my excessive thirst. And that you may not suppose that I am occupying you with words, being unmindful of things, I shall now call to mind the things which were spoken, in which the order of your discussion greatly helps me; for the way in which the things that you said followed by consequence upon one another, and were arranged in a balanced manner, makes them easily recalled to memory by the lines of their order. For the order of sayings is useful for remembering them: for when you begin to follow them point by point in succession, when anything is wanting, immediately the sense seeks for it; and when it has found it, retains it, or at all events, if it cannot discover it, there will be no reluctance to ask it of the master. But not to delay in granting what you demand of me, I shall shortly rehearse what you delivered to me concerning the definition of truth."

Chapter XXIV.-Repetition Continued.

"There always was, there is now, and there ever shall be, that by which the first Will begotten from eternity consists; and from the first Will *proceeds* a second Will. After these came the world; and from the world came time: from this, the multitude of men; from the multitude the election of the beloved, from whose oneness of mind the peaceful kingdom of God is constructed. But the rest, which ought to follow these, you promised to tell me at another time. After this, when you had explained about the creation of the world, you intimated the decree of God, "which He, of His own good pleasure, announced in the presence of all the first angels," and which He ordained as an eternal law to all; and how He established two kingdoms,-I mean that of the present time and that of the future,-and appointed times to each, and decreed that a day of judgment should be expected, which He determined, in which a severance is to be made of things and of souls: so that the wicked indeed shall be consigned to eternal fire for their sins; but those who have lived according to the will of God the Creator, having received a blessing for their good works, effulgent[1] with brightest light, introduced into an eternal abode, and abiding in incorruption, shall receive eternal gifts of ineffable[2] blessings."

Chapter XXV.-Repetition Continued.

---

[1] Shining forth brilliantly; radiant.
[2] Incapable of being expressed or described in words, or not to be spoken because of its sacredness.

Source: *Dictionary.com Unabridged (v 1.1)*.

While I was going on thus, Peter, enraptured with joy, and anxious for me as if I had been his son, lest perhaps I should fail in recollection of the rest, and be put to shame on account of those who were present, said: "It is enough, O Clement; for you have stated these things more clearly than I myself explained them." Then said I, "Liberal learning has conferred upon me the power of orderly narration, and of stating those things clearly for which there is occasion. And if we use learning in asserting the errors of antiquity, we ruin ourselves by gracefulness and smoothness of speech; but if we apply learning and grace of speech to the assertion of the truth, I think that not a little advantage is thereby gained. Be that as it may, my lord Peter, you can but imagine with what thankfulness I am transported for all the rest of your instruction indeed, but especially for the statement of that doctrine which you gave: There is one God, whose work the world is, and who, because He is in all respects righteous, shall render to every one according to his deeds. And after that you added: For the assertion of this dogma countless thousands of words will be brought forward; but in those to whom is granted knowledge of the true Prophet, all this forest of words is cut down. And on this account, since you have delivered to me a discourse concerning the true Prophet, you have strengthened me with all confidence of your assertions." And then, having perceived that the sum of all religion and piety consists in this, I immediately replied: "You have proceeded most excellently, O Peter: wherefore, in future, expound unhesitatingly, as to one who already knows what are the foundations of faith and piety, the traditions of the true Prophet, who alone, as has been clearly proved, is to be believed. But that exposition which requires assertions and arguments, reserve for the unbelievers, to whom you have not yet judged it proper to commit the indubitable[1] faith of prophetic grace." When I had said this, I added: "You promised that you would give at the proper time two things: first this exposition, at once simple and entirely free from error; and then an exposition of each individual point as it

---

[1] Cannot be doubted; patently evident or certain; unquestionable. *Dictionary.com Unabridged (v 1.1)*.

may be evolved in the course of the various questions which shall be raised. And after this you expounded the sequence of things in order from the beginning of the world, even to the present time; and if you please, I can repeat the whole from memory."

Chapter XXVI.-Friendship of God; How Secured.

To this Peter answered: "I am exceedingly delighted, O Clement, that I commit my words to so safe a heart; for to be mindful of the things that are spoken is an indication of having in readiness the faith of works. But he from whom the wicked demon steals away the words of salvation, and snatches them away from his memory, cannot be saved, even though he wish it; for he loses the way by which life is reached. Wherefore let us the rather repeat what has been spoken, and confirm it in your heart, that is, in what manner or by whom the world was made, that we may proceed to the friendship of the Creator. But His friendship is secured by living well, and by obeying His will; which will is the law of all that live. We shall therefore unfold these things briefly to you, in order that they may be the more surely remembered.

Chapter XXVII.-Account of the Creation.

"In the beginning, when God had made the heaven and the earth, as one house, the shadow which was cast by the mundane bodies involved in darkness those things which were enclosed in it. But when the will of God had introduced light, that darkness which had been caused by the shadows of bodies was straightway dispelled: then at length light is appointed for the day, darkness for the night. And now the water which was within the world, in the middle space of that first heaven and earth, congealed as if with frost, and solid as crystal, is distended, and the middle spaces of the heaven and earth are separated as by a firmament of this sort; and that firmament the Creator called heaven, so called by the name of that previously made: and so He divided into two portions that fabric of the universe, although it was but one house. The reason of the division was this, that the upper portion might afford a dwelling-place to angels, and the lower to men. After this, the place of the sea and the chaos which had been made received that portion of the water which remained below, by order of the eternal Will; and these flowing down to the sunk and hollow places, the dry land appeared; and the gatherings of the waters were made seas. And after this the earth, which had appeared, produced various species of herbs and shrubs. It gave forth fountains also, and rivers, not only in the plains, but on the mountains. And so all things were prepared, that men who were to dwell in it might have it in their power to use all these things according to their will, that is, either for good or evil."

Chapter XXVIII.-Account of the Creation Continued.

"After this He adorns that visible heaven with stars. He places in it also the sun and the moon, that the day might enjoy the light of the one, the night that of the other; and that at the same time they might be for an indication of things past, present, and future. For they were made for signs of seasons and of days, which, although they are seen indeed by all, are understood only by the learned and intelligent. And when, after this, He had ordered living creatures to be produced from the earth and the waters, He made Paradise, which also He named a place of delights. But after all these things He made man, on whose account He had prepared all things, whose internal species is older, and for whose sake all things that are were made, given up to his service, and assigned to the uses of his habitation."

Chapter XXIX.-The Giants: the Flood.

"All things therefore being completed which are in heaven, and in earth, and in the waters, and the human race also having multiplied, in the eighth generation, righteous men, who had lived the life of angels, being allured by the beauty of women, fell into promiscuous and illicit connections with these; and thenceforth acting in all things without discretion, and disorderly, they changed the state of human affairs and the divinely prescribed order of life, so that either by persuasion or force they compelled all men to sin against God their Creator. In the ninth generation are born the giants, so called from of old, not dragon-footed, as the fables of the Greeks relate, but men of immense bodies, whose bones, of enormous size, are still shown in some places for confirmation. But against these the righteous providence of God brought a flood upon the world, that the earth might be purified from their pollution, and every place might be turned into a sea by the destruction of the wicked. Yet there was then found one righteous man, by the name of Noah, who, being delivered in an ark with his three sons and their wives, became the colonizer of the world after the subsiding of the waters, with those animals and seeds which he had shut up with him."

Chapter XXX.-Noah's Sons.

"In the twelfth generation, when God had blessed men, and they had begun to multiply, they received a commandment that they should not taste blood, for on account of this also the deluge had been sent. In the thirteenth generation, when the second of Noah's three sons had done an injury to his father, and had been cursed by him, he brought the condition of slavery upon his posterity. His elder brother meantime obtained the lot of a dwelling-place in the middle region of the world, in which is the country of Judea; the younger obtained the eastern quarter, and he the western. In the fourteenth generation one of the cursed progeny first erected an altar to demons. for the purpose of magical arts, and offered there bloody sacrifices. In the fifteenth generation, for the first time, men set up an idol and worshipped it. Until that time the Hebrew language, which had been given by God to men, bore sole sway. In the sixteenth generation the sons of men migrated from the east, and, coming to the lands that had been assigned to their fathers, each one marked the place of his own allotment by his own name. In the seventeenth generation

Nimrod I. reigned in Babylonia, and built a city, and thence migrated to the Persians, and taught them to worship fire."

Chapter XXXI.-World After the Flood.

"In the eighteenth generation walled cities were built, armies were organized and armed, judges and laws were sanctioned, temples were built, and the princes of nations were adored as gods. In the nineteenth generation the descendants of him who had been cursed after the flood, going beyond their proper bounds which they had obtained by lot in the western regions, drove into the eastern lands those who had obtained the middle portion of the world, and pursued them as far as Persia, while themselves violently took possession of the country from which they expelled them. In the twentieth generation a son for the first time died before his father, on account of an incestuous crime."

Chapter XXXII.-Abraham.

"In the twenty-first generation there was a certain wise man, of the race of those who were expelled, of the family of Noah's eldest son, by name Abraham, from whom our Hebrew nation is derived. When the whole world was again overspread with errors, and when for the hideousness of its crimes destruction was really for it, this time not by water, but fire, and when already the scourge was hanging over the whole earth, beginning with Sodom, this man, by reason of his friendship with God, who was well pleased with him, obtained from God that the whole world should not equally perish. From the first this same man, being an astrologer, was able, from the account and order of the stars, to recognize the Creator, while all others were in error, and understood that all things are regulated by His providence. Whence also an angel, standing by him in a vision, instructed him more fully concerning those things which he was beginning to perceive. He showed him also what belonged to his race and posterity, and promised him that those districts should be restored rather than given to them.

Chapter XXXIII.-Abraham: His Posterity.

"Therefore Abraham, when he was desirous to learn the causes of things, and was intently pondering upon what had been told him, the true Prophet appeared to him, who alone knows the hearts and purpose of men, and disclosed to him all things which he desired. He taught him the knowledge of the Divinity; intimated the origin of the world, and likewise its end; showed him the immortality of the soul, and the manner of life which was pleasing to God; declared also the resurrection of the dead, the future judgment, the reward of the good, the punishment of the evil,-all to be regulated by righteous judgment: and having given him all this information plainly and sufficiently, He departed again to the invisible abodes. But while Abraham was still in ignorance, as we said to you before, two sons were born to him, of whom the one was called Ismael, and the other Heliesdros. From the one are descended the barbarous nations, from the other the people of the Persians, some of whom have adopted the manner of living and the institutions of their neighbors, the Brachmans. Others settled in Arabia, of whose posterity some also have spread into Egypt. From them some of the Indians and of the Egyptians have learned to be circumcised, and to be of purer observance than others, although in process of time most of them have turned to impiety what was the proof and sign of purity."

Chapter XXXIV.-The Israelites in Egypt.

"Nevertheless, as he had got these two sons during the time while he still lived in ignorance of things, having received the knowledge of God, he asked of the Righteous One that he might merit to have offspring by Sarah, who was his lawful wife, though she was barren. She obtained a son whom he named Isaac, from whom came Jacob, and from him the twelve patriarchs, and from these twelve seventy-two. These, when famine befell came into Egypt with all their family; and in the course of four hundred years, being multiplied by the blessing and promise of God, they were afflicted by the Egyptians. And when they were afflicted the true Prophet appeared to Moses, and struck the Egyptians with ten plagues, when they refused to let the Hebrew people depart from them, and return to their native land; and he brought the people of God out of Egypt. But those of the Egyptians who survived the plagues, being infected with the animosity of their king, pursued after the Hebrews. And when they had overtaken them at the sea-shore, and thought to destroy and exterminate them all, Moses, pouring out prayer to God, divided the sea into two parts, so that the water was held on the right hand and on the left as if it had been frozen, and the people of God passed as over a dry road; but the Egyptians who were pursuing them, rashly entering, were drowned. For when the last of the Hebrews came out, the last of the Egyptians went down into the sea; and straightway the waters of the sea, which by his command were held bound as with frost, were loosed by his command who had bound them, and recovering their natural freedom, inflicted punishment on the wicked nation.

Chapter XXXV.-The Exodus.

"After this, Moses, by the command of God, whose providence is over all, led out the people of the Hebrews into the wilderness; and, leaving the shortest road which leads from Egypt to Judea, he led the people through long windings of the wilderness, that, by the discipline of forty years, the novelty of a changed manner of life might root out the evils which had clung to them by a long-continued familiarity with the customs of the Egyptians. Meantime they came to Mount Sinai, and thence the law was given to them with voices and sights from heaven, written in ten precepts, of which the first and greatest was that they should worship God Himself alone, and not make to themselves any appearance or form to worship. But when Moses had gone up to the mount, and was staying there forty days, the people, although they had seen Egypt struck with the ten plagues, and the sea parted and passed over by them on foot, manna also given to them from heaven for bread, and drink supplied to them out of the rock that followed them, which kind of food was turned into whatever taste any one desired; and although, being placed under the torrid region of heaven, they were shaded by a cloud in the day-time, that they might not be scorched by the heat, and by night were enlightened by a pillar of fire, lest the horror of darkness should be added to the wasteness of the wilderness;-those very people, I say, when Moses stayed in the mount, made and worshipped a golden calf's head, after the fashion of Apis, whom they had seen worshipped in Egypt; and after so many and so great marvels which they had seen, were unable to cleanse and wash out from themselves the defilements of old habit. On this account, leaving the short road which leads from Egypt to Judea, Moses conducted them by an immense circuit of the desert, if perhaps[1] he might be able, as we mentioned before, to shake off the evils of old habit by the change of a new education."

Chapter XXXVI.-Allowance of Sacrifice for a Time.

"When meantime Moses, that faithful and wise steward, perceived that the vice of sacrificing to idols had been deeply ingrained into the people from their association with the Egyptians, and that the root of this evil could not be extracted from them, he allowed them indeed to sacrifice, but permitted it to be done only to God, that by any means he might cut off one half of the deeply ingrained evil, leaving the other half to be corrected by another, and at a future time; by Him, namely, concerning whom he said himself, `A prophet shall the Lord your God raise unto you, whom ye shall hear even as myself, according to all things which He shall say to you. Whosoever shall not hear that prophet, his soul shall be cut off from his people.'

---

[1] Original word used in the text was: **haply**

Chapter XXXVII.-The Holy Place.

"In addition to these things, he also appointed a place in which alone it should be lawful to them to sacrifice to God. And all this was arranged with this view, that when the fitting time should come, and they should learn by means of the Prophet that God desires mercy and not sacrifice, they might see Him who should teach them that the place chosen of God, in which it was suitable that victims should be offered to God, is his Wisdom; and that on the other hand they might hear that this place, which seemed chosen for a time, often harassed as it had been by hostile invasions and plunderings, was at last to be wholly destroyed. And in order to impress this upon them, even before the coming of the true Prophet, who was to reject at once the sacrifices and the place, it was often plundered by enemies and burnt with fire, and the people carried into captivity among foreign nations, and then brought back when they betook themselves to the mercy of God; that by these things they might be taught that a people who offer sacrifices are driven away and delivered up into the hands of the enemy, but they who do mercy and righteousness are without sacrifices freed from captivity, and restored to their native land. But it fell out that very few understood this; for the greater number, though they could perceive and observe these things, yet were held by the irrational opinion of the vulgar: for right opinion with liberty is the prerogative of a few."

Chapter XXXVIII.-Sins of the Israelites.

"Moses, then, having arranged these things, and having set over the people one Auses[1] to bring them to the land of their fathers, himself by the command of the living God went up to a certain mountain, and there died. Yet such was the manner of his death, that till this day no one has found his burial-place. When, therefore, the people reached their fathers' land, by the providence of God, at their first onset

---

[1] Joshua

the inhabitants of wicked races are routed, and they enter upon their paternal inheritance, which was distributed among them by lot. For some time thereafter they were ruled not by kings, but judges, and remained in a somewhat peaceful condition. But when they sought for themselves tyrants rather than kings, then also with regal ambition they erected a temple in the place which had been appointed to them for prayer; and thus, through a succession of wicked kings, the people fell away to greater and still greater impiety."

Chapter XXXIX.-Baptism Instituted in Place of Sacrifices.

"But when the time began to draw near that what was wanting in the Mosaic institutions should be supplied, as we have said, and that the Prophet should appear, of whom he had foretold that He should warn them by the mercy of God to cease from sacrificing; lest perhaps they might suppose that on the cessation of sacrifice there was no remission of sins for them, He instituted baptism by water amongst them, in which they might be absolved from all their sins on the invocation of His name, and for the future, following a perfect life, might abide in immortality, being purified not by the blood of beasts, but by the purification of the Wisdom of God. Subsequently also an evident proof of this great mystery is supplied *in the fact*, that every one who, believing in this Prophet who had been foretold by Moses, is baptized in His name, shall be kept unhurt from the destruction of war which impends over the unbelieving nation, and the place itself; but that those who do not believe shall be made exiles from their place and kingdom, that even against their will they may understand and obey the will of God."

Chapter XL.-Advent of the True Prophet.

"These things therefore having been fore-arranged, He who was expected comes, bringing signs and miracles as His credentials by which He should be made manifest. But not even so did the people believe, though they had been trained during so many ages to the belief of these things. And not only did they not believe, but they added blasphemy to unbelief, saying that He was a gluttonous man and a belly-slave, and that He was actuated by a demon, even He who had come for their salvation. To such an extent does wickedness prevail by the agency of evil ones; so that, but for the Wisdom of God assisting those who love the truth, almost all would have been involved in impious delusion. Therefore He chose us twelve, the first who believed in Him, whom He named apostles; and afterwards other seventy-two most approved disciples, that, at least in this way recognizing the pattern of Moses, the multitude might believe that this is He of whom Moses foretold, the Prophet that was to come."

Chapter XLI.-Rejection of the True Prophet.

"But some one perhaps may say that it is possible for any one to imitate a number; but what shall we say of the signs and miracles which He wrought? For Moses had wrought miracles and cures in Egypt. He also of whom he foretold that He should rise up a prophet like unto himself, though He cured every sickness and infirmity among the people, wrought innumerable miracles, and preached eternal life, was hurried by wicked men to the cross; which deed was, however, by His power turned to good. In short, while He was suffering, all the world suffered with Him; for the sun was darkened, the mountains were torn asunder, the graves were opened, the veil of the temple was rent, as in lamentation for the destruction impending over the place. And yet, though all the world was moved, they themselves are not even now moved to the consideration of these so great things."

Chapter XLII.-Call of the Gentiles.

"But inasmuch as it was necessary that the Gentiles should be called into the room of those who remained unbelieving, so that the number might be filled up which had been shown to Abraham, the preaching of the blessed kingdom of God is sent into all the world. On this account worldly spirits are disturbed, who always oppose those who are in quest of liberty, and who make use of the engines of error to destroy God's building; while those who press on to the glory of safety and liberty, being rendered braver by their resistance to these spirits, and by the toil of great struggles against them, attain the crown of safety not without the palm of victory. Meantime, when He had suffered, and darkness had overwhelmed the world from the sixth even to the ninth hour, as soon as the sun shone out again, and things were returned to their usual course, even wicked men returned to themselves and their former practices, their fear having abated. For some of them, watching the place with all care, when they could not prevent His rising again, said that He was a magician; others pretended that he was stolen away."

Chapter XLIII.-Success of the Gospel.

"Nevertheless, the truth everywhere prevailed; for, in proof that these things were done by divine power, we who had been very few became in the course of a few days, by the help of God, far more than they. So that the priests at one time were afraid, lest perhaps, by the providence of God, to their confusion, the whole of the people should come over to our faith. Therefore they often sent to us, and asked us to discourse to them concerning Jesus, whether He were the Prophet whom Moses foretold, who is the eternal Christ. For on this point only does there seem to be any difference between us who believe in Jesus, and the unbelieving Jews. But while they often made such requests to us, and we sought for a fitting opportunity, a week of years was completed from the passion of the Lord, the Church of the Lord which was constituted in Jerusalem was most plentifully multiplied and grew, being governed with most righteous ordinances by James, who was ordained bishop in it by the Lord."

Chapter XLIV.-Challenge by Caiaphas.

"But when we twelve apostles, on the day of the Passover, had come together with an immense multitude, and entered into the church of the brethren, each one of us, at the request of James, stated briefly, in the hearing of the people, what we had done in every place. While this was going on, Caiaphas, the high priest, sent priests to us, and asked us to come to him, that either we should prove to him that Jesus is the eternal Christ, or he to us that He is not, and that so all the people should agree upon the one faith or the other; and this he frequently entreated us to do. But we often put it off, always seeking for a more convenient time." Then I, Clement, answered to this: "I think that this very question, whether He is the Christ, is of great importance for the establishment of the faith; otherwise the high priest would not so frequently ask that he might either learn or teach concerning the Christ." Then Peter: "You have answered rightly, O Clement; for as no one can see without eyes, nor hear without ears, nor smell without nostrils, nor taste without a tongue, nor handle anything without hands, so it is impossible, without the true Prophet, to know what is pleasing to God." And I answered: "I have already learned from your instruction that this true prophet is *the Christ*; but I should wish to learn what *the Christ* means, or why He is so called, that a matter of so great importance may not be vague and uncertain to me."

Chapter XLV.-The True Prophet: Why Called the Christ.

Then Peter began to instruct me in this manner: "When God had made the world, as Lord of the universe, He appointed chiefs over the several creatures, over the trees even, and the mountains, and the fountains, and the rivers, and all things which He had made, as we have told you; for it were too long to mention them one by one. He set, therefore, an angel as chief over the angels, a spirit over the spirits, a star over the stars, a demon over the demons, a bird over the birds, a beast over the beasts, a serpent over the serpents, a fish over the fishes, a man over men, who is

Christ Jesus. But He is called *Christ* by a certain excellent rite of religion; for as there are certain names common to kings, as Arsaces among the Persians, Caesar among the Romans, Pharaoh among the Egyptians, so among the Jews a king is called *Christ*. And the reason of this title[1] is this: Although indeed He was the Son of God, and the beginning of all things, He became man; Him first God anointed with oil which was taken from the wood of the tree of life: from that anointing therefore He is called *Christ*. Thence, moreover, He Himself also, according to the appointment of His Father, anoints with similar oil every one of the pious when they come to His kingdom, for their refreshment after their labors, as having got over the difficulties of the way; so that their light may shine, and being filled with the Holy Spirit, they may be endowed with immortality. But it occurs to me that I have sufficiently explained to you the whole nature of that branch from which that ointment is taken."

Chapter XLVI.-Anointing.

"But now also I shall, by a very short representation, recall you to the recollection of all these things. In the present life, Aaron, the first high priest, was anointed with a composition of chrism[2], which was made after the pattern of that spiritual ointment of which we have spoken before. He was prince of the people, and as a king received first-fruits and tribute from the people, man by man; and having undertaken the office of judging the people, he judged of things clean and things unclean. But if any one else was anointed with the same ointment, as deriving virtue from it, he became either king, or prophet, or priest. If, then, this temporal grace, compounded by men, had such efficacy, consider now how potent was that ointment extracted by God from a branch of the tree of life, when that which was made by men could confer so excellent dignities among men. For what in the present age is more glorious than a

---

[1] Original word used in the text was: **appellation**
[2] A consecrated oil, usually mixed with balsam or balsam and spices. Source: *Dictionary.com Unabridged (v 1.1)*.

prophet, more illustrious than a priest, more exalted than a king?"

Chapter XLVII.-Adam Anointed a Prophet.

To this, I replied: "I remember, Peter, that you told me of the first man that he was a prophet; but you did not say that he was anointed. If then there be no prophet without anointing, how could the first man be a prophet, since he was not anointed? "Then Peter, smiling, said: "If the first man prophesied, it is certain that he was also anointed. For although he who has recorded the law in his pages is silent as to his anointing, yet he has evidently left us to understand these things. For as, if he had said that he was anointed, it would not be doubted that he was also a prophet, although it were not written in the law; so, since it is certain that he was a prophet, it is in like manner certain that he was also anointed, because without anointing he could not be a prophet. But you should rather have said, If the chrism was compounded by Aaron, by the perfumer's art, how could the first man be anointed before Aaron's time, the arts of composition not yet having been discovered? "Then I answered, "Do not misunderstand me, Peter; for I do not speak of that compounded *ointment* and temporal oil, but of that simple and eternal ointment, which you told me was made by God, after whose likeness you say that that other was compounded by men."

Chapter XLVIII.-The True Prophet, a Priest.

Then Peter answered, with an appearance of indignation: "What! do you suppose, Clement, that all of us can know all things before the time? But not to be drawn aside now from our proposed discourse, we shall at another time, when your progress is more manifest, explain these things more distinctly.

"Then, however, a priest or a prophet, being anointed with the compounded ointment, putting fire to the altar of God, was held illustrious in all the world. But after Aaron, who was a priest, another is taken out of the waters. I do not speak of Moses, but of Him who, in the waters of baptism, was called by God His Son. For it is Jesus who has put out, by the grace of baptism, that fire which the priest kindled for sins; for, from the time when He appeared, the chrism has ceased, by which the priesthood or the prophetic or the kingly office was conferred."

Chapter XLIX.-Two Comings of Christ.

"His coming, therefore, was predicted by Moses, who delivered the law of God to men; but by another also before him, as I have already informed you. He therefore intimated that He should come, humble indeed in His first coming, but glorious in His second. And the first, indeed, has been already accomplished; since He has come and taught, and He, the Judge of all, has been judged and slain. But at His second coming He shall come to judge, and shall indeed condemn the wicked, but shall take the pious into a share and association with Himself in His kingdom. Now the faith of His second coming depends upon His first. For the prophets-especially Jacob and Moses-spoke of the first, but some also of the second. But the excellency of prophecy is chiefly shown in this, that the prophets spoke not of things to come, according to the sequence of things; otherwise they might seem merely as wise men to have conjectured what the sequence of things pointed out."

Chapter L.-His Rejection by the Jews.

"But what I say is this: It was to be expected that Christ should be received by the Jews, to whom He came, and that they should believe on Him who was expected for the salvation of the people, according to the traditions of the fathers; but that the Gentiles should be averse to Him, since neither promise nor announcement concerning Him had been made to them, and indeed he had never been made known to them even by name. Yet the prophets, contrary to the order and sequence of things, said that He should be the expectation of the Gentiles, and not of the Jews. And so it happened. For when He came, he was not at all acknowledged by those who seemed to expect Him, in consequence of the tradition of their ancestors; whereas those who had heard nothing at all of Him, both believe that He has come, and hope that he is to come. And thus in all things prophecy appears faithful, which said that He was the expectation of the Gentiles. The Jews, therefore, have erred concerning the first coming of the Lord; and on this point only there is disagreement betwixt us and them. For they themselves know and expect that Christ shall come; but that he has come already in humility-even he who is called Jesus-they do not know. And this is a great confirmation of His coming, that all do not believe on Him."

Chapter LI.-The Only Saviour.

"Him, therefore, has God appointed in the end of the world; because it was impossible that the evils of men could be removed by any other, provided that the nature of the human race were to remain entire, i.e., the liberty of the will being preserved. This condition, therefore, being preserved inviolate, He came to invite to His kingdom all righteous ones, and those who have been desirous to please Him. For these He has prepared unspeakable good things, and the heavenly city Jerusalem, which shall shine above the brightness of the sun, for the habitation of the saints. But the unrighteous, and the wicked and those who have despised God, and have devoted the life given them to diverse wickedness, and have given to the practice of evil the time which was given them for the work of righteousness He shall hand over to fitting and condign vengeance. But the rest of the things which shall then be done, it is neither in the power of angels nor of men to tell or to describe. This only it is enough for us to know, that God shall confer upon the good an eternal possession of good things."

Chapter LII.-The Saints Before Christ's Coming.

When he had thus spoken, I answered: "If those shall enjoy the kingdom of Christ, whom His coming shall find righteous, shall then those be wholly deprived of the kingdom who have died before His coming? "Then Peter says: "You compel me, O Clement, to touch upon things that are unspeakable. But so far as it is allowed to declare them, I shall not shrink from doing so. Know then that Christ, who was from the beginning, and always, was ever present with the pious, though secretly, through all their generations: especially with those who waited for Him, to whom He frequently appeared. But the time was not yet that there should be a resurrection of the bodies that were dissolved; but this seemed rather to be their reward from God, that whoever should be found righteous, should remain longer in the body; or, at least, as is clearly related in the writings of the law concerning a certain righteous man, that God translated him. In like manner others were dealt with, who pleased His will, that, being translated to Paradise, they should be kept for the kingdom. But as to those who have not been able completely to fulfill the rule of righteousness, but have had some remnants of evil in their flesh, their bodies are indeed dissolved, but their souls are kept in good and blessed abodes, that at the resurrection of the dead, when they shall recover their own bodies, purified even by the dissolution, they may obtain an eternal inheritance in proportion to their good deeds. And therefore blessed are all those who shall attain to the kingdom of Christ; for not only shall they escape the pains of hell, but shall also remain incorruptible, and shall be the first to see God the Father, and shall obtain the rank of honor among the first in the presence of God."

Chapter LIII.-Animosity of the Jews.

"Wherefore there is not the least doubt concerning Christ; and all the unbelieving Jews are stirred up with boundless rage against us, fearing lest perhaps He against whom they have sinned should be He. And their fear grows all the greater, because they know that, as soon as they fixed Him on the cross, the whole world showed sympathy with Him; and that His body, although they guarded it with strict care, could nowhere be found; and that innumerable multitudes are attaching themselves to His faith. Whence they, together with the high priest Caiaphas, were compelled to send to us again and again, that an inquiry might be instituted concerning the truth of His name. And when they were constantly entreating that they might either learn or teach concerning Jesus, whether He were the Christ, it seemed good to us to go up into the temple, and in the presence of all the people to bear witness concerning Him, and at the same time to charge the Jews with many foolish things which they we re doing. For the people was now divided into many parties, ever since the days of John the Baptist."

Chapter LIV.-Jewish Sects.

"For when the rising of Christ was at hand for the abolition of sacrifices, and for the bestowal of the grace of baptism, the enemy, understanding from the predictions that the time was at hand, wrought various schisms among the people, that, if perhaps it might be possible to abolish the former sin, the latter fault might be incorrigible. The first schism, therefore, was that of those who were called Sadducees, which took their rise almost in the time of John. These, as more righteous than others, began to separate themselves from the assembly of the people, and to deny the resurrection of the dead, and to assert that by an argument of infidelity, saying that it was unworthy that God should be worshipped, as it were, under the promise of a reward. The first author of this opinion was Dositheus; the second was Simon. Another schism is that of the Samaritans; for they deny the resurrection of the dead, and assert that God is not to be worshipped in Jerusalem, but on Mount Gerizim. They indeed rightly, from the predictions of Moses, expect the one true Prophet; but by the wickedness of Dositheus they were hindered from believing that Jesus is He whom they were expecting. The scribes also, and

Pharisees, are led away into another schism; but these, being baptized by John, and holding the word of truth received from the tradition of Moses as the key of the kingdom of heaven, have hid it from the hearing of the people. Yea, some even of the disciples of John, who seemed to be great ones, have separated themselves from the people, and proclaimed their own master as the Christ. But all these schisms have been prepared, that by means of them the faith of Christ and baptism might be hindered."

Chapter LV.-Public Discussion.

"However, as we were proceeding to say, when the high priest had often sent priests to ask us that we might discourse with one another concerning Jesus; when it seemed a fit opportunity, and it pleased all the Church, we went up to the temple, and, standing on the steps together with our faithful brethren, the people kept perfect silence; and first the high priest began to exhort the people that they should hear patiently and quietly, and at the same time witness and judge of those things that were to be spoken. Then, in the next place, exalting with many praises the rite or sacrifice which had been bestowed by God upon the human race for the remission of sins, he found fault with the baptism of our Jesus, as having been recently brought in opposition to the sacrifices. But Matthew, meeting his propositions, showed clearly, that whosoever shall not obtain the baptism of Jesus shall not only be deprived of the kingdom of heaven, but shall not be without peril at the resurrection of the dead, even though he be for-titled by the prerogative of a good life and an upright disposition. Having made these and such like statements, Matthew stopped."

Chapter LVL.-Sadducees Refuted.

"But the party of the Sadducees, who deny the resurrection of the dead, were in a rage, so that one of them cried out from amongst the people, saying that those greatly err who think that the dead ever arise. In opposition to him,

Andrew, my brother, answering, declared that it is not an error, but the surest matter of faith, that the dead rise, in accordance with the teaching of Him of whom Moses foretold that He should come the true Prophet. `Or if, 'says he, `you do not think that this is He whom Moses foretold, let this first be inquired into, so that when this is clearly proved to be He, there may be no further doubt concerning the things which He taught.' These, and many such like things, Andrew proclaimed, and then stopped."

Chapter LVII.-Samaritan Refuted.

"But a certain Samaritan, speaking against the people and against God, and asserting that neither are the dead to rise, nor is that worship of God to be maintained which is in Jerusalem, but that Mount Gerizim is to be reverenced, added also this in opposition to us, that our Jesus was not He whom Moses foretold as a Prophet to come into the world. Against him, and another who supported him in what he said, James and John, the sons of Zebedee, strove vigorously; and although they had a command not to enter into their cities, nor to bring the word of preaching to them, yet, lest their discourse, unless it were confined, should hurt the faith of others, they replied so prudently and so powerfully, that they put them to perpetual silence. For James made an oration concerning the resurrection of the dead, with the approbation of all the people; while John showed that if they would abandon the error of Mount Gerizim, they should consequently acknowledge that Jesus was indeed He who, according to the prophecy of Moses, was expected to come; since, indeed, as Moses wrought signs and miracles, so also did Jesus. And there is no doubt but that the likeness of the signs proves Him to be that prophet of whom he said that He should come, `like himself.' Having declared these things, and more to the same effect, they ceased."

Chapter LVIII.-Scribes Refuted.

"And, behold, one of the scribes, shouting silt from the midst of the people, says: 'The signs and miracles which your Jesus wrought, he wrought not as a prophet, but as a magician.' Him Philip eagerly encounters, showing that by this argument he accused Moses also. For when Moses wrought signs and miracles in Egypt, in like manner as Jesus also did in Judea, it cannot be doubted that what was said of Jesus might as well be said of Moses. Having made these and such like protestations, Philip was silent."

Chapter LIX.-Pharisees Refuted.

"Then a certain Pharisee, hearing this, chided Philip because he put Jesus on a level with Moses. To whom Bartholomew, answering, boldly declared that we do not only say that Jesus was equal to Moses, but that He was greater than he, because Moses was indeed a prophet, as Jesus was also, but that Moses was not the Christ, as Jesus was, and therefore He is doubtless greater who is both a prophet and the Christ, than he who is only a prophet. After following out this train of argument, he stopped. After him James the son of Alphaeus gave an address to the people, with the view of showing that we are not to believe on Jesus on the ground that the prophets foretold concerning Him, but rather that we are to believe the prophets, that they were really prophets, because the Christ bears testimony to them; for it is the presence and coming of Christ that show that they are truly prophets: for testimony must be borne by the superior to his inferiors, not by the inferiors to their superior. After these and many similar statements, James also was silent. After him Lebbaeus began vehemently to charge it upon the people that they did not believe in Jesus, who had done them so much good by teaching them the things that are of God, by comforting the afflicted, healing the sick, relieving the poor; yet for all these benefits their return had been hatred and death. When he had declared these and many more such things to the people, he ceased."

Chapter LX.-Disciples of John Refuted.

"And, behold, one of the disciples of John asserted that John was the Christ, and not Jesus, inasmuch as Jesus Himself declared that John was greater than all men and all prophets. `If, then, 'said he, `he be greater than all, he must be held to be greater than Moses, and than Jesus himself. But if he be the greatest of all, then must he be the Christ.' To this Simon the Canaanite, answering, asserted that John was indeed greater than all the prophets, and all who are born of women, yet that he is not greater than the Son of man. Accordingly Jesus is also the Christ, whereas John is only a prophet: and there is as much difference between him and Jesus, as between the forerunner and Him whose forerunner he is; or as between Him who gives the law, and him who keeps the law. Having made these and similar statements, the Canaanite also was silent. After him Barnabas, who also is called Matthias, who was substituted as an apostle in the place of Judas, began to exhort the people that they should not regard Jesus with hatred, nor speak evil of Him. For it were far more proper, even for one who might be in ignorance or in doubt concerning Jesus, to love than to hate Him. For God has affixed a reward to love, a penalty to hatred. `For the very fact, 'said he, `that He assumed a Jewish body, and was born among the Jews, how has not this incited us all to love Him? 'When he had spoken this, and more to the same effect, he stopped."

Chapter LXI.-Caiaphas Answered.

"Then Caiaphas attempted to impugn[1] the doctrine of Jesus, saying that He spoke vain things, for He said that the poor are blessed; and promised earthly rewards; and placed the chief gift in an earthly inheritance; and promised that those who maintain righteousness shall be satisfied with meat and drink; and many things of this sort He is charged with teaching. Thomas, in reply, proves that his accusation is

---

[1] To challenge as false (another's statements, motives, etc.); cast doubt upon. *Source: Dictionary.com Unabridged (v 1.1)*.

frivolous; showing that the prophets, in whom Caiaphas believes, taught these things much more, and did not show in what manner these things are to be, or how they are to be understood; whereas Jesus pointed out how they are to be taken. And when he had spoken these things, and others of like kind, Thomas also held his peace."

Chapter LXLI.-Foolishness of Preaching.

"Therefore Caiaphas, again looking at me, and sometimes in the way of warning and sometimes in that of accusation, said that, I ought for the future to refrain from preaching Christ Jesus, lest I should do it to my own destruction, and lest, being deceived myself, I should also deceive others. Then, moreover, he charged me with presumption, because, though I was unlearned, a fisherman, and a rustic, I dared to assume the office of a teacher. As he spoke these things, and many more of like kind, I said in reply, that I incurred less danger, if, as he said, this Jesus were not the Christ, because I received Him as a teacher of the law; but that he was in terrible danger if this be the very Christ, as assuredly He is: for I believe in Him who has appeared; but for whom else, who has never appeared, does he reserve his faith? But if I, an unlearned and uneducated man, as you say, a fisherman and a rustic, have more understanding than wise elders, this, said I, ought the more to strike terror into you. For if I disputed with any learning, and won over you wise and learned men, it would appear that I had acquired this power by long learning, and not by the grace of divine power; but now, when, as I have said, we unskilled men convince and overcome you wise men, who that has any sense does not perceive that this is not a work of human subtlety, but of divine will and gift? "

Chapter LXIII.-Appeal to the Jews.

"Thus we argued and bore witness; and we who were unlearned men and fishermen, taught the priests concerning the one only God of heaven; the Saducees, concerning the resurrection of the dead; the Samaritans, concerning the sacredness of Jerusalem (not that we entered into their cities, but disputed with them in public); the scribes and Pharisees, concerning the kingdom of heaven; the disciples of John, that they should not suffer John to be a stumbling-block to them; and all the people, that Jesus is the eternal Christ. At last, however, I warned them, that before we should go forth to the Gentiles, to preach to them the knowledge of God the Father, they should themselves be reconciled to God, receiving His Son; for I showed them that in no way else could they be saved, unless through the grace of the Holy Spirit they hasted to be washed with the baptism of threefold invocation, and received the sacrament[1] of Christ the Lord, whom alone they ought to believe concerning those things which He taught, that so they might merit to attain eternal salvation; but that otherwise it was utterly impossible for them to be reconciled to God, even if they should kindle a thousand altars and a thousand high altars to Him."

Chapter LXIV.-Temple to Be Destroyed.

"`For we.' said I, `have ascertained beyond doubt that God is much rather displeased with the sacrifices which you offer, the time of sacrifices having now passed away; and because ye will not acknowledge that the time for offering victims is now past, therefore the temple shall be destroyed, and the abomination of desolation shall stand in the holy place; and then the Gospel shall be preached to the Gentiles for a testimony against you, that your unbelief may be judged by their faith. For the whole world at different times suffers under divers maladies, either spreading generally over all, or affecting specially. Therefore it needs a physician to visit it for its salvation. We therefore bear witness to you, and declare to you what has been hidden from every one of you. It is for you to consider what is for your advantage.'"

---

[1] Original word used in the text was: **Eucharist**

Chapter LXV.-Tumult Stilled by Gamaliel.

"When I had thus spoken, the whole multitude of the priests were in a rage, because I had foretold to them the overthrow of the temple. Which when Gamaliel, a chief of the people, saw-who was secretly our brother in the faith, but by our advice remained among them-because they were greatly enraged and moved with intense fury against us, he stood up, and said, 'Be quiet for a little, O men of Israel, for ye do not perceive the trial which hangs over you. Wherefore refrain from these men; and if what they are engaged in be of human counsel, it will soon come to an end; but if it be from God, why will you sin without cause, and prevail nothing? For who can overpower the will of God? Now therefore, since the day is declining towards evening. I shall myself dispute with these men to-morrow, in this same place, in your hearing, so that I may openly oppose and clearly confute every error.' By this speech of his their fury was to some extent checked, especially in the hope that next day we should be publicly convicted of error; and so he dismissed the people peacefully."

Chapter LXVI.-Discussion Resumed.

"Now when we had come to our James, while we detailed to him all that had been said and done, we supped, and remained with him, spending the whole night in supplication to Almighty God, that the discourse of the approaching disputation might show the unquestionable truth of our faith. Therefore, on the following day, James the bishop went up to the temple with us, and with the whole church. There we found a great multitude, who had been waiting for us from the middle of the night. Therefore we took our stand in the same place as before, in order that, standing on an elevation, we might be seen by all the people. Then, when profound silence was obtained, Gamaliel, who, as we have said, was of our faith, but who by a dispensation remained amongst them, that if at any time they should attempt anything unjust or wicked against us, he might either check them by skillfully adopted counsel, or might warn us, that we might either be on our guard or might turn it aside;-he therefore, as if acting against us, first of all looking to James the bishop, addressed him in this manner:-

Chapter LXVII.-Speech of Gamaliel.

"`If I, Gamaliel, deem it no reproach either to my learning or to my old age to learn something from babes and unlearned ones, if perhaps there be anything which it is for profit or for safety to acquire (for he who lives reasonably knows that nothing is more precious than the soul), ought not this to be the object of love and desire to all, to learn what they do not know, and to teach what they have learned? For it is most certain that neither friendship, nor kindred, nor lofty power, ought to be more precious to men than truth. Therefore you, O brethren, if ye know anything more, shrink not from laying it before the people of God who are present, and also before your brethren; while the whole people shall willingly and in perfect quietness hear what you say. For why should not the people do this, when they see even me equally with themselves willing to learn from you, if haply God has revealed something further to you? But if you in anything are deficient, be not ye ashamed in like manner to be taught by us, that God may fill up whatever is wanting on either side. But if any fear now agitates you on account of some of our people whose minds are prejudiced against you, and if through fear of their violence you dare not openly speak your sentiments, in order that I may deliver you from this fear, I openly swear to you by Almighty God, who liveth for ever, that I will suffer no one to lay hands upon you. Since, then, you have all this people witnesses of this my oath, and you hold the covenant of our sacrament as a fitting pledge, let each one of you, without any hesitation, declare what he has learned; and let us, brethren, listen eagerly and in silence.'"

Chapter LXVIII.-The Rule of Faith.

"These sayings of Gamaliel did not much please Caiaphas; and holding him in suspicion, as it seemed, he began to insinuate himself cunningly into the discussions: for, smiling at what Gamaliel had said, the chief of the priests asked of James, the chief of the bishops, that the discourse concerning Christ should not be drawn but from the Scriptures; 'that we may know, 'said he, 'whether Jesus be the very Christ or no.' Then said James, 'We must first inquire from what Scriptures we are especially to derive our discussion.' Then he, with difficulty, at length overcome by reason, answered, that it must be derived from the law; and afterwards he made mention also of the prophets."

Chapter LXIX.-Two Comings of Christ.

"To him our James began to show, that whatsoever things the prophets say they have taken from the law, and what they have spoken is in accordance with the law. He also made some statements respecting the books of the Kings in: what way, and when, and by whom they were written, and how they ought to be used. And when he had discussed most fully concerning the law, and had, by a most clear exposition, brought into light whatever things are in it concerning Christ, he showed by most abundant proofs that Jesus is the Christ, and that in Him are fulfilled all the prophecies which related to His humble advent. For he showed that two advents of Him are foretold: one in humiliation, which He has accomplished; the other in glory, which is hoped for to be accomplished, when He shall come to give the kingdom to those who believe in Him, and who observe all things which He has commanded. And when he had plainly taught the people concerning these things, he added this also: That unless a man be baptized in water, in the name of the threefold blessedness, as the true Prophet taught, he can neither receive remission of sins nor enter into the kingdom of heaven; and he declared that this is the prescription of the unbegotten God. To which he added this also: `Do not think that we speak of two unbegotten Gods, or that one is divided into two, or that the same is made male and female. But we speak of the only-begotten Son of God, not sprung from another source, but ineffably self-originated; and in like manner we speak of the Holy Spirit.'[1] But when he had spoken some things also concerning baptism, through seven successive days he persuaded all the people and the high priest that they should hasten straightway to receive baptism."

Chapter LXX.-Tumult Raised by Saul.

"And when matters were at that point that they should come and be baptized, some one of our enemies, entering the temple with a few men, began to cry out, and to say, `What mean ye, O men of Israel? Why are you so easily hurried on? Why are ye led headlong by most miserable men, who are deceived by Simon, a magician?' While he was thus speaking, and adding more to the same effect, and while James the bishop was refuting him, he began to excite the people and to raise a tumult so that the people might not be able to hear what was said. Therefore he began to drive all into confusion with shouting, and to undo what had been arranged with much labor, and at the same time to reproach the priests, and to enrage them with revilings and abuse, and, like a madman, to excite every one to murder, saying, `What do ye? Why do ye hesitate? Oh sluggish and inert, why do we not lay hands upon them, and pull all these fellows to pieces?' When he had said this, he first, seizing a strong brand from the altar, set the example of smiting. Then others also, seeing him, were carried away with like readiness. Then ensued a tumult on either side, of the beating and the beaten. Much blood is shed; there is a confused flight, in the midst of which that enemy attacked James, and threw him headlong from the top of the steps; and supposing him to be dead, he cared not to inflict further violence upon him."

---

[1] Original word used in the text was: **Paraclete**

Chapter LXXI.-Flight to Jericho.

"But our friends lifted him up, for they were both more numerous and more powerful than the others; but, from their fear of God, they rather suffered themselves to be killed by an inferior force, than they would kill others. But when the evening came the priests shut up the temple, and we returned to the house of James, and spent the night there in prayer. Then before daylight we went down to Jericho, to the number of 5000 men. Then after three days one of the brethren came to us from Gamaliel, whom we mentioned before, bringing to us secret tidings that that enemy had received a commission from Caiaphas, the chief priest, that he should arrest all who believed in Jesus, and should go to Damascus with his letters, and that there also, employing the help of the unbelievers, he should make havoc among the faithful; and that he was hastening to Damascus chiefly on this account, because he believed that Peter had fled thither. And about thirty days thereafter he stopped on his way while passing through Jericho going to Damascus. At that time we were absent, having gone out to the sepulchers of two brethren which were whitened of themselves every year, by which miracle the fury of many against us was restrained, because they saw that our brethren were had in remembrance before God."

Chapter LXXII.-Peter Sent to Caesarea.

"While, therefore, we abode in Jericho, and gave ourselves to prayer and fasting, James the bishop sent for me, and sent me here to Caesarea, saying that Zacchaeus had written to him from Caesarea, that one Simon, a Samaritan magician, was subverting many of our people, asserting that he was one *Stans*, -that is, in other words, the Christ, and the great power of the high God, which is superior to the Creator of the world; at the same time that he showed many miracles, and made some doubt, and others fall away to him. He informed me of all things that had been ascertained respecting this man from those who had formerly been either his associates or his disciples, and had afterwards been converted to Zacchaeus. `Many therefore there are, O Peter, 'said James, `for whose safety's sake it behooves you to go and to refute the magician, and to teach the word of truth. Therefore make no delay; nor let it grieve you that you set out alone, knowing that God by Jesus will go with you, and will help you, and that soon, by His grace, you will have many associates and sympathizers. Now be sure that you send me in writing every year an account of your sayings and doings, and especially at the end of every seven years.' With these expressions he dismissed me, and in six days I arrived at Caesarea."

Chapter LXXIII.-Welcomed by Zacchaeus.

"When I entered the city, our most beloved brother Zacchaeus met me; and embracing me, brought me to this lodging, in which he himself stayed, inquiring of me concerning each of the brethren, especially concerning our honorable brother James. And when I told him that he was still lame on one foot, on his immediately asking the cause of this, I related to him all that I have now detailed to you, how we had been called by the priests and Caiaphas the high priest to the temple, and how James the archbishop, standing on the top of the steps, had for seven successive days shown the whole people from the Scriptures of the Lord that Jesus is the Christ; and how, when all were acquiescing that they should be baptized by him in the name of Jesus, an enemy did all those things which I have already mentioned, and which I need not repeat."

Chapter LXXIV.-Simon Magus Challenges Peter.

"When Zacchaeus had heard these things, he told me in return of the doings of Simon; and in the meantime Simon himself-how he heard of my arrival I do not know-sent a message to me, saying, `Let us dispute to-morrow in the hearing of the people.' To which I answered, `Be it so, as it pleaseth you.' And this promise of mine was known over the whole city, so that even you, who arrived on that very day, learned that I was to hold a discussion with Simon on the following day, and having found out my abode, according to the directions which yon had received from Barnabas, came to me. But I so rejoiced at your coming, that my mind, moved I know not how, hastened to expound all things quickly to you, yet especially that which is the main point in our faith, concerning the true Prophet, which alone, I doubt not, is a sufficient foundation for the whole of our doctrine. Then, in the next place, I unfolded to you the more secret meaning of the written law, through its several heads, which there was occasion to unfold; neither did I conceal from you the good things of the traditions. But what remains, beginning from tomorrow, you shall hear from day to day in connection with the questions which will be raised in the discussion with Simon, until by God's favor we reach that city of Rome to which we believe that our journey is to be directed."

I then declared that I owed him all thanks for what he had told me, and promised that I would most readily do all that he commanded. Then, having taken food, he ordered me to rest, and he also betook himself to rest."

Book II.

Chapter I.-Power of Habit.

When the day dawned which had been fixed for the discussion with Simon, Peter, rising at the first cock-crowing, aroused us also: for we were sleeping in the same apartment, thirteen of us in all; of whom, next to Peter, Zacchaeus was first, then Sophonius, Joseph and Michaeas, Eliesdrus, Phineas, Lazarus, and Elisaeus: after these I (Clement) and Nicodemus; then Niceta and Aquila, who had formerly been disciples of Simon, and were converted to the faith of Christ under the teaching of Zacchaeus. Of the women there was no one present. As the evening light was still lasting, we all sat down; and Peter, seeing that we were awake, and that we were giving attention to him, having saluted us, immediately began to speak, as follows:-

"I confess, brethren, that I wonder at the power of human nature, which I see to be fit and suited to every call upon it. This, however, it occurs to me to say of what I have found by experience, that when the middle of the night is passed, I awake of my own accord, and sleep does not come to me again. This happens to me for this reason, that I have formed the habit of recalling to memory the words of my Lord, which I heard from Himself; and for the longing I have towards them, I constrain my mind and my thoughts to be roused, that, awaking to them, and recalling and arranging them one by one, I may retain them in my memory. From this, therefore, whilst I desire to cherish the sayings of the Lord with all delight in my heart, the habit of waking has come upon me, even if there be nothing that I wish to think of. Thus, in some unaccountable way, when any custom is established, the old custom is changed, provided indeed you do not force it above measure, but as far as the measure of nature admits. For it is not possible to be altogether without sleep; otherwise night would not have been made for rest."

Chapter II.-Curtailment of Sleep.

Then I, when I heard this, said: "You have very well said, O Peter; for one custom is superseded by another. For when I was at sea, I was at first distressed, and all my system was disordered, so that I felt as if I had been beaten, and could not bear the tossing and tumult of the sea; but after a few days, when I had got accustomed to it, I began to bear it tolerably, so that I was glad to take food immediately in the morning along with the sailors, whereas before it was not my custom to eat anything before the seventh hour. Now, therefore, simply from the custom which I then acquired, hunger reminds me about that time at which I used to eat with the sailors; which, however, I hope to get rid of, when once another custom shall have been formed. I believe, therefore, that you also have acquired the habit of wakefulness, as yon state; and you have wished at a fitting time to explain this to us, that we also may not grudge to throw off and dispense with some portion of our sleep, that we may be able to take in the precepts of the living doctrine. For when the food is digested, and the mind is under the influence of the silence of night, those things which are seasonably taught abide in it."

Chapter III.-Need of Caution.

Then Peter, being pleased to hear that I understood the meaning[1] of his preface, that he had delivered it for our advantage; and commending me, doubtless for the purpose of encouraging, and stimulating me, began to deliver the following discourse: "It seems to me to be seasonable and necessary to have some discussion relating to those things that are near at hand; that is, concerning Simon. For I should wish to know of what character and of what conduct he is. Wherefore, if any one of you has any knowledge of him, let him not fail to inform me; for it is of consequence to know these things beforehand. For if we have it in charge, that when we enter into a city we should first learn

---

[1] Original word used in the text was: **purport**.

who in it is worthy, that we may eat with him, how much more is it proper for us to ascertain who or what sort of man he is to whom the words of immortality are to be committed! For we ought to be careful, yea, extremely careful, that we cast not our pearls before swine.

Chapter IV.-Prudence in Dealing with Opponents.

"But for other reasons also it is of importance that I should have some knowledge of this man. For if I know that in those things concerning which it cannot be doubted that they are good, he is faultless and irreproachable,-that is to say, if he is sober, merciful, upright, gentle, and humane, which no one doubts to be good qualities,-then it will seem to be fitting, that upon him who possesses these good virtues, that which is lacking of faith and knowledge should be conferred; and so his life, which is in other respects worthy of approbation[1], should be amended in those points in which it shall appear to be imperfect. But if he remains wrapped up and polluted in those sins which are manifestly such, it does not become me to speak to him at all of the more secret and sacred things of divine knowledge, but rather to protest and confront him, that he cease from sin, and cleanse his actions from vice. But if he insinuate himself, and lead us on to speak what he, while he acts improperly, ought not to hear, it will be our part to parry him cautiously. For not to answer him at all does not seem proper, for the sake of the hearers, lest perhaps they may think that we decline the contest through want of ability to answer him, and so their faith may be injured through their misunderstanding of our purpose."

Chapter V.-Simon Magus, a Formidable Antagonist.

When Peter had thus spoken to us, Niceta asks permission to say something to him; and Peter having granted permission, he says: "With your pardon, I beseech you, my lord Peter, to hear me, who am very anxious for thee, and

---

[1] Approval or commendation.
Source: Dictionary.com Unabridged (v 1.1).

who am afraid lest, in the contest which you have in band with Simon, you should seem to be overmatched. For it very frequently happens that he who defends the truth does not gain the victory, since the hearers are either prejudiced, or have no great interest in the better cause. But over and above all this, Simon himself is a most vehement orator, trained in the dialectic[1] art, and in the meshes of syllogisms; and what is worse than all, he is greatly skilled in the magic art. And therefore I fear, lest perhaps, being so strongly fortified on every side, he shall be thought to be defending the truth, whilst he is alleging falsehoods, in the presence of those who do not know him. For neither should we ourselves have been able to escape from him, and to be converted to the Lord, had it not been that, while we were his assistants, and the sharers of his errors, we had ascertained that he was a deceiver and a magician."

Chapter VI.-Simon Magus: His Wickedness.

When Niceta had thus spoken, Aquila also, asking that he might be permitted to speak, proceeded in manner following: "Receive, I entreat thee, most excellent Peter, the assurance of my love towards thee; for indeed I also am extremely anxious on thy account. And do not blame us in this, for indeed to be concerned for any one cometh of affection; whereas to be indifferent is no less than hatred. But I call God to witness that I feel for thee, not as knowing thee to be weaker in debate,-for indeed I was never present at any dispute in which thou wert engaged,-but because I well know the impieties of this man, I think of thy reputation, and at the same time the souls of the hearers, and above all, the interests of the truth itself. For this magician is vehement towards all things that he wishes, and wicked above measure. For in all things we know him well, since from boyhood we have been assistants and ministers of his wickedness; and had not the love of God rescued us from him, we should even now be engaged in the same evil deeds with him. But a certain inborn love towards God

---

[1] Pertaining to, or of the nature of logical argumentation.
Source: Dictionary.com Unabridged (v 1.1).

rendered his wickedness hateful to us, and the worship of God attractive to us. Whence I think also that it was the work of Divine Providence, that we, being first made his associates, should take knowledge in what manner or by what art he effects the prodigies which he seems to work. For who is there that would not be astonished at the wonderful things which he does? Who would not think that he was a god come down from heaven for the salvation of men? For myself, I confess, if I had not known him intimately, and had taken part in his doings, I would easily have been carried away with him. Whence it was no great thing for us to be separated from his society, knowing as we did that he depends upon magic arts and wicked devices. But if thou also thyself wish to know all about him-who, what, and whence he is, and how he contrives what he does-then listen."

Chapter VII.-Simon Magus: His History.

"This Simon's father was Antonius, and his mother Rachel. By nation he is a Samaritan, from a village of the Gettones; by profession a magician yet exceedingly well trained in the Greek literature; desirous of glory, and boasting above all the human race, so that he wishes himself to be believed to be an exalted power, which is above God the Creator, and to be thought to be the Christ, and to be called the *Standing One*. And he uses this name as implying that he can never be dissolved, asserting that his flesh is so compacted by the power of his divinity, that it can endure to eternity. Hence, therefore, he is called the *Standing One*, as though he cannot fall by any corruption."

Chapter VIII.-Simon Magus: His History.

"For after that John the Baptist was killed, as you yourself also know, when Dositheus had broached his heresy, with thirty other chief disciples, and one woman, who was called *Luna* -whence also these thirty appear to have been appointed with reference to the number of the days, according to the course of the moon-this Simon ambitious of evil glory, as we have said, goes to Dositheus, and pretending friendship, entreats him, that if any one of those thirty should die, he should straightway substitute him in room of the dead: for it was contrary to their rule either to exceed the fixed number, or to admit any one who was unknown, or not yet proved; whence also the rest, desiring to become worthy of the place and number, are eager in every way to please, according to the institutions of their sect each one of those who aspire after admittance into the number, hoping that he may be deemed worthy to be put into the place of the deceased, when, as we have said, any one dies. Therefore Dositheus, being greatly urged by this man, introduced Simon when a vacancy occurred among the number."

Chapter IX.-Simon Magus: His Profession.

"But not long after he fell in love with that woman whom they call Luna; and he confided all things to us as his friends: how he was a magician, and how he loved Luna, and how, being desirous of glory, he was unwilling to enjoy her ingloriously, but that he was waiting patiently till he could enjoy her honorably; yet so if we also would conspire with him towards the accomplishment of his desires. And he promised that, as a reward of this service, he would cause us to be invested with the highest honors, and we should be believed by men to be gods; `Only, however, on condition, 'says he, `that you confer the chief place upon me, Simon, who by magic art am able to show many signs and prodigies, by means of which either my glory or our sect may be established. For I am able to render myself invisible to those who wish to lay hold of me, and again to be visible when I am willing to be seen. If I wish to flee, I can dig through the mountains, and pass through rocks as if they were clay. If I should throw myself headlong from a lofty mountain, I should be borne unhurt to the earth, as if I were held up; when bound, I can loose myself, and bind those who had bound me; being shut up in prison, I can make the barriers open of their own accord; I can render statues animated, so that those who see suppose that they are men. I can make new trees suddenly spring up, and produce sprouts at once. I can throw myself into the fire, and not be burnt; I can change my countenance, so that I cannot be recognized; but I can show people that I have two faces. I shall change myself into a sheep or a goat; I shall make a beard to grow upon little boys; I shall ascend by flight into the air; I shall exhibit abundance of gold, and shall make and unmake kings. I shall be worshipped as God; I shall have divine honors publicly assigned to me, so that an image of me shall be set up, and I shall be worshipped and adored as God. And what need of more words? Whatever I wish, that I shall be able to do. For already I have achieved many things by way of experiment. In short, 'says he, `once when my mother Rachel ordered me to go to the field to reap, and I saw a sickle lying, I ordered it to go and reap; and it reaped ten times more than the others. Lately, I produced many new sprouts from the earth, and made them bear leaves and produce fruit in a moment; and the nearest mountain I successfully bored through.'"

Chapter X.-Simon Magus: His Deception.

"But when he spoke thus of the production of sprouts and the perforation of the mountain, I was confounded on this account, because he wished to deceive even us, in whom he seemed to place confidence; for we knew that those things had been from the days of our fathers, which he represented as having been done by himself lately. We then, although we heard these atrocities from him, and worse than these, yet we followed up his crimes, and suffered others to be deceived by him, telling also many lies on his behalf; and this before he did any of the things which he had promised, so that while as yet he had done nothing, he was by some thought to be God."

Chapter XI.-Simon Magus, at the Head of the Sect of Dositheus .

"Meantime, at the outset, as soon as he was reckoned among the thirty disciples of Dositheus, he began to depreciate Dositheus himself, saying that he did not teach purely or perfectly, and that this was the result not of ill intention, but of ignorance. But Dositheus, when he perceived that Simon was depreciating him, fearing lest his reputation among men might be obscured (for he himself was supposed to be the *Standing One*), moved with rage, when they met as usual at the school, seized a rod, and began to beat Simon; but suddenly the rod seemed to pass through his body, as if it had been smoke. On which Dositheus, being astonished, says to him, `Tell me if thou art the *Standing One*, that I may adore thee.' And when Simon answered that he was, then Dositheus, perceiving that he himself was not the Standing One, fell down and worshipped him, and gave up his own place as chief to Simon, ordering all the rank of thirty men to obey him; himself taking the inferior place which Simon formerly occupied. Not long after this he died."

Chapter XII.-Simon Magus and Luna.

"Therefore, after the death of Dositheus Simon took Luna to himself; and with her he still goes about, as you see, deceiving multitudes, and asserting that he himself is a certain power which is above God the Creator, while Luna, who is with him, has been brought down from the higher heavens, and that she is Wisdom, the mother of all things, for whom, says he, the Greeks and barbarians contending, were able in some measure to see an image of her; but of herself, as she is, as the dweller with the first and only God, they were wholly ignorant. Propounding these and other things of the same sort, he has deceived many. But I ought also to state this, which I remember that I myself saw. Once, when this Luna of his was in a certain tower, a great multitude had assembled to see her, and were standing around the tower on all sides; but she was seen by all the people to lean forward, and to look out through all the windows of that tower. Many other wonderful things he did and does; so that men, being astonished at them, think that he himself is the great God."

Chapter XIII.-Simon Magus: Secret of His Magic.

"Now when Niceta and I once asked him to explain to us how these things could be effected by magic art, and what was the nature of that thing, Simon began thus to explain it to us as his associates. `I have, 'said he, `made the soul of a boy, unsullied[1] and violently slain, and invoked by unutterable adjurations[2], to assist me; and by it all is done that I command.' `But, 'said I `is it possible for a soul to do these things? 'He answered: `I would have you know this, that the soul of man holds the next place after God, when once it is set free from the darkness of his body. And immediately it acquires prescience: wherefore it is invoked for necromancy.' Then I answered: `Why, then, do not the souls of persons who are slain take vengeance on their slayers? "Do you not remember, 'said he, `that I told you, that when it goes out of the body it acquires knowledge of the future? "I remember, 'said I. `Well, then, 'said he, `as soon as it goes out of the body, it immediately knows that there is a judgment to come, and that every one shall suffer punishment for those evils that he hath done; and therefore they are unwilling to take vengeance on their slayers, because they themselves are enduring torments for their own evil deeds which they had done here, and they know that severer punishments await them in the judgment. Moreover, they are not permitted by the angels who preside over them to go out, or to do anything.' `Then' I replied, `if the angels do not permit them to come hither, or to do what they please, how can the souls obey the magician who invokes them? "It is not, 'said he, `that they grant indulgence to the souls that are willing to come: but when

---

[1] Spotlessly clean and fresh, free from blemishes.
[2] An earnest, solemn appeal.

Source: Dictionary.com Unabridged (v 1.1).

the presiding angels are adjured by one greater than themselves, they have the excuse of our violence who adjure them, to permit the souls which we invoke to go out: for they do not sin who suffer violence, but we who impose necessity upon them.' Thereupon Niceta, not able longer to refrain, hastily answered, as indeed I also was about to do, only I wished first to get information from him on several points; but, as I said, Niceta, anticipating me, said: `And do you not fear the day of judgment, who do violence to angels, and invoke souls, and deceive men, and bargain for divine honor to yourself from then? And how do you persuade us that there shall be no judgment, as some of the Jews confess, and that souls are not immortal, as many suppose, though you see them with your very eyes, and receive from them assurance of the divine judgment?'"

Chapter XIV.-Simon Magus, Professes to Be God.

"At those sayings of his Simon grew pale; but after a little, recollecting himself, he thus answered: `Do not think that I am a man of your race. I am neither magician, nor lover of Luna, nor son of Antonius. For before my mother Rachel and he came together, she, still a virgin, conceived me, while it was in my power to be either small or great, and to appear as a man among men. Therefore I have chosen you first as my friends, for the purpose of trying you, that I may place you first in my heavenly and unspeakable places when I shall have proved you. Therefore I have pretended to be a man, that I might more clearly ascertain if you cherish entire affection towards me.' But when I heard that, judging him indeed to be a wretch, yet wondering at his impudence; and blushing for him, and at the same time fearing lest he should attempt some evil against us, I beckoned to Niceta to feign for a little along with me, and said to him: `Be not angry with us, corruptible men, O thou incorruptible God, but rather accept our affection, and our mind willing to know who God is; for we did not till now know who thou art, nor did we perceive that thou art he whom we were seeking.'"

Chapter XV.-Simon Magus, Professed to Have Made a Boy of Air.

"As we spoke these and such like words with looks suited to the occasion, this most vain fellow believed that we were deceived; and being thereby the more elated, he added also this: `I shall now be propitious[1] to you, for the affection which you bear towards me as God; for you loved me while you did not know me, and were seeking me in ignorance. But I would not have you doubt that this is truly to be God, when one is able to become small or great as he pleases; for I am able to appear to man in whatever manner I please. Now, then, I shall begin to unfold to you what is true. Once on a time, I, by my power, turning air into water, and water again into blood, and solidifying it into flesh, formed a new human creature-a boy-and produced a much nobler work than God the Creator. For He created a man from the earth, but I from air-a far more difficult matter; and again I unmade him and restored him to air, but not until I had placed his picture and image in my bed-chamber, as a proof and memorial of my work.' Then we understood that he spake concerning that boy, whose soul, after he had been slain by violence, he made use of for those services which he required."

Chapter XVI.-Simon Magus: Hopelessness of His Case.

But Peter, hearing these things, said with tears: "Greatly do I wonder at the infinite patience of God, and, on the other hand, at the audacity of human rashness in some. For what further reason can be found to persuade Simon that God judges the unrighteous, since he persuades himself that he employs the obedience of souls for the service of his crimes? But, in truth, he is deluded by demons. Yet, although he is sure by these very things that souls are immortal, and are judged for the deeds which they have done, and although he thinks that he really sees those things which we believe by faith; though, as I said, he is deluded

---

[1] Favorably inclined; disposed to bestow favors or forgive.
Source: Dictionary.com Unabridged (v 1.1).

by demons, yet he thinks that he sees the very substance of the soul. How shall such a man, I say, be brought to confess either that he acts wickedly while he occupies such an evil position, or that he is to be judged for those things which he hath done, who, knowing the judgment of God, despises it, and shows himself an enemy to God, and dares commit such horrid things? Wherefore it is certain, my brethren, that some oppose the truth and religion of God, not because it appears to them that reason can by no means stand with faith, but because they are either involved in excess of wickedness, or prevented by their own evils, or elated by the swelling of their heart, so that they do not even believe those things which they think that they see with their own eyes."

Chapter XVII.-Men Enemies to God.

"But, inasmuch as inborn affection towards God the Creator seemed to suffice for salvation to those who loved Him, the enemy studies to pervert this affection in men, and to render them hostile and ungrateful to their Creator. For I call heaven and earth to witness, that if God permitted the enemy to rage as much as he desires, all men should have perished long ere now; but for His mercy's sake God doth not suffer him. But if men would turn their affection towards God, all would doubtless be saved, even if for some faults they might seem to be corrected for righteousness But now the most of men have been made enemies of God, whose hearts the wicked one has entered, and has turned aside towards himself the affection which God the Creator had implanted in them, that they might have it towards Him. But of the rest, who seemed for a time to be watchful, the enemy, appearing in a phantasy of glory and splendor, and promising them certain great and mighty things, has caused their mind and heart to wander away from God; yet it is for some just reason that he is permitted to accomplish these things."

Chapter XVIII.-Responsibility of Men.

"To this Aquila answered: "How, then, are men in fault, if the wicked one, transforming himself into the brightness of light, promises to men greater things than the Creator Himself does? "Then Peter answered: "I think," says he "that nothing is more unjust than this; and now listen while I tell you how unjust it is. If your son, whom you have trained and nourished with all care, and brought to man's estate, should be ungrateful to you, and should leave you and go to another, whom perhaps he may have seen to be richer, and should show to him the honor which he owed to you, and, through hope of greater profit, should deny his birth, and refuse you your paternal rights, would this seem to you right or wicked? "Then Aquila answered: "It is manifest to all that it would be wicked." Then Peter said: "If you say that this would be wicked among men, how much more so is it in the case of God, who, above all men, is worthy of honor from men; whose benefits we not only enjoy, but by whose means and power it is that we began to be when we were not, and whom, if we please, we shall obtain from Him to be for ever in blessedness! In order, therefore, that the unfaithful may be distinguished from the faithful, and the pious from the impious, it has been permitted to the wicked one to use those arts by which the affections of every one towards the true Father may be proved. But if there were in truth some strange God, were it right to leave our own God, who created us, and who is our Father and our Maker, and to pass over to another? ""God forbid!" said Aquila. Then said Peter: "How, then, shall we say that the wicked one is the cause of our sin, when this is done by permission of God, that those may be proved and condemned in the day of judgment, who, allured by greater promises, have abandoned their duty towards their true Father and Creator; while those who have kept the faith and the love of their own Father, even with poverty, if so it has befallen, and with tribulation, may enjoy heavenly gifts and immortal dignities in His kingdom But we shall expound these things more carefully at another time. Meantime I desire to know what Simon did after this."

Chapter XIX.-Disputation Begun.

And Niceta answered: "When he perceived that we had found him out, having spoken to one another concerning his crimes we left him, and came to Zacchaeus, telling him those same things which we have now told to you. But he, receiving us most kindly, and instructing us concerning the faith of our Lord Jesus Christ, enrolled us in the number of the faithful." When Niceta had done speaking, Zacchaeus, who had gone out a little before, entered, saying, "It is time, O Peter, that yon proceed to the disputation; for a great crowd, collected in the court of the house, is awaiting you, in the midst of whom stands Simon, supported by many attendants." Then Peter, when he heard this, ordering me to withdraw for the sake of prayer (for I had not yet been washed from the sins which I had committed in ignorance), said to the rest, "Brethren, let its pray that God, for His unspeakable mercy through His Christ, would help me going out on behalf of the salvation of men who have been created by Him." Having said this, and having prayed, he went forth to the court of the house, in which a great multitude of people were assembled; and when he saw them all looking intently on him in profound silence, and Simon the magician standing in the midst of them like a standard-bearer, he began in manner following.

Chapter XX.-The Kingdom of God and His Righteousness.

"Peace be to all of you who are prepared to give your right hands to truth: for whosoever are obedient to it seem indeed themselves to confer some favor upon God; whereas they do themselves obtain from Him the gift of His greatest bounty, walking in His paths of righteousness. Wherefore the first duty of all is to inquire into the righteousness of God and His kingdom; His righteousness, that we may be taught to act rightly; His kingdom, that we may know what is the reward appointed for labor and patience; in which kingdom there is indeed a bestowal of eternal good things upon the good, but upon those who have acted contrary to the will of God, a worthy infliction of penalties in proportion to the doings of every one. It becomes you, therefore, whilst you are here,-that is, whilst you are in the present life,-to ascertain the will of God, while there is opportunity also of doing it. For if any one, before he amends his doings, wishes to investigate concerning things which he cannot discover, such investigation will be foolish and ineffectual. For the time is short, and the judgment of God shall be occupied with deeds, not questions. Therefore before all things let us inquire into this, what or in what manner we must act that we may merit to obtain eternal life.

Chapter XXI.-Righteousness the Way to the Kingdom.

"For if we occupy the short time of this life with vain and useless questions, we shall without doubt go into the presence of God empty and void of good works, when, as I have said, our works shall be brought into judgment. For everything has its own time and place. This is the place, this the time of works; the world to come, that of recompenses. That we may not therefore be entangled, by changing the order of places and times, let us inquire, in the first place, what is the righteousness of God; so that, like persons going to set out on a journey, we may be filled with good works as with abundant provision, so that we may be able to come to the kingdom of God, as to a very great city. For to those who think aright, God is manifest even by the operations of the world which He has made, using the evidence of His creation; and therefore, since there ought to be no doubt about God, we have now to inquire only about His righteousness and His kingdom. But if our mind suggest to us to make any inquiry concerning secret and hidden things before we inquire into the works of righteousness, we ought to render to ourselves a reason, because if acting well we shall merit to obtain salvation: then, going to God chaste and clean, we shall be filled with the Holy Spirit, and shall know all things that are secret and hidden, without any caviling[1] of questions; whereas now,

---

[1] To raise irritating and trivial objections; find fault with unnecessarily.
Source: Dictionary.com Unabridged (v 1.1).

even if any one should spend the whole of his life in inquiring into these things, he not only shall not be able to find them, but shall involve himself in greater errors, because he did not first enter through the way of righteousness, and strive to reach the haven of life."

Chapter XXII.-Righteousness; What It is.

"And therefore I advise that His righteousness be first inquired into, that, pursuing our journey through it, and placed in the way of truth, we may be able to find the true Prophet, running not with swiftness of foot, but with goodness of works, and that, enjoying His guidance, we may be under no danger of mistaking the way. For if under His guidance we shall merit to enter that city to which we desire to come, all things concerning which we now inquire we shall see with our eyes, being made, as it were, heirs of all things. Understand, therefore, that the way is this course of our life; the travelers are those who do good works; the gate is the true Prophet, of whom we speak; the city is the kingdom in which dwells the Almighty Father, whom only those can see who are of pure heart. Let us not then think the labor of this journey hard, because at the end of it there shall be rest. For the true Prophet Himself also from the beginning of the world, through the course of time, hastens to rest. For He is present with us at all times; and if at any time it is necessary, He appears and corrects us, that He may bring to eternal life those who obey Him. Therefore this is my judgment, as also it is the pleasure of the true Prophet, that inquiry should first be made concerning righteousness, by those especially who profess that they know God. If therefore any one has anything to propose which he thinks better, let him speak; and when he has spoken, let him hear, but with patience and quietness: for in order to this at the first, by way of salutation, I prayed for peace to you all."

Chapter XXIII.-Simon Refuses Peace.

To this Simon answered: "We have no need of your peace; for if there be peace and concord, we shall not be able to make any advance towards the discovery of truth. For robbers and debauchees have peace among themselves, and every wickedness agrees with itself; and if we have met with this view, that for the sake of peace we should give assent to all that is said, we shall confer no benefit upon the hearers; but on the contrary, we shall impose upon them, and shall depart friends. Wherefore, do not invoke peace, but rather battle, which is the mother of peace; and if you can, exterminate errors. And do not seek for friendship obtained by unfair admissions; for this I would have you know, above all, that when two fight with each other, then there will be peace when one has been defeated and has fallen. And therefore fight as best you can, and do not expect peace without war, which is impossible; or if it can be attained, show us how."

Chapter XXIV.-Peter's Explanation.

To this Peter answered: "Hear with all attention, O men, what we say. Let us suppose that this world is a great plain, and that from two states, whose kings are at variance with each other, two generals were sent to fight: and suppose the general of the good king gave this counsel, that both armies should without bloodshed submit to the authority of the better king, whereby all should be safe without danger; but that the opposite general should say, No, but we must fight; that not he who is worthy, but who is stronger, may reign, with those who shall escape;-which, I ask you, would you rather choose? I doubt not but that you would give your hands to the better king, with the safety of all. And I do not now wish, as Simon says that I do, that assent should be given, for the sake of peace, to those things that are spoken amiss but that truth be sought for with quietness and order.

Chapter XXV.-Principles on Which the Discussion Should Be Conducted.

"For some, in the contest of disputations, when they perceive that their error is confuted, immediately begin, for the sake of making good their retreat, to create a disturbance, and to stir up strife, that it may not be manifest to all that they are defeated; and therefore I frequently entreat that the investigation of the matter in dispute may be conducted with all patience and quietness, so that if perchance anything seem to be not rightly spoken, it may be allowed to go back over it, and explain it more distinctly. For sometimes a thing may be spoken in one way and heard in another, while it is either advanced too obscurely, or not attended to with sufficient care; and on this account I desire that our conversation should be conducted patiently, so that neither should the one snatch it away from the other, nor should the unseasonable speech of one contradicting interrupt the speech of the other; and that we should not cherish the desire of finding fault, but that we should be allowed, as I have said, to go over again what has not been clearly enough spoken, that by fairest examination the knowledge of the truth may become clearer. For we ought to know, that if any one is conquered by the truth, it is not he that is conquered, but the ignorance which is in him, which is the worst of all demons; so that he who can drive it out receives the palm of salvation. For it is our purpose to benefit the hearers, not that we may conquer badly, but that we may be well conquered for the acknowledgment of the truth. For if our speech be actuated by the desire of seeking the truth, even although we shall speak anything imperfectly through human frailty, God in His unspeakable goodness will fill up secretly in the understandings of the hearers those things that are lacking. For He is righteous; and according to the purpose of every one, He enables some to find easily what they seek, while to others He renders even that obscure which is before their eyes. Since, then, the way of God is the way of peace, let us with peace seek the things which are God's. If any one has anything to advance in answer to this, let him do so; but if there is no one who wishes to answer, I shall begin to speak, and I myself shall bring forward what another may object to me, and shall refute it."

Chapter XXVI.-Simon's Interruption.

When therefore Peter had begun to continue his discourse, Simon, interrupting his speech, said: "Why do you hasten to speak whatever you please? I understand your tricks. You wish to bring forward those matters whose explanation you have well studied, that you may appear to the ignorant crowd to be speaking well; but I shall not allow you this subterfuge. Now therefore, since you promise, as a brave man, to answer to all that any one chooses to bring forward, be pleased to answer me in the first place." Then Peter said: "I am ready, only provided that our discussion may be with peace." Then Simon said: "Do not you see, O simpleton, that in pleading for peace *you act* in opposition to your Master, and that what you propose is not suitable to him who promises that he will overthrow ignorance? Or, if you are right in asking peace from the audience, then your Master was wrong in saying, `I have not come to send peace on earth, but a sword.' For either you say well, and he not well; or else, if your Master said well, then you not at all well: for you do not understand that your statement is contrary to his, whose disciple you profess yourself to be."

Chapter XXVII.-Questions and Answers.

Then Peter: "Neither He who sent me did amiss in sending a sword upon the earth, nor do I act contrary to Him in asking peace of the hearers. But you both unskillfully and rashly find fault with what you do not understand: for you have heard that the Master came not to send peace on earth; but that He also said, `Blessed are the peace-makers, for they shall be called the very sons of God, ' you have not heard. Wherefore my sentiments are not different from those of the Master when I recommend peace, to the keepers of which He assigned blessedness." Then Simon said: "In your desire to answer for your Master, O Peter, you have brought a much more serious charge against him, if he himself came not to make peace, yet enjoined upon others to keep it. Where, then, is the consistency of that other saying of his, `it is enough for the disciple that he be as his master?'"

Chapter XXVIII.-Consistency of Christ's Teaching.

To this Peter answered: "Our Master, who was the true Prophet, and ever mindful of Himself, neither contradicted Himself, nor enjoined upon us anything different from what Himself practiced. For whereas He said, `I am not come to send peace on earth, but a sword; and henceforth you shall see father separated from son, son from father, husband from wife and wife from husband, mother from daughter and daughter from mother, brother from brother, father-in-law from daughter-in-law friend from friend, 'all these contain the doctrine of peace; and; will tell you how. At the beginning of His preaching, as wishing to invite and lead all to salvation, and induce them to bear patiently labors and trials, He blessed the poor, and promised that they should obtain the kingdom of heaven for their endurance of poverty, in order that under the influence of such a hope they might bear with peace[1] the weight of poverty, despising covetousness; for covetousness is one, and the greatest, of most pernicious sins. But He promised also that the hungry and the thirsty should be satisfied with the eternal blessings of righteousness, in order that they might bear poverty patiently, and not be led by it to undertake any unrighteous work. In like manner also, He said that the pure in heart are blessed, and that thereby they should see God, in order that every one desiring so great a good might keep himself from evil and polluted thoughts."

Chapter XXIX.-Peace and Strife.

"Thus, therefore, our Master, inviting His disciples to patience, impressed upon them that the blessing of peace

---

[1] Original word used in the text was: **equanimity**.

was also to be preserved with the labor of patience. But, on the other hand, He mourned over those who lived in riches and luxury, who bestowed nothing upon the poor; proving that they must render an account, because they did not pity their neighbors, even when they were in poverty, whom they ought to love as themselves. And by such sayings as these He brought some indeed to obey Him, but others He rendered hostile. The believers therefore, and the obedient, He charges to have peace among themselves, and says to them, `Blessed are the peacemakers, for they shall be called the very sons of God.' But to those who not only did not believe, but set themselves in opposition to His doctrine, He proclaims the war of the word and of confutation, and says that `henceforth ye shall see son separated from father, and husband from wife, and daughter from mother, and brother from brother, and daughter-in-law from mother-in-law, and a man's foes shall be they of his own house.' For in every house, when there begins to be a difference betwixt believer and unbeliever, there is necessarily a contest: the unbelievers, on the one hand. fighting against the faith; and the believers on the other, confuting the old error and the vices of sins in them."

Chapter XXX.-Peace to the Sons of Peace.

"In like manner, also, during the last period of His teaching, He wages war against the scribes and Pharisees, charging them with evil deeds and unsound doctrine, and with hiding the key of knowledge which they had handed down to them from Moses, by which the gate of the heavenly kingdom might be opened. But when our Master sent us forth to preach, He commanded as, that into whatsoever city or house we should enter, we should say, `Peace be to this house.' `And if, 'said He, `a son of peace be there, your peace shall come upon him; but if there be not, your peace shall return to you.' Also that, going out from that house or city, we should shake off upon them the very dust which adhered to our feet. `But it shall be more tolerable for the land of Sodom and Gomorrah in the day of judgment than for that city or house.' This indeed He commanded to be done at length, if first the word of truth be preached in the city or house, whereby they who receive the faith of the truth may become sons of peace and sons of God; and those who will not receive it may be convicted as enemies of peace and of God."

Chapter XXXI.-Peace and War.

"Thus, therefore, we, observing the commands of our Master, first offer peace to our hearers, that the way of salvation may be known without any tumult. But if any one do not receive the words of peace, nor acquiesce in the truth, we know how to direct against him the war of the word, and to rebuke him sharply by confuting his ignorance and charging home upon him his sins. Therefore of necessity we offer peace, that if any one is a son of peace, our peace may come upon him; but from him who makes himself an enemy of peace, our peace shall return to ourselves. We do not therefore, as you say, propose peace by agreement with the wicked, for indeed we should straightway have given you the right hand; but only in order that, through our discussing quietly and patiently, it might be more easily ascertained by the hearers which is the true speech. But if you differ and disagree with yourself, how shall you stand? He must of necessity fall who is divided in himself; `for every kingdom divided against itself shall not stand.' If you have aught to say to this, say on."

Chapter XXXII.-Simon's Challenge.

Then said Simon: "I am astonished at your folly. For you so propound the words of your Master, as if it were held to be certain concerning him that he is a prophet; while I can very easily prove that he often contradicted himself. In short, I shall refute you from those words which you have yourself brought forward. For you say, that he said that every kingdom or every city divided in itself shall not stand; and elsewhere you say, that he said that he would send a sword, that he might separate those who are in one house, so that son shall be divided from father, daughter from mother, brother from brother; so that if there be five in one house, three shall be divided against two, and two against three. if, then, everything that is divided falls, he who makes divisions furnishes causes of falling; and if he is such, assuredly he is wicked. Answer this if you can."

Chapter XXXIII.-Authority.

Then Peter: "Do not rashly take exception, O Simon, against the things which you do not understand. In the first place, I shall answer your assertion, that I set forth the words of my Master, and from them resolve matters about which there is still doubt. Our Lord, when He sent us apostles to preach, enjoined us to teach all nations the things which were committed to us. We cannot therefore speak those things as they were spoken by Himself. For our commission is not to *speak*, but to *teach* those things, and from them to show how every one of them rests upon truth. Nor, again, are we permitted to speak anything of our own. For we are sent; and of necessity he who is sent delivers the message as he has been ordered, and sets forth the will of the sender. For if I should speak anything different from what He who sent me enjoined me, I should be a false apostle, not saying what I am commanded to say, but what seems good to myself. Whoever does this, evidently wishes to show himself to be better than he is by whom he is sent, and without doubt is a traitor. If, on the contrary, he keeps by the things that he is commanded, and brings forward most clear assertions of them, it will appear that he is accomplishing the work of an apostle; and it is by striving to fulfill this that I displease you. Blame me not, therefore, because I bring forward the words of Him who sent me. But if there is aught in them that is not fairly spoken, you have liberty to confute me; but this can in no wise be done, for He is a prophet, and cannot be contrary to Himself. But if you do not think that He is a prophet, let this be first inquired into."

Chapter XXXIV.-Order of Proof.

Then said Simon: "I have no need to learn this from you, but how these things agree with one another. For if he shall be shown to be inconsistent, he shall be proved at the same time not to be a prophet." Then says Peter: "But if I first show Him to be a prophet, it will follow that what seems to be inconsistency is not such. For no one can be proved to be a prophet merely by consistency, because it is possible for many to attain this; but if consistency does not make a prophet, much more inconsistency does not. Because, therefore, there are many things which to some seem inconsistent, which yet have consistency in them on a more profound investigation; as also other things which seem to have consistency, but which, being more carefully discussed, are found to be inconsistent; for this reason I do not think there is any better way to judge of these things than to ascertain in the first instance whether He be a prophet who has spoken those things which appear to be inconsistent. For it is evident that, if He be found a prophet, those things which seem to be contradictory must have consistency, but are misunderstood. Concerning these things, therefore, proofs will be properly demanded. For we apostles are sent to expound the sayings and affirm the judgments of Him who has sent us; but we are not commissioned to say anything of our own, but to unfold the truth, as I have said, of His words."

Chapter XXXV.-How Error Cannot Stand with Truth.

Then Simon said: "Instruct us, therefore, how it can be consistent that he who causes divisions, which divisions cause those who are divided to fall, can either seem to be good, or to have come for the salvation of men." Then Peter said: "I will tell you how our Master said that every, kingdom and every house divided against itself cannot stand; and whereas He Himself did this, see how it makes for salvation. By the word of truth He certainly divides the kingdom of the world, which is founded in error, and every home in it, that error may fall, and truth may reign. But if it happen to any house, that error, being introduced by any one, divides the truth, then, where error has gained a footing, it is certain that truth cannot stand." Then Simon said: "But it is uncertain whether your master divides error or truth." Then Peter: "That belongs to another question; but if you are agreed that everything which is divided falls, it remains that I show, if only you will hear in peace, that our Jesus has divided and dispelled error by teaching truth."

Chapter XXXVI.-Altercation.

Then said Simon: "Do not repeat again and again your talk of peace, but expound briefly what it is that you think or believe." Peter answered: "Why are you afraid of hearing frequently of peace? for do you not know that peace is the perfection of law? For wars and disputes spring from sins; and where there is no sin, there is peace of soul; but where there is peace, truth is found in disputations, righteousness in works." Then Simon: "You seem to me not to be able to profess what you think." Then Peter: "I shall speak, but according to my own judgment, not under constraint of your tricks. For I desire that what is salutary[1] and profitable be brought to the knowledge of all and therefore I shall not delay to state it as briefly as possible. There is one God; and He is the creator of the world, a righteous judge, rendering to every one at some time or other according to his deeds. But now for the assertion of these things I know that countless thousands of words can be called forth."

Chapter XXXVII.-Simon's Subtlety.

Then Simon said: "I admire, indeed, the quickness of your wit, yet I do not embrace the error of your faith. For you have wisely foreseen that you may be contradicted; and you have even politely confessed, that for the assertion of these things countless thousands of words will be called forth, for no one agrees with the profession of your faith. In short, as

---

[1] Favorable to or promoting health, conducive to some beneficial purpose. *Source: Dictionary.com Unabridged (v 1.1)*.

to there being one God, and the world being His work, who can receive this doctrine? Neither, I think, any one of the Pagans, even if he be an unlearned man, and certainly no one of the philosophers; but not even the rudest and most wretched of the Jews, nor I myself, who am well acquainted with their law." Then Peter said: "Put aside the opinions of those who are not here, and tell us face to face what is your own." Then Simon said: "I can state what I really think; but this consideration makes me reluctant to do so, that if I say what is neither acceptable to you, nor seems right to this unskilled rabble, you indeed, as confounded, will straightway shut your ears, that they may not he polluted with blasphemy, indeed[1], and will take to flight because you cannot find an answer; while the unreasoning populace will assent to you, and embrace you as one teaching those things which are commonly received among them; and will curse me, as professing things new and unheard of, and instilling my error into the minds of others."

Chapter XXXVIII.-Simon's Creed.

Then Peter: "Are not you making use of long preambles, as you accused us of doing, because you have no truth to bring forward? For if you have, begin without circumlocution[2], if you have so much confidence. And if, indeed, what you say be displeasing to any one of the hearers, he will withdraw; and those who remain shall be compelled by your assertion to approve what is true. Begin, therefore, to expound what seemeth to you to be right." Then Simon said: "I say that there are many gods; but that there is one incomprehensible and unknown to all, and that He is the God of all these gods." Then Peter answered: "This God whom you assert to be incomprehensible and unknown to all, can you prove His existence from the Scriptures of the Jews, which are

---

[1] Original word used in the text was: **forsooth**.
[2] A roundabout or indirect way of speaking; the use of more words than necessary to express an idea.
Source: Dictionary.com Unabridged (v 1.1).

held to be of authority, or from some others of which we are all ignorant, or from the Greek authors, or from your own writings? Certainly you are at liberty to speak from whatever writings you please, yet so that you first show that they are prophetic; for so their authority will be held without question."

Chapter XXXIX.-Argument for Polytheism.

Then Simon said: "I shall make use of assertions from the law of the Jews only. For it is manifest to all who take interest in religion, that this law is of universal authority, yet that every one receives the understanding of this law according to his own judgment. For it has so been written by Him who created the world, that the faith of things is made to depend upon it. Whence, whether any one wishes to bring forward truth, or any one to bring forward falsehood, no assertion will be received without this law. Inasmuch, therefore, as my knowledge is most fully in accordance with the law, I rightly declared that there are many gods, of whom one is more eminent than the rest, and incomprehensible, even He who is God of gods. But that there are many gods, the law itself informs me. For, in the first place, *it says this in the passage* where one in the figure of a serpent speaks to Eve, the first woman, `On the day ye eat of the tree of the knowledge of good and evil, ye shall be as gods, ' that is, as those who made man; and after they have tasted of the tree, God Himself testifies, saying to the rest of the gods, `Behold, Adam is become as one of us; ' thus, therefore, it is manifest that there were many gods engaged in the making of man. Also, whereas at the first God said to the other gods, `Let us make man after our image and likeness; ' also His saying, `Let us drive him out; ' and again, `Come, let us go down, and confound their language; ' all these things indicate that there are many gods. But this also is written, `Thou shalt not curse the gods, nor curse the chief of thy people; and again this writing, `God alone led them, and there was no strange god with them, shows that there are many gods. There are also many other testimonies which might be adduced from the law, not only obscure, but plain, by which it is taught that there are many gods. One of these was chosen by lot, that he might be the god of the Jews. But it is not of him that I speak, but of that God who is also his God, whom even the Jews themselves did not know. For he is not their God, but the God of those who know him."

Chapter XL.-Peter's Answer.

When Peter had heard this, he answered: "Fear nothing, Simon: for, behold, we have neither shut our ears, nor fled; but we answer with words of truth to those things which you have spoken falsely, asserting this first, that there is one God, even the God of the Jews, who is the only God, the Creator of heaven and earth, who is also the God of all those whom you call gods. If, then, I shall show you that none is superior to Him, but that He Himself is above all, you will confess that your error is above all." Then Simon said: "Why, indeed, though I should be unwilling to confess it, would not the hearers who stand by charge me with unwillingness to profess the things that are true?"

Chapter XLI.-The Answer, Continued.

"Listen, then," says Peter, "that you may know, first of all, that even if there are many gods, as you say, they are subject to the God of the Jews, to whom no one is equal, than whom no one can be greater; for it is written that the prophet Moses thus spoke to the Jews: `The Lord your God is the God of gods, and the Lord of lords, the great God.' Thus, although there are many that are called gods, yet He who is the God of the Jews is alone called the God of gods. For not every one that is called God is necessarily God. Indeed, even Moses is called a god to Pharaoh, and it is certain that he was a man; and judges were called gods, and it is evident that they were mortal. The idols also of the Gentiles are called gods, and we all know that they are not; but this has been inflicted as a punishment on the wicked, that because they would not acknowledge the true God, they should regard as God whatever form or image should occur to them. Because they refused to receive the knowledge of the One who, as I said, is God of all, therefore it is permitted to them to have as gods those who can do nothing for their worshippers. For what can either dead images or living creatures confer upon men, since the power of all things is with One?

Chapter XLII.-Guardian Angels.

"Therefore the name *God* is applied in three ways: either because he to whom it is given is truly God, or because he is the servant of him who is truly; and for the honor of the sender, that his authority may be full, he that is sent is called by the name of him who sends, as is often done in respect of angels: for when they appear to a man, if he is a wise and intelligent man, he asks the name of him who appears to him, that he may acknowledge at once the honor of the sent, and the authority of the sender. For every nation has an angel, to whom God has committed the government of that nation; and when one of these appears, although he be thought and called God by those over whom he presides, yet, being asked, he does not give such testimony to himself. For the Most High God, who alone holds the power of all things, has divided all the nations of the earth into seventy-two parts, and over these He hath appointed angels as princes. But to the one among the archangels who is greatest, was committed the government of those who, before all others, received the worship and knowledge of the Most High God. But holy men also, as we have said, are made gods to the wicked, as having received the power of life and death over them, as we mentioned above with respect to Moses and the judges. Wherefore it is also written concerning them, 'Thou shalt not curse the gods, and thou shalt not curse the prince of thy people.' Thus the princes of the several nations are called gods. But Christ is God of princes, who is Judge of all. Therefore neither angels, nor men, nor any creature, can be truly gods, forasmuch as they are placed under authority, being created and changeable: angels, for they were not, and are; men, for they are mortal; and every creature, for it is capable of dissolution, if only He dissolve it who made it. And therefore He alone is the true God, who not only Himself lives, but also bestows life upon others, which He can also take away when it pleases Him.

Chapter XLIII.-No God But Jehovah.

"Wherefore the Scripture exclaims in name of the God of the Jews, saying, `Behold, behold, seeing that I am God, and there is none else besides me, I will kill, and I will make alive; I will smite, and I will heal; and there is none who can deliver out of my hands.' See therefore how, by some ineffable virtue, the Scripture, opposing the future errors of those who should affirm that either in heaven or on earth there is any other god besides Him who is the God of the Jews, decides thus: `The Lord your God is one God, in heaven above, and in the earth beneath; and besides Him there is none else.' How, then, hast thou dared to say that there is any other God besides Him who is the God of the Jews? And again the Scripture says, `Behold, to the Lord thy God belong the heaven, and the heaven of heavens, the earth, and all things that are in them: nevertheless I have chosen your fathers, that I might love them, and you after them.' Thus that judgment is supported by the Scripture on every side, that He who created the world is the true and only God.

Chapter XLIV.-The Serpent, the Author of Polytheism.

"But even if there be others, as we have said, who are called gods, they are under the power of the God of the Jews; for thus saith the Scripture to the Jews, `The Lord our God, He is God of gods, and Lord of lords.' Him alone the Scripture also commands to be worshipped, saying, `Thou shall worship the Lord thy God, and Him only shall thou serve; ' and, `Hear, O Israel: the Lord thy God is one God.' Yea, also the saints, filled with the Spirit of God, and bedewed with the drops of His mercy, cried out, saying, `Who is like unto Thee among the gods? O Lord, who is like unto Thee?' And again, `Who is God, but the Lord; and who is God, but our Lord?' Therefore Moses, when he saw that the people were advancing, by degrees initiated them in the understanding of the monarchy and the faith of one God, as he says in the following words: 'Thou shalt not make negation of the names of other gods;' doubtless remembering with what penalty the serpent was visited, which had first named *gods*. For it is condemned to feed upon dust, and is judged worthy of such food, for this cause, that it first of all introduced the name of *gods* into the world. But if you also wish to introduce many gods, see that you partake not the serpent's doom.

Chapter XLV.-Polytheism Inexcusable.

"For be sure of this, that you shall not have us participators in this attempt; nor will we suffer ourselves to be deceived by you. For it will not serve us for an excuse in the judgment, if we say that you deceived us; because neither could it excuse the first woman, that she had unhappily believed the serpent; but she was condemned to death, because she believed badly. For this cause therefore, Moses, also commending the faith of one God to the people, says, 'Take heed to thyself, that thou be not seduced from the Lord thy God.' Observe that he makes use of the same word which the first woman also made use of in excusing herself, saying that she was seduced; but it profited her nothing. But over and above all this, even if some true prophet should arise, who should perform signs and miracles, but should wish to persuade us to worship other gods besides the God of the Jews, we should never be able to believe him. For so the divine law has taught us, handing down a secret injunction more purely by means of tradition, for thus it saith: 'If there arise among you a prophet, or one dreaming a dream, and give you signs or wonders, and these signs or wonders come to pass, and he say to you, Let us go and worship strange gods, whom ye know not; ye shall not hear the words of that prophet, nor the dream of that dreamer, because proving he hath proved you, that he may see if ye love the 'Lord your God.'

Chapter XLVI.-Christ Acknowledged the God of the Jews.

"Wherefore also our Lord, who wrought signs and wonders, preached the God of the Jews; and therefore we are right in believing what He preached. But as for you, even if you were really a prophet, and performed signs and wonders, as you promise to do, if you were to announce other gods besides Him who is the true God, it would be manifest that you were raised up as a trial to the people of God; and therefore you can by no means be believed. For He alone is the true God, who is the God of the Jews; and for this reason our Lord Jesus Christ did not teach them that they must inquire after God, for Him they knew well already, but that they must seek His kingdom and righteousness, which the scribes and Pharisees, having received the key of knowledge, had not shut in, but shut out. For if they had been ignorant of the true God, surely He would never have left the knowledge of this thing, which was the chief of all, and blamed them for small and little things, as for enlarging their fringes, and claiming the uppermost rooms in feasts, and praying standing in the highways, and such like things; which assuredly, in comparison of this great charge, ignorance of God, seem to be small and insignificant matters."

Chapter XLVII.-Simon's Cavil.

To this Simon replied: "From the words of your master I shall refute you, because even he introduces to all men a certain God who was known. For although both Adam knew the God who was his creator, and the maker of the world; and Enoch knew him, inasmuch as he was translated by him; and Noah, since he was ordered by him to construct the ark; and although Abraham, and Isaac, and Jacob, and Moses, and all, even every people and all nations, know the maker of the world, and confess him to be a God, yet your Jesus, who appeared long after the patriarchs, says: 'No one knows the Son, but the Father; neither knoweth any one the Father, but the Son, and he to whom the Son has been pleased to reveal Him.' Thus, therefore, even your Jesus confesses that there is another God, incomprehensible and unknown to all."

Chapter XLVIII.-Peter's Answer.

Then Peter says: "You do not perceive that you are making statements in opposition to yourself. For if our Jesus also knows Him whom ye call the unknown God, then He is not known by you alone. Yea, if our Jesus knows Him, then Moses also, who prophesied that Jesus should come, assuredly could not himself be ignorant of Him. For he was a prophet; and he who prophesied of the Son doubtless knew the Father. For if it is in the option of the Son to reveal the Father to whom He will, then the Son, who has been with the Father from the beginning, and through all generations, as He revealed the Father to Moses, so also to the other prophets; but if this be so, it is evident that the Father has not been unknown to any of them. But how could the Father be revealed to you, who do not believe in the Son, since the Father is known to none except him to whom the Son is pleased to reveal Him? But the Son reveals the Father to those who honor the Son as they honor the Father."

Chapter XLIX.-The Supreme Light.

Then Simon said: "Remember that you said that God has a son, which is doing Him wrong; for how can He have a son, unless He is subject to passions, like men or animals? But on these points there is not time now to show your profound folly, for I hasten to make a statement concerning the immensity of the supreme light; and so now listen. My opinion is that there is a certain power of immense and ineffable light, whose greatness may be held to be incomprehensible, of which power even the maker of the world is ignorant, and Moses the lawgiver, and Jesus your master."

Chapter L.-Simon's Presumption.

Then Peter: "Does it not seem to you to be madness, that any one should take upon himself to assert that there is another God than the God of all; and should say that he supposes there is a certain power, and should presume to affirm this to others, before he himself is sure of what he says? Is any one so rash as to believe your words, of which he sees that you are yourself doubtful, and to admit that there is a certain power unknown to God the Creator, and to Moses, and the prophets, and the law, and even to Jesus our Master, which power is so good, that it will not make itself known to any but to one only, and that one such an one as thou! Then, further, if that is a new power, why does it not confer upon us some new sense, in addition to those five which we possess, that by that new sense, bestowed upon us by it, we may be able to receive and understand itself which is new? Or if it cannot bestow such a sense upon us, how has it bestowed it upon you? Or if it has revealed itself to you, why not also to us? But if you of yourself understand things which not even the prophets were able to perceive or understand, come, tell us what each one of us is thinking now; for if there is such a spirit in you that you know those things which are above the heavens, which are unknown to all, and incomprehensible by all, much more easily do you know the thoughts of men upon the earth. But if you cannot know the thoughts of us who are standing here, how can you say that you know those things which, you assert, are known to none? "

Chapter LI.-The Sixth Sense.

"But believe me, that you could never know what light is unless you had received both vision and understanding from light itself; so also in other things. Hence, having received understanding, you are framing in imagination something greater and more sublime, as if dreaming, but deriving all your hints from those five senses, to whose Giver you are unthankful. But be sure of this, that until you find some new sense which is beyond those five which we all enjoy, you cannot assert the existence of a new God." Then Simon answered: "Since all things that exist are in accordance with those five senses, that power which is more excellent than all cannot add anything new." Then Peter said: "It is false; for there is also a sixth sense, namely that of foreknowledge: for those five senses are capable of knowledge, but the sixth is that of foreknowledge: and this the prophets possessed. How, then, can you know a God who is unknown to all, who do not know the prophetic sense, which is that of prescience? "Then Simon began to say: "This power of which I speak, incomprehensible and more excellent than all, ay, even than that God who made the world, neither any of the angels has known, nor of the demons, nor of the Jews, nay, nor any creature which subsists by means of God the creator. How, then, could that creator's law teach me that which the creator himself did not know, since neither did the law itself know it, that it might teach it? "

Chapter LII.-Reductio a.d. Absurdum.

Then Peter said: "I wonder how you have been able to learn more from the law than the law was able to know or to teach; and how you say that you adduce[1] proofs from the law of those things which you are pleased to assert, when you declare that neither the law, nor He who gave the law- that is, the Creator of the world-knows those things of which you speak! But this also I wonder at, how you, who alone know these things, should be standing here now with us all, circumscribed by the limits of this small court." Then Simon, seeing Peter and all the people laughing, said: "Do you laugh, Peter, while so great and lofty matters are under discussion? "Then said Peter: "Be not enraged, Simon, for we are doing no more than keeping our promise: for we are neither shutting our ears, as you said, nor did we take to flight as soon as we heard you propound your unutterable things; but we have not even stirred from the place. For indeed you do not even propound things that

---

[1] To bring forward in argument or as evidence.
Source: Dictionary.com Unabridged (v 1.1).

have any resemblance to truth, which might to a certain extent frighten us. Yet, at all events, disclose to us the meaning of this saying, how from the law you have learned of a God whom the law itself does not know, and of whom He who gave the law is ignorant." Then Simon said: "If you have done laughing, I shall prove it by clear assertions." Then Peter said: "Assuredly I shall give over, that I may learn from you how you have learned from the law what neither the law nor the God of the law Himself knows."

Chapter LIII.-Simon's Blasphemy.

Then says Simon: "Listen: it is manifest to all, and ascertained in a manner of which no account can be given, that there is one God, who is better than all, from whom all that is took its beginning; whence also of necessity, all things that are after him are subject to him, as the chief and most excellent of all. When, therefore, I had ascertained that the God who created the world, according to what the law teaches, is in many respects weak, whereas weakness is utterly incompatible with a perfect God, and I saw that he is not perfect, I necessarily concluded that there is another God who is perfect. For this God, as I have said, according to what the writing of the law teaches, is shown to be weak in many things. In the first place, because the man whom he formed was not able to remain such as be had intended him to be; and because he cannot be good who gave a law to the first man, that he should eat of all the trees of paradise, but that he should not touch the tree of knowledge; and if he should eat of it, he should die. For why should he forbid him to eat, and to know what is good and what evil, that, knowing, he might shun the evil and choose the good? But this he did not permit; and because he did eat in violation of the commandment, and discovered what is good, and learned for the sake of honor to cover his nakedness (for he perceived it to be unseemly to stand naked before his Creator), he condemns to death him who had learned to do honor to God, and curses the serpent who had shown him these things. But truly, if man was to be injured by this means, why did he place the cause of injury in paradise at all? But if that which he placed in paradise was good, it is not the part of one that is good to restrain another from good."

Chapter LIV.-How Simon Learned from the Law What the Law Does Not Teach.

"Thus then, since he who made man and the world is, according to what the law relates, imperfect, we are given to understand, without doubt, that there is another who is perfect. For it is of necessity that there be one most excellent of all, on whose account also every creature keeps its rank. Whence also I, knowing that it is every way necessary that there be some one more benignant and more powerful than that imperfect God who gave the law, understanding what is perfect from comparison of the imperfect, understood even from the Scripture that God who is not mentioned there. And in this way I was able, O Peter, to learn from the law what the law did not know. But even if the law had not given indications from which it might be gathered that the God who made the world is imperfect, it was still possible for me to infer from those evils which are done in this world, and are not corrected, either that its creator is powerless, if he cannot correct what is done amiss; or else, if he does not wish to remove the evils, that he is himself evil; but if he neither can nor will, that he is neither powerful nor good. And from this it cannot but be concluded that there is another God more excellent and more powerful than all. If you have aught to say to this, say on."

Chapter LV.-Simon's Objections Turned Against Himself.

Peter answered: "O Simon, they are wont to conceive such absurdities against God who do not read the law with the instruction of masters, but account themselves teachers, and think that they can understand the law, though he has not explained it to them who has learned of the Master. Nevertheless now, that we also may seem to follow the book of the law according to your apprehension of it;

inasmuch as you say that the creator of the world is shown to be both impotent and evil, how is it that you do not see that that power of yours, which you say is superior to all, fails and lies under the very same charges? For the very same thing may be said of it, that it is either powerless, since it does not correct those things which here are done amiss; or if it can and will not, it is evil; or if it neither can nor will, then it is both impotent and imperfect. Whence that new power of yours is not only found liable to a similar charge, but even to a worse one, if, in addition to all these things, it is believed to be, when it is not. For He who created the world, His existence is manifest by His very operation in creating the world, as you yourself also confess. But this power which you say that you alone know, affords no indication of itself, by which we might perceive, at least, that it is, and subsists."

Chapter LVI.-No God Above the Creator.

"What kind of conduct, then, would it be that we should forsake God, in whose world we live and enjoy all things necessary for life, and follow I know not whom, from whom we not only obtain no good, but cannot even know that he exists? Nor truly does he exist. For whether you call him light, and brighter than that light which we see, you borrow that very name from the Creator of the world; or whether you say that he is a substance above all, you derive from Him the idea with enlargement of speech. Whether you make mention of mind, or goodness, or life, or whatever else, you borrow the words from Him. Since, then, you have nothing new concerning that power you speak of, not only as regards understanding, but even in respect of naming him, how do you introduce a new God, for whom you cannot even find a new name? For not only is the Creator of the world called a Power, but even the ministers of His glory, and all the heavenly host. Do you not then think it better that we should follow our Creator God, as a Father who trains us and endows us as He knows how? But if, as you say, there be some God more benignant than all, it is certain that he will not be angry with us; or if he be angry, he is evil. For if our God is angry and punishes, He is not evil, but righteous, for He corrects and amends His own sons. But he who has no concern with us, if he shall punish us, how should he be good? Inflicting punishments upon us because we have not been drawn by vain imaginations to forsake our own Father and follow him, how can you assert that he is so good, when he cannot be regarded as even just? "

Chapter LVII.-Simon's Inconsistency.

Then Simon: "Do you so far err, Peter, as not to know that our souls were made by that good God, the most excellent of all, but they have been brought down as captives into this world? "To this Peter answered: "Then he is not unknown by all, as you said a little while ago; and yet how did the good God permit his souls to be taken captive, if he be a power over all?" Then Simon said: "He sent God the creator to make the world; and he, when he had made it, gave out that himself was God." Then Peter said: "Then he is not, as you said, unknown to Him who made the world; nor are souls ignorant of him, if indeed they were stolen away from him. To whom, then, can he be unknown, if both the Creator of the world know him, as having been sent by him; and all souls know him, as having been violently withdrawn from him? Then, further, I wish you would tell us whether he who sent the creator of the world did not know that he would not keep faith? For if he did not know it, then he was not prescient; while if he foreknew it, and suffered it, he is himself guilty of this deed, since he did not prevent it; but if he could not, then he is not omnipotent. But if, knowing it as good, he did not prohibit it, he is found to be better, who presumed to do that which he who sent him did not know to be good."

Chapter LVIII.-Simon's God Unjust.

Then Simon said: "He receives those who will come to him, and does them good." Peter answered: "But there is nothing new in this; for He whom you acknowledge to be the Creator of the world also does so." Then Simon: "But the good God bestows salvation if he is only acknowledged; but the creator of the world demands also that the law be fulfilled." Then said Peter: "He saves adulterers and men-slayers, if they know him; but good, and sober, and merciful persons, if they do not know him, in consequence of their having no information concerning him, he does not save! Great and good truly is he whom you proclaim, who is not so much the savior of the evil, as he is one who shows no mercy to the good." Then Simon: "It is truly very difficult for man to know him, as long as he is in the flesh; for blacker than all darkness, and heavier than all clay, is this body with which the soul is surrounded." Then says Peter: "That good God of yours demands things which are difficult; but He who is truly God seeks easier things. Let him then, since he is so good, leave us with our Father and Creator; and when once we depart from the body, and leave that darkness that you speak of, we shall more easily know Him; and then the soul shall better understand that God is its Creator, and shall remain with Him, and shall no more be harassed with diverse imaginations; nor shall wish to betake itself to another power, which is known to none but Simon only, and which is of such goodness that no one can come to it, unless he be first guilty of impiety towards his own father! I know not how this power can be called either good or just, which no one can please except by acting impiously towards him by whom he was made!"

Chapter LIX.-The Creator Our Father,

Then Simon: "It is not impious for the sake of greater profit and advantage to flee to him who is of richer glory." Then Peter: "If, as you say, it is not impious to flee to a stranger, it is at all events much more pious to remain with our own father, even if he be poor. But if you do not think it impious to leave our father, and flee to another, as being better than he; and you do not believe that our Creator will take this amiss; much more the good God will not be angry, because, when we were strangers to him, we have not fled to him, but have remained with our own Creator. Yea, I think he will rather commend us the more for this, that we have kept faith with God our Creator; for he will consider that, if we had been his creatures, we should never have been seduced by the allurements of any other to forsake him. For if any one, allured by richer promises, shall leave his own father and betake himself to a stranger, it may be that he will leave him in his turn, and go to another who shall promise him greater things, and this the rather because he is not his son, since he could leave even him who by nature was his father." Then Simon said: "But what if souls are from him, and do not know him, and he is truly their father?"

Chapter LX.-The Creator the Supreme God.

Then Peter said: "You represent him as weak enough. For if, as you say, he is more powerful than all, it can never be believed the weaker wrenched the spoils from the stronger. Or if God the Creator was able by violence to bring down souls into this world, how can it be that, when they are separated from the body and freed from the bonds of captivity, the good God shall call them to the sufferance of punishment, on the ground that they, either through his remissness or weakness, were dragged away to this place, and were involved in the body, as in the darkness of ignorance? You seem to me not to know what a father and a God is: but I could tell you both whence souls are, and when and how they were made; but it is not permitted to me now to disclose these things to you, who are in such error in respect of the knowledge of God." Then said Simon: "A time will come when you shall be sorry that you did not understand me speaking of the ineffable power." Then said Peter: "Give us then, as I have often said, as being yourself a new God, or as having yourself come down from him, some new sense, by means of which we may know that new God of whom you speak; for those five senses, which God our Creator has given us, keep faith to their own Creator, and do not perceive that there is any other God, for so their nature necessitates them."

Chapter LXI.-Imagination.

To this Simon answered: "Apply your mind to those things which I am going to say, and cause it, walking in peaceable paths, to attain to those things which I shall demonstrate. Listen now, therefore. Did you never in thought reach forth your mind into regions or islands situated far away, and remain so fixed in them, that you could not even see the people that were before you, or know where yourself were sitting, by reason of the delightfulness of those things on which yon were gazing? "And Peter said: "It is true, Simon, this has often occurred to me." Then Simon said: "In this way now reach forth your sense into heaven, yea above the heaven, and behold that there must be some place beyond the world, or outside the world, in which there is neither heaven nor earth, and where no shadow of these things produces darkness; and consequently, since there are neither bodies in it, nor darkness occasioned by bodies, there must of necessity be immense light; and consider of what sort that light must be, which is never succeeded by darkness. For if the light of this sun fills this whole world, how great do you suppose that bodiless and infinite light to be? So great, doubtless, that this light of the sun would seem to be darkness and not light, in comparison."

Chapter LXII.-Peter's Experience of Imagination.

When Simon thus spoke, Peter answered: "Now listen patiently concerning both these matters, that is, concerning the example of stretching out the senses, and concerning the immensity of light. I know that I myself, O Simon, have sometimes in thought extended my sense, as you say, into regions and islands situated afar off, and have seen them with my mind not less than if it had been with my eyes. When I was at Capernaum, occupied in the taking of fishes, and sat upon a rock, holding in my hand a hook attached to a line, and fitted for deceiving the fishes, *I was so absorbed* that I did not feel a fish adhering to it while my mind eagerly ran through my beloved Jerusalem, to which I had frequently gone up, waking, for the sake of offerings and prayers. But I was accustomed also to admire this Caesarea, hearing of it from others, and to long to see it; and I seemed to myself to see it, although I had never been in it; and I thought of it what was suitable to be thought of a great city, its gates, walls, baths, streets, lanes, markets, and the like, in accordance with what I had seen in other cities; and to such an extent was I delighted with the intentness of such inspection, that, as you said, neither saw one who was present and standing by me, nor knew where myself was sitting." Then said Simon: "Now you say well."

Chapter LXIII.-Peter's Reverie.

Then Peter: "In short, when I did not perceive, through the occupation of my mind, that I had caught a very large fish which was attached to the hook, and that although it was dragging the hook-line from my hand, my brother Andrew, who was sitting by me, seeing me in a reverie and almost ready to fall, thrusting his elbow into my side as if he would awaken me from sleep, said: `Do you not see, Peter, what a large fish you have caught? Are you out of your senses, that you are thus in a stupor of astonishment? Tell me, what is the matter with you?' But I was angry with him for a little, because he had withdrawn me from the delight of those things which I was contemplating; then I answered that I was not suffering from any malady, but that I was mentally gazing on the beloved Jerusalem, and at the same time on Caesarea; and that, while I was indeed with him in the body, in my mind I was wholly carried away thither. But he, I know not whence inspired, uttered a hidden and secret word of truth."

Chapter LXIV.-Andrew's Rebuke.

"`Give over, 'says he, `O Peter. What is it that you are doing? For those who are beginning to be possessed with a demon, or to be disturbed in their minds, begin in this way. They are first carried away by fancies to some pleasant and delightful things, then they are poured out in vain and fond motions towards things which have no existence. Now this happens from a certain disease of mind, by reason of which they see not the things which are, but long to bring to their sight those which are not. But thus it happens also to those who are suffering derangement[1], and seem to themselves to see many images, because their soul, being torn and withdrawn from its place by excess of cold or of heat, suffers a failure of its natural service. But those also who are in distress through thirst, when they fall asleep, seem to themselves to see rivers and fountains, and to drink; but this befalls them through being distressed by the dryness of the unmoistened body. Wherefore it is certain that this occurs through some ailment either of the soul or body.'

Chapter LXV.-Fallacy of Imagination.

"In short, that you may receive the faith of the matter; concerning Jerusalem, which I had often seen, I told my brother what places and what gatherings of people I had seemed to myself to see. But also concerning Caesarea, which I had never seen, I nevertheless contended that it was such as I had conceived it in my mind and thought. But when I came hither, and saw nothing at all like to those things which I had seen in phantasy, I blamed myself, and observed distinctly, that I had assigned to it gates, and walls, and buildings from others which I had seen, taking the likeness in reality from others. Nor indeed can any one imagine anything new, and of which no form has ever existed. For even if any one should fashion from his imagination bulls with five heads, he only forms them with five heads out of those which he has seen with one head. And you therefore, now, if truly you seem to yourself to perceive anything with your thought, and to look above the heavens, there is no doubt but that you imagine them from those things which you see, placed as you are upon the earth. But if you think that there is easy access for your mind above the heavens, and that you are able to conceive the things that are there, and to apprehend knowledge of that immense light, I think that for him who can

---

[1] Original word used in the text was: **phrenzy**.

comprehend these things, it were easier to throw his sense, which knows how to ascend thither, into the heart and breast of some one of us who stand by, and to tell what thoughts he is cherishing in his breast. If therefore you can declare the thoughts of the heart of any one of us, who is not pre-engaged in your favor, we shall perhaps be able to believe you, that you are able to know those things that are above the heavens, although these are much loftier."

Chapter LXVI.-Existence and Conception.

To this Simon replied: "O thou who hast woven a web of many frivolities, listen now. It is impossible that anything which comes into a man's thoughts should not also subsist in truth and reality. For things that do not subsist, have no appearances; but things that have no appearances, cannot present themselves to our thoughts." Then said Peter: "If everything that can come into our thoughts has a subsistence, then, with respect to that place of immensity which you say is outside the world, if one thinks in his heart that it is light, and another that it is darkness, how can one and the same place be both light and darkness, according to their different thoughts concerning it?" Then said Simon: "Let pass for the present what I have said; and tell us what you suppose to be above the heavens."

Chapter LXVII.-The Law Teaches of Immensity.

Then said Peter: "If you believed concerning the true fountain of light, I could instruct you what and of what sort is that which is immense, and should render, not a vain fancy, but a consistent and necessary account of the truth, and should make use, not of sophistical assertions, but testimonies of the law and nature, that you might know that the law especially contains what we ought to believe in regard to immensity. But if the doctrine of immensity is not unknown to the law, then assuredly, naught else can be unknown to it; and therefore it is a false supposition of yours, that there is anything of which the law is not cognizant. Much more shall nothing be unknown to Him who gave the law. Yet I cannot speak anything to you of immensity and of those things which are without limit, unless first you either accept our account of those heavens which are bounded by a certain limit, or else propound your own account of them. But if you cannot understand concerning those which are comprehended within fixed boundaries, much more can you neither know nor learn anything concerning those which are without limit."

Chapter LXVIII.-The Visible and the Invisible Heaven.

To this Simon answered: "It seems to me to be better to believe simply that God is, and that the heaven which we see is the only heaven in the whole universe." But Peter said: "Not so; but it is proper to confess one God who truly is; but that there are heavens, which were made by Him, as also the law says, of which one is the higher, in which also is contained the visible firmament; and that that higher heaven is perpetual and eternal, with those who dwell in it; but that this visible heaven is to be dissolved and to pass away at the end of the world, in order that that heaven which is older and higher may appear after the judgment to the holy and the worthy." To this Simon answered: "That these things are so, as you say, may appear to those who believe them; but to him who seeks for reasons of these things, it is impossible that they can be produced from the law, and especially concerning the immensity of light."

Chapter LXIX.-Faith and Reason.

Then Peter: "Do not think that we say that these things are only to be received by faith, but also that they are to be asserted by reason. For indeed it is not safe to commit these things to bare faith without reason, since assuredly truth cannot be without reason. And therefore he who has received these things fortified by reason, call never lose them; whereas he who receives them without proofs, by an assent to a simple statement of them, can neither keep them safely, nor is certain if they are true; because he who easily believes, also easily yields. But he who has sought reason for those things which he has believed and received, as though bound by chains of reason itself, can never be torn away or separated from those things which he hath believed. And therefore, according as any one is more anxious in demanding a reason, by so much will he be the firmer in preserving his faith."

Chapter LXX.-Adjournment.

To this Simon replied: "It is a great thing which you promise, that the eternity of boundless light can be shown from the law." And when Peter said, "I shall show it whenever you please," Simon answered: "Since now it is a late hour, I shall stand by you and oppose you to-morrow; and if you can prove that this world was created, and that souls are immortal, you shall have me to assist you in your preaching." When he had said thus, he departed, and was followed by a third part of all the people who had come with him, who were about one thousand men. But the rest with bended knees prostrated themselves before Peter; and he, invoking upon them the name of God, cured some who had demons, healed others who were sick, and so dismissed the people rejoicing, commanding them to come early the next day. But Peter, when the crowds had withdrawn, commanded the table to be spread on the ground, in the open air, in the court where the disputation had been held, and sat down together with those eleven; but I dined reclining with some others who also had made a beginning of hearing the word of God, and were greatly beloved.

Chapter LXXI.-Separation from the Unclean.

But Peter, most benignantly regarding me, lest perhaps that separation might cause me sorrow, says to me: "It is not from pride, O Clement, that I do not eat with those who have not yet been purified; but I fear lest perhaps I should injure myself, and do no good to them. For this I would have you know for certain, that every one who has at any time worshipped idols, and has adored those whom the pagans call gods, or has eaten of the things sacrificed to them, is not without an unclean spirit; for he has become a guest of demons, and has been partaker with that demon of which he has formed the image in his mind, either through fear or love. And by these means he is not free from an unclean spirit, and therefore needs the purification of baptism, that the unclean spirit may go out of him, which has made its abode in the inmost affections of his soul, and what is worse, gives no indication that it lurks within, for fear it should be exposed and expelled."

Chapter LXXII.-The Remedy.

"For these unclean spirits love to dwell in the bodies of men, that they may fulfill their own desires by their service, and, inclining the motions of their souls to those things which they themselves desire, may compel them to obey their own lusts, that they may become wholly vessels of demons. One of whom is this Simon, who is seized with such disease, and cannot now be healed, because he is sick in his will and purpose. Nor does the demon dwell in him against his will; and therefore, if any one would drive it out of him, since it is inseparable from himself, and, so to speak, has now become his very soul, he should seem rather to kill him, and to incur the guilt of manslaughter. Let no one of you therefore be saddened at being separated from eating with us, for every one ought to observe that it is for just so long a time as he pleases. For he who wishes soon to be baptized is separated but for a little time, but he for a longer who wishes to be baptized later. Every one therefore has it in his own power to demand a shorter or a longer time for his repentance; and therefore it lies with you, when you wish it, to come to our table; and not with us, who are not permitted to take food with any one who has not been baptized. It is rather you, therefore, who hinder us from eating with you, if you interpose delays in the way of your purification, and defer your baptism." Having said thus, and having blessed, he took food. And afterwards, when he had given thanks to God, he went into the house and went to bed; and we all did the like, for it was now night.

Book III.

Chapter I.-Pearls Before Swine.

Meantime Peter, rising at the crowing of the cock, and wishing to rouse us, found us awake, the evening light still burning; and when, according to custom, he had saluted us, and we had all sat down, he thus began. "Nothing is more difficult, thy brethren, than to reason concerning the truth in the presence of a mixed multitude of people. For that which is may not be spoken to all as it is, on account of those who hear wickedly and treacherously; yet it is not proper to deceive, on account of those who desire to hear the truth sincerely. What, then, shall he do who has to address a mixed multitude? Shall he conceal what is true? How, then, shall he instruct those who are worthy? But if he set forth pure truth to those who do not desire to obtain salvation, he does injury to Him by whom he has been sent, and from whom he has received commandment not to throw the pearls of His words before swine and dogs, who, striving against them with arguments and sophisms,[1] roll them in the rand of carnal understanding, and by their barkings and base answers break and weary the preachers of God's word. Wherefore I also, for the most part, by using a certain circumlocution,[2] endeavor to avoid publishing the chief knowledge concerning the Supreme Divinity to unworthy ears." Then, beginning from the Father, and the Son, and the Holy Spirit, he briefly and plainly expounded to us, so that all of us hearing him wondered that men have forsaken the truth, and have turned themselves to vanity.

---

[1] Deceptive or fallacious argumentation.
[2] A roundabout or indirect way of speaking.

Source: Dictionary.com Unabridged (v 1.1)

Chapter XII. -Second Day's Discussion.

But when the day had dawned, some one came in and said: "There is a very great multitude waiting in the court, and in the midst of them stands Simon, endeavoring to preoccupy the ears of the people with most wicked persuasions." Then Peter, immediately going out, stood in the place where he had disputed the day before, and all the people turning to him with joy, gave heed to him. But when Simon perceived that the people rejoiced at the sight of Peter, and were moved to love him, he said in confusion: "I wonder at the folly of men, who call me a magician, and love Peter; whereas, having knowledge of me of old, they ought to love me rather. And therefore from this sign those who have sense may understand that Peter may rather seem to be the magician, since affection is not borne to me, to whom it is almost due from acquaintance, but is abundantly expended upon him, to whom it is not due by any familiarity."

Chapter XIII.-Simon a Seducer.

While Simon was talking on in this style, Peter, having saluted the people in his usual way thus answered: "O Simon, his own conscience is sufficient for every one to disprove[1] him; but if you wonder at this, that those who are acquainted with you not only do not love you but even hate you, learn the reason from me. Since you are a seducer you profess to proclaim the truth; and on this account you had many friends who had a desire to learn the truth. But when they saw in you things contrary to what you professed, they being, as I said, lovers of truth, began not only not to love you, but even to hate you. But yet they did not immediately forsake you, because you still promised that you could show them what is true. As long, therefore, as no one was present who could show them, they bore with you; but since the hope of better instruction has dawned upon them, they despise you, and seek to know what they understand to

---

[1] Original word used in the text was: **confute**

be better. And you indeed, acting by nefarious arts, thought at first that you should escape detection. But you are detected. For you are driven into a corner, and, contrary to your expectation, you are made notorious, not only as being ignorant of the truth, but as being unwilling to hear it from those who know it. For if you had been willing to hear, that saying would have been exemplified in you, of Him who said that 'there is nothing hidden which shall not be known, nor covered which shall not be disclosed.'"

Chapter XIV.-Simon Claims the Fulfillment of Peter's Promise.

While Peter spoke these words, and others to the same effect, Simon answered: "I will not have you detain me with long speeches, Peter; I claim from you what you promised yesterday. You then said that you could show that the law teaches concerning the immensity of the eternal light, and that there are only two heavens, and these created, and that the higher is the abode of that light, in which the ineffable Father dwells alone for ever; but that after the pattern of that heaven is made this visible heaven, which you asserted is to pass away. You said, therefore, that the Father of all is one, because there cannot be two infinites; else neither of them would be infinite, because in that in which the one subsists, he makes a limit of the subsistence of the other. Since then you not only promised this, but are able to show it from the law, leave off other matters and set about this." Then Peter said: "If I were asked to speak of these things only on your account, who come only for the purpose of contradicting, you should never hear a single discourse from me; but seeing it is necessary that the husbandman, wishing to sow good ground, should sow some seeds, either in stony places, or places that are to be trodden of men, or in places filled with brambles and briers (as our Master also set forth, indicating by these the diversities of the purposes of several souls), I shall not delay."

Chapter XV.-Simon's Arrogance.

Then said Simon: "You seem to me to be angry; but if it be so, it is not necessary to enter into the conflict." Then Peter: "I see that you perceive that you are to be convicted, and you wish politely to escape from the contest; for what have you seen to have made me angry against you, a man desiring to deceive so great a multitude, and when you have nothing to say, pretending moderation, who also command, indeed,[1] by your authority that the controversy shall be conducted as you please, and not as order demands?" Then Simon: "I shall enforce myself to bear patiently your unskillfulness, that I may show that you indeed wish to seduce the people, but that I teach the truth. But now I refrain from a discussion concerning that boundless light. Answer me, therefore, what I ask of you. Since God, as you say, made all things, whence comes evil?" Then said Peter: "To put questions in this way is not the part of an opponent, but of a learner. If therefore you wish to learn, confess it; and I shall first teach you how you ought to learn, and when you have learned to listen, then straightway I shall begin to teach you. But if you do not wish to learn, as though you knew all things, I shall first set forth the faith which I preach, and do you also set forth what you think to be true; and when the profession of each of us has been disclosed, let our hearers judge whose discourse is supported by truth." To this Simon answered: "This is a good joke: behold a fellow who offers to teach me! Nevertheless I shall suffer you, and bear with your ignorance and your arrogance. I confess, then, I do wish to learn; let us see how you can teach me."

Chapter XVI.-Existence of Evil.

Then Peter said: "If you truly wish to learn, then first learn this, how unskillfully you have framed your question; for you say, Since God has created all things, whence is evil? But before you asked this, three sorts of questions should

---

[1] Original word used in the text was: **forsooth**

have had the precedence: *First,* Whether there be evil? *Secondly,* What evil is? *Thirdly,* To whom it is, and whence? "To this Simon answered: "Oh thou most unskillful and unlearned, is there any man who does not confess that there is evil in this life? Whence I also, thinking that you had even the common sense of all men, asked, whence evil is; not as wishing to learn, since I know all things, least of all from you, who know nothing, but that I might show you to be ignorant of all things. And that you may not suppose that it is because I am angry that I speak somewhat sternly, know that I am moved with compassion for those who are present, whom you are attempting to deceive." Then Peter said: "The more wicked are you, if you can do such wrong, not being angry; but smoke must rise where there is fire. Nevertheless I shall tell you, lest I should seem to take you up with words, so as not to answer to those things which you have spoken disorderly. You say that all confess the existence of evil, which is verily false; for, first of all, the whole Hebrew nation deny its existence."

Chapter XVII.-Not Admitted by All.

Then Simon, interrupting his discourse, said: "They do rightly who say that there is no evil." Then Peter answered: "We do not propose to speak of this now, but only to state the fact that the existence of evil is not universally admitted. But the second question that you should have asked is, What is evil?-a substance, an accident, or an act? And many other things of the same sort. And after that, towards what, or how it is, or to whom it is evil,-whether to God, or to angels, or to men, to the righteous or the wicked, to all or to some, to one's self or to no one? And then you should inquire, Whence it is?-whether from God, or from nothing; whether it has always been, or has had its beginning in time; whether it is useful or useless? and many other things which a proposition of this sort demands." To this Simon answered: "Pardon me; I was in error concerning the first question; but suppose that I now ask first, whether evil is or not?"

Chapter XVIII.-Manner of Conducting the Discussion.

Then Peter said: "In what way do you put the question; as wishing to learn, or to teach or for the sake of raising the question? If indeed as wishing to learn, I have something to teach you first, that coining by consequence and the right order of doctrine, you may understand from yourself what evil is. But if you put the question as an instructor, I have no need to be taught by you, for I have a Master from whom I have learned all things. But if you ask merely for the sake of raising a question and disputing, let each of us first set forth his opinion, and so let the matter be debated. For it is not reasonable that you should ask as one wishing to learn, and contradict as one teaching, so that after my answer it should be in your discretion to say whether I have spoken well or ill. Wherefore you cannot stand in the place of a gainsayer and be judge of what we say. And therefore, as I said, if a discussion is to be held, let each of us state his sentiments; and while we are placed in conflict, these religious hearers will be just judges."

Chapter XIX.-Desire of Instruction.

Then Simon said: "Does it not seem to you to be absurd that an unskilled people should sit in judgment upon our sayings?" Then Peter: "It is not so; for what perhaps is less clear to one, can be investigated by many, for oftentimes even a popular rumor has the aspect of a prophecy. But in addition to all this, all these people stand here constrained by the love of God, and by a desire to know the truth, and therefore all these are to be regarded as one, by reason of their affection being one and the same towards the truth; as, on the other hand, two are many and diverse, if they disagree with each other. But if you wish to receive an indication how all these people who stand before us are as one man, consider from their very silence and quietness how with all patience, as you see, they do honor to the truth of God, even before they learn it, for they have not yet learned the greater observance which they owe to it. Wherefore I hope, through the mercy of God, that He will accept the religious purpose of their mind towards Him, and will give the palm of victory to him who preaches the truth, that He may make manifest to them the herald of truth."

Chapter XX.-Common Principles.

Then Simon: "On what subject do you wish the discussion to be held? Tell me, that I also may define what I think, and so the inquiry may begin." And Peter answered: "If indeed, you will do as I think right, I would have it done according to the precept of my Master, who first of all commanded the Hebrew nation, whom He knew to have knowledge of God, and that it is He who made the world, not that they should inquire about Him whom they knew, but that, knowing Him, they should investigate His will and His righteousness; because it is placed in men's power that, searching into these things, they may find, and do, and observe those things concerning which they are to be judged. Therefore He commanded us to inquire, not whence evil cometh, as you asked just now, but to seek the righteousness of the good God, and His kingdom; and all these things, says He, shall be added to you." Then Simon said: "Since these things are commanded to Hebrews, as having a right knowledge of God, and being of opinion that every one has it in his power to do these things concerning which he is to be judged,-but my opinion differs from theirs,-where do you wish me to begin? "

Chapter XXI.-Freedom of the Will.

Then said Peter: "I advise that the first inquiry be, whether it be in our power to know whence we are to be judged." But Simon said: "Not so; but concerning God, about whom all who are present are desirous to hear." Then Peter: "You admit, then, that something is in the power of the will: only confess this, if it is so, and let us inquire, as you say, concerning God." To this Simon answered: "By no means" Then Peter said: "If, then, nothing is in our power, it is useless for us to inquire anything concerning God, since it is not in the power of those who seek to find; hence I said well, that this should be the first inquiry, whether anything is in the power of the will." Then said Simon: "We cannot even understand this that you say, if there is anything in the power of the will." But Peter, seeing that he was turning to contention, and, through fear of being overcome, was confounding all things as being in general uncertain, answered: "How then do you know that it is not in the power of man to know anything, since this very thing at least you know? "

Chapter XXII.-Responsibility.

Then Simon said: "I know not whether I know even this; for every one, according as it is decreed to him by fate, either does, or understands, or suffers." Then Peter said: "See, my brethren, into what absurdities Simon has fallen, who before my coming was teaching that men have it in their power to be wise and to do what they will, but now, driven into a corner by the force of my arguments, he denies that man has any power either of perceiving or of acting; and yet he presumes to profess himself to be a teacher! But tell me how then God judges according to truth every one for his doings, if men have it not in their own power to do anything? If this opinion he held, all things are torn up by the roots; vain will be the desire of following after goodness; yea, even in vain do the judges of the world administer laws and punish those who do amiss, for they had it not in their power not to sin; vain also will be the laws of nations which assign penalties to evil deeds. Miserable also will those be who laboriously keep righteousness; but blessed those who, living in pleasure, exercise tyranny, living in luxury and wickedness. According to this, therefore, there can be neither righteousness, nor goodness, nor any virtue, nor, as you would have it, any God. But, O Simon, I know why you have spoken thus: truly because you wished to avoid inquiry, lest you should be openly confuted; and therefore you say that it is not in the power of man to perceive or to discern anything. But if this had really been your opinion, you would not surely, before my coming, have professed yourself before the people to be a teacher. I say, therefore, that man is under his own control." Then said Simon: "What is the meaning of being under his own control? Tell us." To this Peter: "If nothing can be learned, why do you wish to hear?" And Simon said: "You have nothing to answer to this."

Chapter XXIII.-Origin of Evil.

Then said Peter: "I shall speak, not as under compulsion from you, but at the request of the hearers. The power of choice is the sense of the soul, possessing a quality by which it can be inclined towards what acts it wills." Then Simon, applauding Peter for what he had spoken, said: "Truly you have expounded it magnificently and incomparably, for it is my duty to bear testimony to your speaking well. Now if you will explain to me this which I now ask you, in all things else I shall submit to you. What I wish to learn, then, is this: if what God wishes to be, is; and what He does not wish to be, is not. Answer me this." Then Peter: "If you do not know that you are asking an absurd and incompetent question, I shall pardon you and explain; but if you are aware that yon are asking inconsequently, you do not well." Then Simon said: "I swear by the Supreme Divinity, whatsoever that may be, which judges and punishes those who sin, that I know not what I have said inconsequently, or what absurdity there is in my words, that is, in those that I have just uttered."

Chapter XXIV.-God the Author of Good, Not of Evil.

To this Peter answered: "Since, then, you confess that you are ignorant, now learn. Your question demanded our deliverance on two matters that are contrary to one another. For every motion is divided into two parts, so that a certain part is moved by necessity, and another by will; and those things which are moved by necessity are always in motion, those which are moved by will, not always. For example, the sun's motion is performed by necessity to complete its appointed circuit, and every state and service of heaven depends upon necessary motions. But man directs the voluntary motions of his own actions. And thus there are some things which have been created for this end, that in their services they should be subject to necessity, and should be unable to do aught else than what has been assigned to them; and when they have accomplished this service, the Creator of all things, who thus arranged them according to His will, preserves them. But there are other things, in which there is a power of will, and which have a free choice of doing what they will. These, as I have said, do not remain always in that order in which they were created: but according as their will leads them, and the judgment of their mind inclines them, they effect either good or evil; and therefore He hath proposed rewards to those who do well, and penalties to those who do evil.

Chapter XXV.-"Who Hath Resisted His Will? "

You say, therefore, if God wishes anything to be, it is; and if He do not wish it, it is not. But if I were to answer that what He wishes is, and what He wishes not is not, you would say that then He wishes the evil things to be which are done in the world, since everything that He wishes is, and everything that He wishes not is not. But if I had answered that it is not so that what God wishes is, and what He wishes not is not, then you would retort upon me that God must then be powerless, if He cannot do what He wills; and you would be all the more petulant, as thinking that you had got a victory, though had said nothing to the point. Therefore you are ignorant, O Simon, yea very ignorant, how the will of God acts in each individual case. For some things, as we have said, He has so willed to be, that they cannot be otherwise than as they are ordained by Him; and to these He has assigned neither rewards nor punishments; but those which He has willed to be so that they have it in their power to do what they will, He has assigned to them according to their actions and their wills, to earn either rewards or punishments. Since, therefore, as I have informed you, all things that are moved are divided into two parts, according to the distinction that I formerly stated, everything that God wills is, and everything that He wills not is not.

Chapter XXVI.-No Goodness Without Liberty

To this Simon answered: "Was not He able to make us all such that we should be good, and that we should not have it in our power to be otherwise?" Peter answered: "This also is an absurd question. For if He had made us of an unchangeable nature and incapable of being moved away from good, we should not be really good, because we could not be aught else; and it would not be of our purpose that we were good; and what we did would not be ours, but of the necessity of our nature. But how can that be called good which is not done of purpose? And on this account the world required long periods, until the number of souls which were predestined to fill it should be completed, and then that visible heaven should be folded up like a scroll, and that which is higher should appear, and the souls of the blessed, being restored to their bodies, should be ushered into light; but the souls of the wicked, for their impure actions being surrounded with fiery spirit, should be plunged into the abyss of unquenchable fire, to endure punishments through eternity. Now that these things are so, the true Prophet has testified to us; concerning whom, if you wish to know that He is a prophet, I shall instruct you by innumerable declarations. For of those things which were spoken by Him, even now everything that He said is being fulfilled; and those things which He spoke with respect to the future are believed to be about to be fulfilled, for faith is given to the future from those things which have already come to pass."

Chapter XXVII.-The Visible Heaven: Why Made.

But Simon, perceiving that Peter was clearly assigning a reason from the head of prophecy, from which the whole question is settled, declined that the discourse should take this turn; and thus answered: "Give me an answer to the questions that I put, and tell me, if that visible heaven is, as you say, to be dissolved, why was it made at first? "Peter answered: "It was made for the sake of this present life of men, that there might be some sort of interposition and separation, lest any unworthy one might see the habitation of the celestials and the abode of God Himself, which are prepared in order to be seen by those only who are of pure heart. But now, that is in the time of the conflict, it has pleased Him that those things be invisible, which are destined as a reward to the conquerors." Then Simon said: "If the Creator is good, and the world is good, how shall He who is good ever destroy that which is good? But if He shall destroy that which is good, how shall He Himself be thought to be good? But if He shall dissolve and destroy it as evil, how shall He not appear to be evil, who has made that which is evil? "

Chapter XXVIII.-Why to Be Dissolved.

To this Peter replied: "Since we have promised not to run away from your blasphemies, we endure them patiently, for you shall yourself render an account for the things that you speak. Listen now, therefore. If indeed that heaven which is visible and transient had been made for its own sake, there would have been some reason in what you say, that it ought not to be dissolved. But if it was made not for its own sake, but for the sake of something else, it must of necessity be dissolved, that that for which it seems to have been made may appear. As I might say, by way of illustration, however fairly and carefully the shell of the egg may seem to have been formed, it is yet necessary that it be broken and opened, that the chick may issue from it, and that may appear for which the form of the whole egg seems to have been molded. So also, therefore, it is necessary that the condition of this world pass away, that that sublimer condition of the heavenly kingdom may shine forth."

Chapter XXIX.-Corruptible and Temporary Things Made by the Incorruptible and Eternal.

Then Simon: "It does not seem to me that the heaven, which has been made by God, can be dissolved. For things made by the Eternal One are eternal, while things made by a corruptible one are temporary and decaying." Then Peter: "It is not so. Indeed corruptible and temporary things of all sorts are made by mortal creatures; but the Eternal does not always make things corruptible, nor always incorruptible; but according to the will of God the Creator, so will be the things which He creates. For the power of God is not subject to law, but His will is law to His creatures." Then Simon answered: "I call you back to the first question. You said now that God is visible to no one; but when that heaven shall be dissolved, and that superior condition of the heavenly kingdom shall shine forth, then those who are pure in heart shall see God; which statement is contrary to the law, for there it is written that God said, 'None shall see my face and live.'"

Chapter XXX.-How the Pure in Heart See God.

Then Peter answered: "To those who do not read the law according to the tradition of Moses, my speech appears to be contrary to it; but I will show you how it is not contradictory. God is seen by the mind, not by the body; by the spirit, not by the flesh. Whence also angels, who are spirits, see God; and therefore men, as long as they are men, cannot see Him. But after the resurrection of the dead, when they shall have been made like the angels, they shall be able to see God. And thus my statement is not contrary to the law; neither is that which our Master said, 'Blessed are they of a pure heart, for they shall see God.' For He showed that a time shall come in which of men shall be made angels, who in the spirit of their mind shall see God." After these and many similar sayings, Simon began to assert with many oaths, saying: "Concerning one thing only render me a reason, whether the soul is immortal, and I shall submit to your will in all things. But let it be to-morrow, for to-day it is late." When therefore Peter began to speak, Simon went out, and with him a very few of his associates; and that for shame. But all the rest, turning to Peter, on bended knees prostrated themselves before him; and some of those who were afflicted with diverse sicknesses, or invaded by demons, were healed by the prayer of Peter, and departed rejoicing, as having obtained at once the doctrine of the true God, and also His mercy. When therefore the crowds had withdrawn, and only we his attendants remained with him, we sat down on couches placed on the ground, each one recognizing his accustomed place, and having taken food, and given thanks to God, we went to sleep.

Chapter XXXI.-Diligence in Study.

But on the following day, Peter, as usual, rising before dawn, found us already awake and ready to listen; and thus began: "I entreat you, my brethren and fellow-servants, that if any of you is not able to wake, he should not torment himself through respect to my presence, because sudden change is difficult; but if for a long time one gradually accustoms himself, that will not be distressing which comes of use. For we had not all the same training; although in course of time we shall be able to be molded into one habit, for they say that custom holds the place of a second nature. But I call God to witness that I am not offended, if any one is not able to wake; but rather by this, if, when any one sleeps all through the night, he does not in the course of the day fulfill that which he omitted in the night. For it is necessary to give heed intently and unceasingly, to the study of doctrine, that our mind may be filled with the thought of God only: because in the mind which is filled with the thought of God, no place will be given to the wicked one."

Chapter XXXII.-Peter's Private Instruction.

When Peter spoke thus to us, every one of us eagerly assured him, that ere now we were awake, being satisfied with short sleep, but that we were afraid to arouse him, because it did not become the disciples to command the master; "and yet even this O Peter we had almost ventured to take upon ourselves, because our hearts, agitated with longing for your words, drove sleep wholly from our eyes. But again our affection towards you opposed it, and did not suffer us violently to rouse you." Then Peter said: "Since therefore you assert that you are willingly awake through desire of hearing, I wish to repeat to you more carefully, and to explain in their order, the things that were spoken yesterday without arrangement. And this I propose to do throughout these daily disputations, that by night, when privacy of time and place is afforded, I shall unfold in correct order, and by a straight line of explanation, anything that in the controversy has not been stated with sufficient fullness." And then he began to point out to us how the yesterday's discussion ought to have been conducted, and how it could not be so conducted on account of the contentiousness or the unskillfulness of his opponent; and how therefore he only made use of assertion, and only overthrew what was said by his adversary, but did not expound his own doctrines either completely or distinctly. Then repeating the several matters to us, he discussed them in regular order and with full reason.

Chapter XXXIII.-Learners and Cavillers.

But when the day began to be light, after prayer he went out to the crowds and stood in his accustomed place, for the discussion; and seeing Simon standing in the middle of the crowd, he saluted the people in his usual way, and said to them: "I confess that I am grieved with respect to some men, who come to us in this way that they may learn something, but when we begin to teach them, they profess that they themselves are masters, and while indeed they ask questions as ignorant persons, they contradict as knowing trees. But perhaps some one will say, that he who puts a question, puts it indeed in order that he may learn, but when that which he hears does not seem to him to be right, it is necessary that he should answer, and that seems to he contradiction which is not contradiction, but further inquiry.

Chapter XXXIV.-Against Order is Against Reason.

"Let such a one then hear this: The teaching of all doctrine has a certain order, and there are some things which must be delivered first, others in the second place, and others in the third, and so all in their order; and if these things be delivered in their order, they become plain; but if they be brought forward out of order, they will seem to be spoken against reason. And therefore order is to be observed above all things, if we seek for the purpose of finding what we seek. For he who enters rightly upon the road, will observe the second place in due order, and from the second will more easily find the third; and the further he proceeds, so much the more will the way of knowledge become open to him, even until he arrive at the city of truth, whither he is bound, and which he desires to reach. But he who is unskillful, and knows not the way of inquiry, as a traveler in a foreign country, ignorant and wandering, if he will not employ a native of the country as a guide,-undoubtedly when he has strayed from the way of truth, shall remain outside the gates of life, and so, involved in the darkness of black night, shall walk through the paths of perdition. Inasmuch therefore, as, if those things which are to be sought, be sought in an orderly manner, they can most easily be found, but the unskillful man is ignorant of the order of inquiry, it is right that the ignorant man should yield to the knowing one, and first learn the order of inquiry, that so at length he may find the method of asking and answering."

Chapter XXXV.-Learning Before Teaching.

To this Simon replied: "Then truth is not the property of all, but of those only who know the art of disputation, which is absurd; for it cannot be, since He is equally the God of all, that all should not be equally able to know His will." Then Peter: "All were made equal by Him, and to all He has given equally to be receptive of truth. But that none of those who are born, are born with education, but education is subsequent to birth, no one can doubt. Since, therefore, the birth of men holds equity in this respect, that all are equally capable of receiving discipline, the difference is not in nature, but in education. Who does not know that the things which any one learns, he was ignorant of before he learned them? "Then Simon said "You say truly." Then Peter said · "If then in those arts which are in common use, one first learns and then teaches, how much more ought those who profess to be the educators of souls, first to learn, and so to teach, that they may not expose themselves to ridicule, if they promise to afford knowledge to others, when they themselves are unskillful? "Then Simon: "This is true in respect of those arts which are in common use; but in the word of knowledge, as soon as any one has heard, he has learned."

Chapter XXXVI.-Self-Evidence of the Truth,

Then said Peter: "If indeed one hear in an orderly and regular manner he is able to know what is true; but he who refuses to submit to the rule of a reformed life and a pure conversation, which truly is the proper result of knowledge of the truth, will not confess that he knows what he does know. For this is exactly what we see in the case of some who, abandoning the trades which they learned in their youth, betake themselves to other performances, and by way of excusing their own sloth, begin to find fault with the trade as unprofitable." Then Simon: "Ought all who hear to believe that whatever they hear is true?" Then Peter: "Whoever hears an orderly statement of the truth, cannot by any means gainsay it, but knows that what is spoken is true, provided he also willingly submit to the rules of life. But those who, when they hear, are unwilling to betake themselves to good works, are prevented by the desire of doing evil from acquiescing in those things which they judge to be right. Hence it is manifest that it is in the power of the hearers to choose which of the two they prefer. But if all who hear were to obey, it would be rather a necessity of nature, leading all in one way. For as no one can be persuaded to become shorter or taller, because the force of nature does not permit it; so also, if either all were converted to the truth by a word, or all were not converted, it would be the force of nature which compelled all in the one case, and none at all in the other, to be converted."

Chapter XXXVII.-God Righteous as Well as Good.

Then said Simon: "Inform us, therefore, what he who desires to know the truth must first learn." Then Peter: "Before all things it must be inquired what it is possible for man to find out. For of necessity the judgment of God turns upon this, if a man was able to do good and did it not. And therefore men must inquire whether they have it in their power by seeking to find what is good, and to do it when they have found it; for this is that for which they are to be judged. But more than this there is no occasion for any one but a prophet to know: for what is the need for men to know how the world was made? This, indeed, would be necessary to be learned if we had to enter upon a similar construction. But now it is sufficient for us, in order to the worship of God, to know that He made the world; but how He made it is no subject of inquiry for us, because, as I have said, it is not incumbent upon us to acquire the knowledge of that art, as though we were about to make something similar. But neither are we to be judged for this, why we have not learned how the world was made, but only for that, if we be without knowledge of its Creator. For we shall know that the Creator of the world is the righteous and good God, if we seek Him in the paths of righteousness. For if we only know regarding Him that He is good, such knowledge is not sufficient for salvation. For in the present life not only the worthy, but also the unworthy, enjoy His goodness and His benefits. But if we believe Him to be not only good, but also righteous, and if, according to what we believe concerning God, we observe righteousness in the whole course of our life, we shall enjoy His goodness for ever. In a word, to the Hebrews, whose opinion concerning God was that He is only good, our Master said that they should seek also His righteousness; that is, that they should know that He is good indeed in this present time, that all may live in His goodness, but that He shall be righteous at the day of judgment, to bestow eternal rewards upon the worthy, from which the unworthy shall be excluded.

Chapter XXXVIII.-God's Justice Shown at the Day of Judgment.

Then Simon: "How can one and the same being be both good and righteous?" Peter answered: "Because without righteousness, goodness would be unrighteousness; for it is the part of a good God to bestow His sunshine and rain equally on the just and the unjust; but this would seem to be unjust, if He treated the good and the bad always with equal fortune, and were it not that He does it for the sake of the fruits, which all may equally enjoy who are born in this world. But as the rain given by God equally nourishes the corn and the tares, but at the time of harvest the crops are gathered into the barn, but the chaff or the tares are burnt in the fire, so in the day of judgment, when the righteous shall be introduced into the kingdom of heaven, and the unrighteous shall be cast out, then also the justice of God shall be shown. For if He remained for ever alike to the evil and the good, this would not only not be good, but even unrighteous and unjust; that the righteous and the unrighteous should be held by Him in one order of desert."

Chapter XXXIX.-Immortality of the Soul.

Then said Simon: "The one point on which I should wish to be satisfied is, whether the soul is immortal; for I cannot take up the burden of righteousness unless I know first concerning the immortality of the soul; for indeed if it is not immortal, the profession of your preaching cannot stand." Then said Peter: "Let us first inquire whether God is just; for if this were ascertained, the perfect order of order of religion would straight-way be established." Then Simon: "With all your boasting of your knowledge of the order of discussion, you seem to me now to have answered contrary to order; for when I ask you to show whether the soul is immortal, you say that we must first inquire whether God is just." Then said Peter: "That is perfectly right and regular." Simon: "I should wish to learn how."

Chapter XL.-Proved by the Success of the Wicked in This Life.

"Listen, then," said Peter: "Some men who are blasphemers against God, and who spend their whole life in injustice and pleasure die in their own bed and obtain honorable burial; while others who worship God, and maintain their life frugally with all honesty and sobriety, die in deserted places for their observance of righteousness, so that they are not even thought worthy of burial. Where, then, is the justice of God, if there be no immortal soul to suffer punishment in the future for impious deeds, or enjoy rewards for piety and rectitude? "Then Simon said: "It is this indeed that makes me incredulous, because many well-doers perish miserably, and again many evil-doers finish long lives in happiness."

Chapter XLI.-Cavils of Simon.

Then said Peter: "This very thing which draws you into incredulity, affords to us a certain conviction that there shall be a judgment. For since it is certain that God is just, it is a necessary consequence that there is another world, in which every one receiving according to his deserts, shall prove the justice of God. But if all men were now receiving according to their deserts, we should truly seem to be deceivers when we say that there is a judgment to come; and therefore this very fact, that in the present life a return is not made to every one according to his deeds, affords, to those who know that God is just, an unquestionable[1] proof that there shall be a judgment." Then said Simon: "Why, then, am I not persuaded of it?" Peter: "Because you have

---

[1] The original word used in the text was: **indubitable**.

not heard the true Prophet saying, `Seek first His righteousness, and all these things shall be added to you.' "Then said Simon: "Pardon me if I am unwilling to seek righteousness, before I know if the soul is immortal." Then Peter: "You also pardon me this one thing, because I cannot do otherwise than the Prophet of truth has instructed me." Then said Simon: "It is certain that you cannot assert that the soul is immortal, and therefore you cavil,[1] knowing that if it be proved to be mortal, the whole profession of that religion which you are attempting to propagate will be plucked up by the roots. And therefore, indeed, I commend your prudence, while I do not approve your persuasiveness; for you persuade many to embrace your religion, and to submit to the restraint of pleasure, in hope of future good things; to whom it happens that they lose the enjoyment of things present, and are deceived with hopes of things future. For as soon as they die, their soul shall at the same time be extinguished."

Chapter XLII.-"Full of All Subtlety and All Mischief."

But Peter, when he heard him speak thus, grinding his teeth, and rubbing his forehead with his hand, and sighing with profound grief, said: "Armed with the cunning of the old serpent, you stand forth to deceive souls; and therefore, as the serpent is more subtle than any other beast, you profess that you are a teacher from the beginning. And again, like the serpent you wished to introduce many gods; but now, being confuted in that, you assert that there is no God at all. For by occasion of I know not what unknown God, you denied that the Creator of the world is God, but asserted that He is either an evil being, or that He has many equals, or, as we have said, that He is not God at all. And when you had been overcome in this position, you now assert that the soul is mortal, so that men may not live righteously and uprightly in hope of things to come. For if there be no hope for the future, why should not mercy be given up, and men indulge in luxury and pleasures, from

---

[1] To raise irritating and trivial objections; find fault with unnecessarily. *Source: Dictionary.com Unabridged (v 1.1)*

which it is manifest that all unrighteousness springs? And while you introduce so impious a doctrine into the miserable life of men, you call yourself pious, and me impious, because, under the hope of future good things, I will not suffer men to take up arms and fight against one another, plunder and subvert everything, and attempt whatsoever lust may dictate. And what will be the condition of that life which you would introduce, that men will attack and be attacked, be enraged and disturbed, and live always in fear? For those who do evil to others must expect like evil to themselves. Do you see that you are a leader of disturbance and not of peace, of iniquity and not of equity? But I feigned anger, not because I could not prove that the soul is immortal, but because I pity the souls which you are endeavoring to deceive. I shall speak, therefore, but not as compelled by you; for I know how I should speak; and you will be the only one who wants not so much persuasion as admonition on this subject. But those who are really ignorant of this, I shall instruct as is suitable."

Chapter XLIII.-Simon's Subterfuges.

Then says Simon: "If you are angry, I shall neither ask you any questions, nor do I wish to hear you." Then Peter: "If you are now seeking a pretext for escaping, you have full liberty, and need not use any special pretext. For all have heard you speaking all amiss, and have perceived that you can prove nothing, but that you only asked questions for the sake of contradiction; which any one can do. For what difficulty is there in replying, after the clearest proofs have been adduced, `You have said nothing to the purpose? 'But that you may know that I am able to prove to you in a single sentence that the soul is immortal, I shall ask you with respect to a point which all know; answer me, and I shall prove to you in one sentence that it is immortal." Then Simon, who had thought that he had got, from the anger of Peter, a pretext for departing, stopped on account of the remarkable promise that was made to him, and said: "Ask me then, and I shall answer you what all know, that I may hear in a single sentence, as you have promised, how the soul is immortal."

Chapter XLIV.-Sight or Hearing?

Then Peter: "I shall speak so that it may be proved to you before all the rest. Answer me, therefore, which of the two can better persuade an incredulous man, seeing or hearing? "Then Simon said: "Seeing." Then Peter: "Why then do you wish to learn from me by words, what is proved to you by the thing itself and by sight?" Then Simon: "I know not what you mean." Then Peter: "If you do not know, go now to your house, and entering the inner bed-chamber you will see an image placed, containing the figure of a murdered boy clothed in purple; ask him, and he will inform you either by hearing or seeing. For what need is there to hear from him if the soul is immortal, when you see it standing before you? For if it were not in being, it assuredly could not be seen. But if you know not what image I speak of, let us straightway go to your house, with ten other men, of those who are here present."

Chapter XLV.-A Home-Thrust.

But Simon hearing this, and being smitten by his conscience, changed color and became bloodless; for he was afraid, if he denied it, that his house would be searched, or that Peter in his indignation would betray him more openly, and so all would learn what he was. Thus he answered: "I beseech thee, Peter, by that good God who is in thee, to overcome the wickedness that is in me. Receive me to repentance, and you shall have me as an assistant in your preaching. For now I have learned in very deed that you are a prophet of the true God, and therefore you alone know the secret and hidden things of men." Then said Peter: "You see, brethren, Simon seeking repentance; in a little while you shall see him returning again to his infidelity. For, thinking that I am a prophet, forasmuch as I have disclosed his wickedness, which he supposed to be secret and hidden, he has promised that he will repent. But it is not lawful for me to lie, nor must I deceive, whether this infidel be saved or not saved. For I call heaven and earth to witness, that I spoke not by a prophetic spirit what I said, and what I intimated, as far as was possible, to the listening crowds; but I learned from some who once were his associates in his works, but have now been converted to our faith, what things he did in secret. Therefore I spoke what I knew, not what I foreknew."

Chapter XLVI.-Simon's Rage.

But when Simon heard this, he assailed Peter with curses and reproaches, saying: "Oh most wicked and most deceitful of men, to whom fortune, not truth, hath given the victory. But I sought repentance not for defect of knowledge, but in order that you, thinking that by repentance I should become your disciple, might entrust to me all the secrets of your profession, and so at length, knowing them all, I might confute you. But as you cunningly understood for what reason I had pretended penitence, and acquiesced as if you did not understand my stratagem, that you might first expose me in presence of the people as unskillful, then foreseeing that being thus exposed to the people, I must of necessity be indignant, and confess that I was not truly penitent, you anticipated me, that you might say, that I should, after my penitence, again return to my infidelity, that you might seem to have conquered on all sides, both if I continued in the penitence which I had professed, and if I did not continue; and so you should be believed to be wise, because you had foreseen these things, while I should seem to be deceived, because I did not foresee your trick. But you foreseeing mine, have used subtlety and circumvented me. But, as I said, your victory is the result of fortune, not of truth: yet I know why I did not foresee this; because I stood by you and spoke with you in my, goodness, and bore patiently with you. But now I shall show you the power of my divinity, so that you shall quickly fall down and worship me."

Chapter XLVII.-Simon's Vaunt.

"I am the first power, who am always, and without beginning. But having entered the womb of Rachel, I was born of her as a man, that I might be visible to men. I have flown through the air; I have been mixed with fire, and been made one body with it; I have made statues to move; I have animated lifeless things; I have made stones bread; I have flown from mountain to mountain; I have moved from place to place, upheld by angels' hands, and have lighted on the earth. Not only have I done these things; but even now I am able to do them, that by facts I may prove to all, that I am the Son of God, enduring to eternity, and that I can make those who believe on me endure in like manner for ever. But your words are all vain; nor can you perform any real works *such as I have now mentioned*, as he also who sent you is a magician, who yet could not deliver himself from the suffering of the cross."

Chapter XLVIII.-Attempts to Create a Disturbance.

To this speech of Simon, Peter answered: "Do not meddle with the things that belong to others; for that you are a magician, you have confessed and made manifest by the very deeds that you have done; but our Master, who is the Son of God and of man, is manifestly good; and that he is truly the Son of God has been told, and shall be told to those to whom it is fitting. But if you will not confess that you are a magician, let us go, with all this multitude, to your house, and then it will be evident who is a magician." While Peter was speaking thus, Simon began to assail him with blasphemies and curses, that he might make a riot, and excite all so that he could not be refuted, and that Peter, withdrawing on account of his blasphemy, might seem to be overcome. But he stood fast, and began to charge him more vehemently.

Chapter XLIX.-Simon's Retreat.

Then the people in indignation cast Simon from the court, and drove him forth from the gate of the house; and only one person followed him when he was driven out. Then silence being obtained, Peter began to address the people in this manner: "You ought, brethren, to bear with wicked men patiently; knowing that although God could cut them off, yet He suffers them to remain even till the day appointed, in which judgment shall pass upon all. Why then should not we bear with those whom, God suffers? Why should not we bear with fortitude the wrongs that they do to us, when He who is almighty does not take vengeance on them, that both His own goodness and the impiety of the wicked may be known? But if the wicked one had not found Simon to be his minister, he would doubtless have found another: for it is of necessity that in this life offences come, `but woe to that man by whom they come; ' and therefore Simon is rather to be mourned over, because he has become a choice vessel for the wicked one, which undoubtedly would not have happened had he not received power over him for his former sins. For why should I further say that he once believed in our Jesus, and was persuaded that Souls are immortal? Although in this he is deluded by demons, yet he has persuaded himself that he has the soul of a murdered boy ministering to him in whatever he pleases to employ it in; in which truly, as I have said, he is deluded by demons, and therefore I spoke to him according to his own ideas: for he has learned from the Jews, that judgment and vengeance are to be brought forth against those who set themselves against the true faith, and do not repent. But here are men to whom, as being perfect in crimes, the wicked one appears, that he may deceive them, so that they may never be turned to repentance.

Chapter L.-Peter's Benediction.

"You therefore who are turned to the Lord by repentance, bend to Him your knees." When he had said this, all the multitude bent their knees to God; and Peter, looking towards heaven, prayed for them with tears that God, for His goodness, would deign to receive those betaking themselves to Him. And after he had prayed and had instructed them to meet early the next day, he dismissed the multitude. Then according to custom, having taken food, we went to sleep.

Chapter LI.-Peter's Accessibility.

Peter, therefore, rising at the usual hour of the night, found us waking; and when, saluting us, in his usual manner, he had taken his seat, first of all Niceta, said: "If you will permit me, my lord Peter, I have something to ask of you." Then Peter said: "I permit not only you, but all, and not only now, but always, that every one confess what moves him, and the part in his mind that is pained, in order that he may obtain healing. For things which are covered with silence, and are not made known to us, are cured with difficulty, like maladies of long standing; and therefore, since the medicine of seasonable and necessary discourse cannot easily be applied to those who keep silence, every one ought to declare in what respect his mind is feeble through ignorance. But to him who keeps silence, it belongs to God alone to give a remedy. We indeed also can do it, but by the lapse of a long time. For it is necessary that the discourse of doctrine, proceeding in order from the beginning, and meeting each single question, should disclose all things, and resolve and reach to all things, even to that which every one required in his mind; but that, as I have said, can only be done in the course of a long time. Now, then, ask what you please."

Chapter LII.-False Signs and Miracles.

Then Niceta said: "I give you abundant thanks, O most clement[1] Peter; but this is what I desire to learn, how Simon, who is the enemy of God, is able to do such and so

---

[1] Mild or merciful in disposition or character; lenient; compassionate.
Source: Dictionary.com Unabridged (v 1.1)

great things? For indeed he told no lie in his declaration of what he has done." To this the blessed Peter thus answered: "God, who is one and true, has resolved to prepare good and faithful friends for His first begotten; but knowing that none can be good, unless they have in their power that perception by which they may become good, that they may be of their own intent what they choose to be,-and otherwise they could not be truly good, if they were kept in goodness not by purpose, but by necessity,-has given to every one the power of his own will, that he may be what he wishes to be. And again, foreseeing that that power of will would make some choose good things and others evil, and so that the human race would necessarily be divided into two classes, He has permitted each class to choose both a place and a king, whom they would. For the good King; rejoices in the good, and the wicked one in the evil. And although I have expounded those things more fully to you, O Clement, in that treatise in which I discoursed on predestination and the end, yet it is fitting that I should now make clear to Niceta also, as he asks me, what is the reason than Simon, whose thoughts are against God, is able to do so great marvels.

Chapter LIII.-Self-Love the Foundation of Goodness.

"First of all, then, he is evil, in the judgment of God, who will not inquire what is advantageous to himself. For how can any one love another, if he does not love himself? Or to whom will that man not be an enemy, who cannot be a friend to himself? In order, therefore, that there might be a distinction between those who choose good and those who choose evil, God has concealed that which is profitable to men, i.e., the possession of the kingdom of heaven, and has laid it up and hidden it as a secret treasure, so that no one can easily attain it by his own power or knowledge. Yet He has brought the report of it, under various names and opinions, through successive generations, to the hearing of all: so that whosoever should be lovers of good, hearing it, might inquire and discover what is profitable and healthy[1] to them; but that they should ask it, not from themselves, but from Him who has hidden it, and should pray that access and the way of knowledge might be given to them: which way is opened to those only who love it above all the good things of this world; and on no other condition can any one even understand it, however wise he may seem; but that those who neglect to inquire what is profitable and healthy[2] to themselves, as self-haters and self-enemies, should be deprived of its good things, as lovers of evil things.

Chapter LIV.-God to Be Supremely Loved.

"It behooves, therefore, the good to love that *way* above all things, that is, above riches, glory, rest, parents, relatives, friends, and everything in the world. But he who perfectly loves this possession of the kingdom of heaven, will undoubtedly cast away all practice of evil habit, negligence, sloth, malice, anger, and such like. For if you prefer any of these to it, as loving the vices of your own lust more than God, you shall not attain to the possession of the heavenly kingdom; for truly it is foolish to love anything more than God. For whether they be parents, they die; or relatives, they do not continue; or friends, they change. But God alone is eternal, and abideth unchangeable. He, therefore, who will not seek after that which is profitable to himself, is evil, to such an extent that his wickedness exceeds the very prince of impiety. For he abuses the goodness of God to the purpose of his own wickedness, and pleases himself; but the other neglects the good things of his own salvation, that by his own destruction he may please the evil one."

Chapter LV.-Ten Commandments Corresponding to the Plagues of Egypt.

"On account of those, therefore, who by neglect of their own salvation please the evil one, and those who by study

---

[1] Original word used in the text was: **salutary**
[2] See footnote 1

of their own profit seek to please the good One, ten things have been prescribed as a test to this present age, according to the number of the ten plagues which were brought upon Egypt. For when Moses, according to the commandment of God, demanded of Pharaoh that he should let the people go, and in token of his heavenly commission showed signs, his rod being thrown upon the ground was turned into a serpent. And when Pharaoh could not by these means be brought to consent, as having freedom of will, again the magicians seemed to do similar signs, by permission of God, that the purpose of the king might be proved from the freedom of his will, whether he would rather believe the signs wrought by Moses, who was sent by God, or those which the magicians rather seemed to work than actually wrought. For truly he ought to have understood from their very name that they were not workers of truth, because they were not called messengers of God, but magicians, as the tradition also intimates. Moreover, they seemed to maintain the contest up to a certain point, and afterwards they confessed of themselves, and yielded to their superior. Therefore the last plague is inflicted, the destruction of the first-born, and then Moses is commanded to consecrate the people by the sprinkling of blood; and so, gifts being presented, with much entreaty he is asked to depart with the people.

Chapter LVI.-Simon Resisted Peter, as the Magicians Moses.

"In a similar transaction I see that I am even now engaged. For as then, when Moses exhorted the king to believe God, the magicians opposed him by a pretended exhibition of similar signs, and so kept back the unbelievers from salvation; so also now, when I have come forth to teach all nations to believe in the true God, Simon the magician resists me, acting in opposition to me, as they also did in opposition to Moses; in order that whosoever they be from among the nations that do not use sound judgment, they may be made manifest; but that those may be saved who rightly distinguish signs from signs." While Peter thus spoke, Niceta answered: "I beseech you that you would permit me to state whatever occurs to my mind." Then Peter, being delighted with the eagerness of his disciples, said: "Speak what you will."

Chapter LVII.-Miracles of the Magicians.

Then said Niceta: "In what respect did the Egyptians sin in not believing Moses, since the magicians wrought like signs, even although they were done rather in appearance than in truth? For if I had been there then, should I not have thought, from the fact that the magicians did like things to those which Moses did, either that Moses was a magician, or that the magicians wrought their signs by divine commission? For I should not have thought it likely that the same things could be effected by magicians, even in appearance, which he who was sent by God performed. And now, in what respect do they sin who believe Simon, since they see him do so great marvels? Or is it not marvelous to fly through the air, to be so mixed with fire as to become one body with it, to make statues walk, brazen dogs bark, and other such like things, which assuredly are sufficiently wonderful to those who know not how to distinguish? Yea, he has also been seen to make bread of stones. But if he sins who believes those who do signs, how shall it appear that he also does not sin who has believed our Lord for His signs and works of power?"

Chapter LVIII.-Truth Veiled with Love.

Then said Peter: "I take it well that you bring the truth to the rule, and do not suffer hindrances of faith to lurk in your soul. For thus you can easily obtain the remedy. Do you remember that I said, that the worst of all things is when any one neglects to learn what is for his good? "Niceta answered: "I remember." Then Peter: "And again, that God has veiled His truth, that He may disclose it to those who faithfully follow Him?""Neither," said Niceta, "have I forgotten this." Then said Peter: "What think you then? That God has buried His truth deep in the earth, and has heaped mountains upon it, that it may be found by those only who are able to dig down into the depths? It is not so; but as He has surrounded the mountains and the earth with the expanse of heaven, so hath He veiled the truth with the curtain of His own love, that he alone may be able to reach it, who has first knocked at the gate of divine love.

Chapter LIX.-Good and Evil in Pairs.

"For, as I was beginning to say, God has appointed for this world certain pairs; and he who comes first of the pairs is of evil, he who comes second, of good. And in this is given to every man an occasion of right judgment, whether he is simple or prudent. For if he is simple, and believes him who comes first, though moved thereto by signs and prodigies, he must of necessity, for the same reason, believe him who comes second; for he will be persuaded by signs and prodigies, as he was before. When he believes this second one, he will learn from him that he ought not to believe the first, who comes of evil; and so the error of the former is corrected by the emendation[1] of the latter. But if he will not receive the second, because he has believed the first, he will deservedly be condemned as unjust; for unjust it is, that when he believed the first on account of his signs, he will not believe the second, though he bring the same, or even greater signs. But if he has not believed the first, it follows that he may be moved to believe the second. For his mind has not become so completely inactive but that it may be roused by the redoubling of marvels. But if he is prudent, he can make distinction of the signs. And if indeed he has believed in the first, he will be moved to the second by the increase in the miracles, and by comparison he will apprehend which are better; although clear tests *of miracles* are recognized by all learned men, as we have shown in the regular order of our discussion. But if any one, as being whole and not needing a physician, is not moved to the first, he will be drawn to the second by the very

---

[1] An alteration intended to improve.
Source: Dictionary.com Unabridged (v 1.1)

continuance of the thing, and will make a distinction of signs and marvels after this fashion;-he who is of the evil one, the signs that he works do good to no one; but those which the good man worketh are profitable to men."

Chapter LX.-Uselessness of Pretended Miracles.

"For tell me, I pray you, what is the use of showing statues walking, dogs of brass or stone barking, mountains dancing, of flying through the air, and such like things, which you say that Simon did? But those *signs* which are of the good One, are directed to the advantage of men, as are those which were done by our Lord, who gave sight to the blind and hearing to the deaf, raised up the feeble and the lame, drove away sicknesses and demons, raised the dead, and did other like things, as you see also that I do. Those signs, therefore, which make for the benefit of men, and confer some good upon them, the wicked one cannot do, excepting only at the end of the world. For then it shall be permitted him to mix up with his signs some good ones, as the expelling of demons or the healing of diseases; by this means going beyond his bounds, and being divided against himself, and fighting against himself, he shall be destroyed. And therefore the Lord has foretold, that in the last times there shall be such temptation, that, if it be possible, the very elect shall be deceived; that is to say, that by the marks of signs being confused, even those must be disturbed who seem to be expert in discovering spirits and distinguishing miracles.

Chapter LXI.-Ten Pairs.

"The ten pairs of which we have spoken have therefore been assigned to this world from the beginning of time. Cain and Abel were one pair. The second was the giants and Noah; the third, Pharaoh and Abraham; the fourth, the Philistines and Isaac; the fifth, Esau and Jacob; the sixth, the magicians and Moses the lawgiver; the seventh, the tempter and the Son of man; the eighth, Simon and I, Peter; the ninth, all nations, and he who shall be sent to sow the word among the nations; the tenth, Antichrist and Christ. Concerning these pairs we shall give you fuller information at another time." When Peter spoke thus, Aquila said: "Truly there is need of constant teaching, that one may learn what is true about everything."

Chapter LXII.-The Christian Life.

But Peter said: "Who is he that is earnest toward instruction, and that studiously inquires into every particular, except him who loves his own soul to salvation, and renounces all the affairs of this world, that he may have leisure to attend to the word of God only? Such is he whom alone the true Prophet deems wise, even he who sells all that he has and buys the one true pearl, who understands what is the difference between temporal things and eternal, small and great, men and God. For he understands what is the eternal hope in presence of the true and good God. But who is he that loves God, save him who knows His wisdom? And how can any one obtain knowledge of God's wisdom, unless he is constant in hearing His word? Whence it comes, that he conceives a love for Him, and venerates Him with worthy honor, pouring out hymns and prayers to Him, and most pleasantly resting in these, accounteth it his greatest damage if at any time he speak or do aught else even for a moment of time; because, in reality, the soul which is filled with the love of God can neither look upon anything except what pertains to God, nor, by reason of love of Him, can be satisfied with meditating upon those things which it knows to be pleasing to Him. But those who have not conceived affection for Him, nor bear His love lighted up in their mind, are as it were placed in darkness and cannot see light; and therefore, even before they begin to learn anything of God, they immediately faint as though worn out by labor; and filled with weariness, they are straightway hurried by their own peculiar habits to those words with which they are pleased. For it is wearisome and annoying to such persons to hear anything about God; and that for the reason I have stated, because their mind has received no sweetness of divine love."

Chapter LXIII.-A Deserter from Simon's Camp.

While Peter was thus speaking, the day dawned; and, behold, one of the disciples of Simon came, crying out: "I beseech thee, O Peter, receive me, a wretch, who have been deceived by Simon the magician, to whom I gave heed as to a heavenly God, by reason of those miracles which I saw him perform. But when I heard your discourses, I began to think him a man, and indeed a wicked man; nevertheless, when he went out from this I alone followed him, for I had not yet clearly perceived his impieties. But when he saw me following him, he called me blessed, and led me to his house; and about the middle of the night he said to me, `I shall make you better than all men, if you will remain with me even till the end.' When I had promised him this, he demanded of me an oath of perseverance; and having got this, he placed upon my shoulders some of his polluted and accursed secret things, that I might carry them, and ordered me to follow him. But when we came to the sea, he went aboard a boat which happened to be there, and took from my neck what he had ordered me to carry. And as he came out a little after, bringing nothing with him, he must have thrown it into the sea. Then he asked me to go with him, saying that he was going to Rome, and that there he would please the people so much, that he should be reckoned a god, and publicly gifted with divine honors. `Then, 'said he, `if you wish to return hither, I shall send you back, loaded with all riches, and upheld by various services.' When I heard this, and saw nothing in him in accordance with this profession, but perceived that he was a magician and a deceiver, I answered: `Pardon me, I pray you; for I have a pain in my feet, and therefore I am not able to leave Caesarea. Besides, I have a wife and little children, whom I cannot leave by any means.' When he heard this, he charged me with sloth, and set out towards Dora, saying, `You will be sorry, when you hear what glory I shall get in the city of Rome.' And after this he set out for Rome, as he said; but I hastily returned hither, entreating you to receive me to penitence, because I have been deceived by him."

Chapter LXIV.-Declaration of Simon's Wickedness.

When he who had returned from Simon had thus spoken, Peter ordered him to sit down in the court. And he himself going forth, and seeing immense crowds, far more than on the previous days, stood in his usual place; and pointing out him who had come, began to discourse as follows: "This man whom I point out to you, brethren, has just come to me, telling me of the wicked practices of Simon, and how he has thrown the implements of his wickedness into the sea, not induced to do so by repentance, but being afraid lest, being detected, he should be subjected to the public laws. And he asked this man, as he tells me, to remain with him, promising him immense gifts; and when he could not persuade him to do so, he left him, reproaching him for sluggishness, and set out for Rome." When Peter had intimated this to the crowd, the man himself who had returned from Simon stood up, and began to state to the people everything relating to Simon's crimes. And when they were shocked by the things which they heard that Simon had done by his magical acts, Peter said:

Chapter LXV.-Peter Resolves to Follow Simon.

"Be not, my brethren, distressed by those things that have been done, but give heed to the future: for what is passed is ended; but the things which threaten are dangerous to those who shall fall in with them. For offences shall never be wanting in this world, so long as the enemy is permitted to act according to his will; in order that the prudent and those who understood his wiles may be conquerors in the contests which he raises against them; but that those who neglect to learn the things that pertain to the salvation of their souls, may be taken by him with merited deceptions. Since, therefore, as you have heard, Simon has gone forth to preoccupy the ears of the Gentiles who are called to salvation, it is necessary that I also follow upon his track, so that whatever disputations he raises may be corrected by us. But inasmuch as it is right that greater anxiety should be felt concerning you who are already received within the walls of life,-for if that which has been actually acquired perish, a positive loss is sustained; while with respect to that which has not yet been acquired, if it can be got, there is so much gain; but if not, the only loss is that there is no gain;-in order, therefore, that you may be more and more confirmed in the truth, and the nations who are called to salvation may in no way be prevented by the wickedness of Simon, I have thought good to ordain Zacchaeus as pastor over you, and to remain with you myself for three months; and so to go to the Gentiles, lest through our delaying longer, and the crimes of Simon stalking in every direction, they should become incurable."

Chapter LXVI.-Zacchaeus Made Bishop of Caesarea; Presbyters and Deacons Ordained.

At this announcement all the people wept, hearing that he was going to leave them; and Peter, sympathizing with them, himself also shed tears; and looking up to heaven, he said: "To Thee, O God, who hast made heaven and earth, and all things that are in them, we pour out the prayer of supplication, that Thou wouldest comfort those who have recourse to Thee in their tribulation. For by reason of the affection that they have towards Thee, they do love me who have declared to them Thy truth. Wherefore guard them with the right hand of Thy compassion; for neither Zacchaeus nor any other man can be a sufficient guardian to them." When he had said this, and more to the same effect, he laid his hands upon Zacchaeus, and prayed that he might blamelessly discharge the duty of his bishopric. Then he ordained twelve presbyters and four deacons, and said: "I have ordained you this Zacchaeus as a bishop, knowing that he has the fear of God, and is expert in the Scriptures. You ought therefore to honor him as holding the place of Christ, obeying him for your salvation, and knowing that whatever honor and whatever injury is done to him, redounds[1] to Christ, and from Christ to God. Hear him therefore with all attention, and receive from him the doctrine of the faith; and from the presbyters the admonitions[2] of life; and from the deacons the order of discipline. Have a religious care of widows; vigorously assist orphans; take pity on the poor; teach the young modesty;-and in a word, sustain one another as circumstances shall demand; worship God, who created heaven and earth; believe in Christ; love one another; be compassionate to all; and fulfill charity not only in word, but in act and deed."

Chapter LXVII.-Invitation to Baptism.

When he had given them these and such like precepts, he made proclamation to the people, saying: "Since I have resolved to stay three months with you, if any one desires it, let him be baptized; that, stripped of his former evils, he may for the future, in consequence of his own conduct, become heir of heavenly blessings, as a reward for his good actions. Whosoever will, then, let him come to Zacchaeus and give his name to him, and let him hear from him the mysteries of the kingdom of heaven. Let him attend to frequent fastings, and approve himself in all things, that at the end of these three months he may be baptized on the day of the festival. But every one of you shall be baptized in ever flowing waters, the name of the Threefold[3] Beatitude being invoked over him; he being first anointed with oil sanctified by prayer, that so at length, being consecrated by these things, he may attain a perception of holy things."

Chapter LXVIII.-Twelve Sent Before Him.

And when he had spoken at length on the subject of baptism, he dismissed the crowd, and betook himself to his

---

[1] To have an effect or consequence.
Source: Dictionary.com Unabridged (v 1.1)
[2] Original word used in the text was: **monitions**
[3] Original word used in the text was: **Trine**

usual place of abode; and there, while the twelve stood around him (viz. Zacchaeus and Sophonias, Joseph and Michaeus, Eleazar and Phineas, Lazarus and Eliseus, I Clement and Nicodemus, Niceta and Aquila), he addressed us to the following effect: "Let us, my brethren, consider what is right; for it is our duty to bring some help to the nations, which are called to salvation. You have yourselves heard that Simon has set out, wishing to anticipate our journey. Him we should have followed step by step, that wheresoever he tries to subvert any, we might immediately confute him. But since it appears to me to be unjust to forsake those who have been already converted to God, and to bestow our care upon those who are still afar off, I think it right that I should remain three months with those in this city who have been turned to the faith, and should strengthen them; and yet that we should not neglect those who are still far off, lest perhaps, if they be long infected with the power of pernicious doctrine, it be more difficult to recover them. Therefore I wish (only, however, if you also think it right), that for Zacchaeus, whom we have now ordained bishop, Benjamin the son of Saba be substituted; and for Clement (whom I have resolved to have always by me, because, coming from the Gentiles, he has a great desire to hear the word of God) there be substituted Ananias the son of Safra; and for Niceta and Aquila, who have been but lately converted to the faith of Christ, Rubelus the brother of Zacchaeus, and Zacharias the builder. I wish, therefore, to complete the number of twelve by substituting these four for the other four, that Simon may feel that I in them am always with him."

Chapter LXIX.-Arrangements Approved by All the Brethren.

Having therefore separated me, Clement, and Niceta and Aquila, he said to those twelve: "I wish you the day after to-morrow to proceed to the Gentiles, and to follow in the footsteps of Simon, that you may inform me of all his proceedings. You will also inquire diligently the sentiments of every one, and announce to them that I shall come to them without delay; and, in short, in all places instruct the Gentiles to expect my coming." When he had spoken these things, and others to the same effect, he said: "You also, my brethren, if you have anything to say to these things, say on, lest perhaps it be not right which seems good to me alone." Then all, with one voice applauding him, said: "We ask you rather to arrange everything according to your own judgment, and to order what seems good to yourself; for this we think to be the perfect work of piety, if we fulfill what you command."

Chapter LXX.-Departure of the Twelve.

Therefore, on the day appointed, when they had ranged themselves before Peter, they said: "Do not think, O Peter, that it is a small grief to us that we are to be deprived of the privilege of hearing you for three months; but since it is good for us to do what you order, we shall most readily obey. We shall always retain in our hearts the remembrance of your face; and so we set out actively, as you have commanded us." Then he, having poured out a prayer to the Lord for them, dismissed them. And when those twelve who had been sent forward had gone, Peter entered, according to custom, and stood in the place of disputation. And a multitude of people had come together, even a larger number than usual; and all with tears gazed upon him, by reason of what they had heard from him the day before, that he was about to go forth on account of Simon. Then, seeing them weeping, he himself also was similarly affected, although he endeavored to conceal and to restrain his tears. But the trembling of his voice, and the interruption of his discourse, betrayed that he was distressed by similar emotion.

Chapter LXXI.-Peter Prepares the Caesareans for His Departure.

However, rubbing his forehead with his hand, he said: "Be of good courage, my brethren, and comfort your sorrowful hearts by means of counsel, referring all things to God, whose will alone is to be fulfilled and to be preferred in all things. For let us suppose for a moment, that by reason of the affection that we have towards you, we should act against His will, and remain with you, is He not able, by sending death upon me, to appoint to me a longer separation from you? And therefore it is better for us to carry out this shorter separation with His will, as those to whom it is prescribed to obey God in all things. Hence you also ought to obey Him with like submission, inasmuch as you love me from no other reason than on account of your love of Him. As friends of God, therefore, acquiesce in His will; but also judge yourselves what is right. Would it not have seemed wicked, if, when Simon was deceiving you, I had been detained by the brethren in Jerusalem, and had not come to you, and that although you had Zacchaeus among you, a good and eloquent man? So now also consider that it would be wicked, if, when Simon has gone forth to assail the Gentiles, who are wholly without a defender, I should be detained by you, and should not follow him. Wherefore let us see to it, that we do not, by an unreasonable affection, accomplish the will of the wicked one."

Chapter LXXII.-More Than Ten Thousand Baptized.

"Meantime I shall remain with you three months, as I promised. Be ye constant in hearing the word; and at the end of that time, if any are able and willing to follow us, they may do so, if duty will admit of it. And when I say *if duty will admit* I mean that no one by his departure must sadden any one who ought not to be saddened, as by leaving parents who ought not to be left, or a faithful wife, or any other person to whom he is bound to afford comfort for God's sake." Meantime, disputing and teaching day by day, he filled up the tithe appointed with the labor of teaching; and when the festival day arrived, upwards of ten thousand were baptized.

Chapter LXXIII.-Tidings of Simon.

But in those days a letter was received from the brethren who had gone before, in which were detailed the crimes of Simon, how going from city to city he was deceiving multitudes, and everywhere maligning Peter, so that, when he should come, no one might afford him a hearing. For he asserted that Peter was a magician, a godless man, injurious, cunning, ignorant, and professing impossible things. "For," says he, "he asserts that the dead shall rise again, which is impossible. But if any one attempts to confute him, he is cut off by secret snares by him, through means of his attendants. Wherefore, I also," says he, "when I had vanquished him and triumphed over him, fled for fear of his snares, lest he should destroy me by incantations, or compass my death by plots." They intimated also that he mainly stayed at Tripolis.

Chapter LXXIV.-Farewell to Caesarea.

Peter therefore ordered the letter to be read to the people; and after the reading of it, he addressed them and gave them full instructions about everything, but especially that they should obey Zacchaeus, whom he had ordained bishop over them. Also he commended the presbyters and the deacons to the people, and not less the people to them. And then, announcing that he should spend the winter at Tripolis, he said: "I commend you to the grace of God, being about to depart to-morrow, with God's will. But during the whole three months which he spent at Caesarea, for the sake of instruction, whatever he discoursed of in the presence of the people in the day-time, he explained more fully and perfectly in the night, in private to us, as more faithful and completely approved by him. And at the same time he commanded me, because he understood that I carefully stored in my memory what I heard, to commit to writing whatever seemed worthy of record, and to send it to you, my lord James, as also I did, in obedience to his command."

Chapter LXXV.-Contents of Clement's Despatches to James.

The first book, therefore, of those that I formerly sent to you, contains an account of the true Prophet, and of the peculiarity of the understanding of the law, according to what the tradition of Moses teaches. The second contains an account of the beginning, and whether there be one beginning or many, and that the law of the Hebrews knows what immensity is. The third, concerning God, and those things that have been ordained by Him. The fourth, that though there are many that are called gods, there is but one true God, according to the testimonies of the Scriptures. The fifth, that there are two heavens, one of which is that visible firmament which shall pass away, but the other is eternal and invisible. The sixth, concerning good and evil; and that all things are subjected to good by the Father; and why, and how, and whence evil is, and that it co-operates with good, but not with a good purpose; and what are the signs of good, and what those of evil; and what is the difference between duality and conjunction[1]. The seventh, what are the things which the twelve apostles treated of in the presence of the people in the temple. The eighth, concerning the words of the Lord which seem to be contradictory, but are not; and what is the explanation of them. The ninth, that the law which has been given by God is righteous and perfect, and that it alone can make pure. The tenth, concerning the carnal birth of men, and concerning the generation which is by baptism; and what is the succession of carnal seed in man; and what is the account of his soul, and how the freedom of the will is in it, which, seeing it is not unbegotten, but made, could not be immoveable from good. Concerning these several subjects, therefore, whatever Peter discoursed at Caesarea, according to his command, as I have said, I have sent you written in ten volumes. But on the next day, as had been determined, we set out from Caeesarea with some faithful men, who had resolved to accompany Peter.

---

[1] The state of being conjoined; union; association.
Source: Dictionary.com Unabridged (v 1.1)

Book IV.

Chapter I.-Halt at Dora.

Having set out from Caesarea on the way to Tripolis, we made our first stoppage at a small town called Dora, because it was not far distant; and almost all those who had believed through the preaching of Peter could scarcely bear to be separated from him, but walked along with us, again and again gazing upon him, again and again embracing him, again and again conversing with him, until we came to the inn. On the following day we came to Ptolemais, where we stayed ten days; and when a considerable number had received the word of God, we signified to some of them who seemed particularly attentive, and wished to detain us longer for the sake of instruction, that they might, if so disposed, follow us to Tripolis. We acted in the same way at Tyre, and Sidon, and Berytus, and announced to those who desired to hear further discourses, that we were to spend the winter at Tripolis. Therefore, as all those who were anxious followed Peter from each city, we were a great multitude of elect ones when we entered into Tripolis. On our arrival, the brethren who had been sent before met us before the gates of the city; and taking us under their charge, conducted us to the various lodgings which they had prepared. Then there arose a commotion in the city, and a great assemblage of persons desirous to see Peter.

Chapter II.-Reception in the House of Maro.

And when we had come to the house of Maro, in which preparation had been made for Peter, he turned to the crowd, and told them that he would address them the day after to-morrow. Therefore the brethren who had been sent before assigned lodgings to all who had come with us. Then, when Peter had entered into the house of Maro, and was asked to partake of food, he answered that he would by no means do so, until he had ascertained whether all those that had accompanied him were provided with lodgings. Then he learned from the brethren who had been sent before, that the citizens had received them not only hospitably, but with all kindness, by reason of their love towards Peter; so much so, that several were disappointed because there were no guests for them; for that all had made such preparations, that even if many more had come, there would still have been a deficiency of guests for the hosts, not of hosts for the guests.

Chapter III.-Simon's Flight.

Thereupon Peter was greatly delighted, and praised the brethren, and blessed them, and requested them to remain with him. Then, when he had bathed in the sea, and had taken food, he went to sleep in the evening; and rising, as usual, at cock-crow, while the evening light was still burning, he found us all awake. Now there were in all sixteen of us, viz. Peter and I, Clement, Niceta and Aquila, and those twelve who had preceded us. Saluting us, then, as was his wont, Peter said: "Since we are not taken up with others to-day, let us be taken up with ourselves. I shall tell you what took place at Caesarea after your departure, and you shall tell us of the doings of Simon here." And while the conversation was going on on these subjects, at daybreak some of the members of the family came in and told Peter that Simon, when he heard of Peter's arrival, departed in the night, on the way to Syria. They also stated that the crowds thought that the day which he had said was to intervene was a very long time for their affection, and that they were standing in impatience before the gate, conversing among themselves about those things which they wished to hear, and that they hoped that they should by all means see him before the time appointed; and that as the day became lighter the multitudes were increasing, and that they were trusting confidently, whatever they might be presuming upon, that they should hear a discourse from him. "Now then" said they "instruct us to tell them what seems good to you; for it is absurd that so great a multitude should have come together, and should depart with sadness, through no answer being returned to them. For they will not consider that it is they that have not waited for; the appointed day but rather they will think that you are slighting them."

Chapter IV.-The Harvest Plenteous,

Then Peter, filled with admiration, said: "You see, brethren, how every word of the Lord spoken prophetically is fulfilled. For I remember that He said, `The harvest indeed is plenteous, but the laborers are few; ask therefore the Lord of the harvest, that He would send out laborers into His harvest.' Behold, therefore, the things which are foretold in a mystery are fulfilled. But whereas He said also, `Many shall come from the east and the west, from the north and the south, and shall recline in the bosom of Abraham, and Isaac, and Jacob; ' this also is, as you see, in like manner fulfilled. Wherefore I entreat you, my fellow-servants and helpers, that you would learn diligently the order of preaching, and the ways of absolutions, that ye may be able to save the souls of men, which by the secret power of God acknowledge whom they ought to love, even before they are taught. For you see that these men, like good servants, long for him whom they expect to announce to them the coming of their Lord, that they may be able to fulfill His will when they have learned it. The desire, therefore, of hearing the word of God, and inquiring into His will, they have from God; and this is the beginning of the gift of God, which is given to the Gentiles, that by this they may be able to receive the doctrine of truth.

Chapter V.-Moses and Christ.

"For so also it was given to the people of the Hebrews from the beginning, that they should love Moses, and believe his word; whence also it is written: `The people believed God, and Moses His servant. What, therefore, was of peculiar gift from God toward the nation of the Hebrews, we see now to be given also to those who are called from among the Gentiles to the faith. But the method of works is put into the power and will of every one, and this is their own; but to have an affection towards a teacher of truth. this is a gift of the heavenly Father. But salvation is in this, that you do His will of whom you have conceived a love and affection through the gift of God; lest that saying of His be addressed to you which He spoke, `Why call ye me Lord, Lord, and do not what I say? ' It is therefore the peculiar gift bestowed by God upon the Hebrews, that they believe Moses; and the peculiar gift bestowed upon the Gentiles is that they love Jesus. For this also the Master intimated, when He said, `I will confess' to Thee, O Father, Lord of heaven and earth, because Thou hast concealed these things from the wise and prudent, and hast revealed them to babes. By which it is certainly declared, that the people of the Hebrews, who were instructed out of the law, did not know Him; but the people of the Gentiles have acknowledged Jesus, and venerate Him; on which account also they shall be saved, not only acknowledging Him, but also doing His will. But he who is of the Gentiles, and who has it of God to believe Moses, ought also to have it of his own purpose to love Jesus also. And again, the Hebrew, who has it of God to believe Moses, ought to have it also of his own purpose to believe in Jesus; so that each of them, having in himself something of the divine gift, and something of his own exertion, may be perfect by both. For concerning such an one our Lord spoke, as of a rich man, `Who brings forth from his treasures things new and old.'

Chapter VI.-A Congregation.

"But enough has been said of these things for time presses, and the religious devotion of the people invites us to address them." And when he had thus spoken, he asked where there was a suitable place for discussion. And Maro said: "I have a very spacious hall which can hold more than five hundred men, and there is also a garden within the house; or if it please you to be in some public place, all would prefer it, for there is nobody who does not desire at least to see your face." Then Peter said: "Show me the hall, or the garden." And when he had seen the hall, he went in to see the garden also; and suddenly the whole multitude, as if some one had called them, rushed into the house, and thence broke through into the garden, where Peter was already standing, selecting a fit place for discussion.

Chapter VII.-The Sick Healed.

But when he saw that the crowds had, like the waters of a great river, poured over the narrow passage, he mounted upon a pillar which happened to stand near the wall of the garden, and first saluted the people in a religious manner. But some of those who were present, and who had been for a long time distressed by demons, threw themselves on the ground, while the unclean spirits entreated that they might be allowed but for one day to remain in the bodies that they had taken possession of. But Peter rebuked them, and commanded them to depart; and they went out without delay. After these, others who had been afflicted with long-standing sicknesses asked Peter that they might receive healing; and he promised that he would entreat the Lord for them as soon as his discourse of instruction was completed. But as soon as he promised, they were freed from their sicknesses; and he ordered them to sit down apart, with those who had been freed from the demons, as after the fatigue of labor. Meantime, while this was going on, a vast multitude assembled, attracted not only by the desire of hearing Peter, but also by the report of the cures which had been accomplished. But Peter, beckoning with his hand to the people to be still, and settling the crowds in tranquility, began to address them as follows:-

Chapter VIII.-Providence Vindicated

"It seems to me necessary, at the outset of a discourse concerning the true worship of God, first of all to instruct those who have not as yet acquired any knowledge of the subject, that throughout the divine providence must be maintained to be without blame, by which the world is ruled and governed. Moreover, the reason of the present undertaking, and the occasion offered by those whom the power of God has healed, suggest this subject for a beginning, viz. to show that for good reason very many persons are possessed of demons, that so the justice of God may appear. For ignorance will be found to be the mother of almost all evils. But now let us come to the reason.

Chapter IX.-State of Innocence a State of Enjoyment.

"When God had made man after His own image and likeness, He grafted into His work a certain breathing and odor of His divinity, that so men, being made partakers of His Only-begotten, might through Him be also friends of God and sons of adoption. Whence also He Himself, as the true Prophet, knowing with what actions the Father is pleased, instructed them in what way they might obtain that privilege. At that time, therefore, there was among men only one worship of God-a pure mind and an uncorrupted spirit. And for this reason every creature kept an inviolable covenant with the human race. For by reason of their reverence of the Creator, no sickness, or bodily disorder, or corruption of food, had power over them; whence it came to pass, that a life of a thousand years did not fall into the frailty of old age.

Chapter X.-Sin the Cause of Suffering.

"But when men, leading a life void of distress, began to think that the continuance of good things was granted them not by the divine bounty, but by the chance of things, and to accept as a debt of nature, not as a gift of God's goodness, their enjoyment without any exertion of the delights of the divine complaisance,-men, being led by these things into contrary and impious thoughts, came at last, at the instigation of idleness, to think that the life of gods was theirs by nature, without any labors or merits on their part. Hence they go from bad to worse, to believe that neither is the world governed by the providence of God, nor is there any place for virtues, since they knew that they themselves possessed the fullness of ease and delights, without the assignment of any works previously, and without any labors were treated as the friends of God.

Chapter XI.-Suffering Salutary.

"By the most righteous judgment of God, therefore, labors and afflictions are assigned as a remedy to men languishing in the vanity of such thoughts. And when labor and tribulations came upon them, they were excluded from the place of delights and amenity. Also the earth began to produce nothing to them without labor; and then men's thoughts being turned in them, they were warned to seek the aid of their Creator, and by prayers and vows to ask for the divine protection. And thus it came to pass, that the worship of God, which they had neglected by reason of their prosperity, they recovered through their adversity; and their thoughts towards God, which indulgence had perverted, affliction corrected. So therefore the divine providence, seeing that this was more profitable to man, removed from them the ways of benignity[1] and abundance, as being hurtful, and introduced the way of vexation and tribulation.

Chapter XII.-Translation of Enoch.

"But that He might show that these things were done on account of the ungrateful, He translated to immortality a certain one[2] of the first race of men, because He saw that he was not unmindful of His grace, and because he hoped to call on the name of God; while the rest, who were so ungrateful that they could not be amended and corrected even by labors and tribulations, were condemned to a terrible death. Yet amongst them also He found a certain one,[3] who was righteous with his house, whom He preserved, having enjoined him to build an ark, in which he and those who were commanded to go with him might

---
[1] The quality or condition of being kind and gentle.
Source: Dictionary.com Unabridged (v 1.1)
[2] Likely speaking of Enoch.
[3] Noah

escape, when all things should be destroyed by a deluge: in order that, the wicked being cut off by the overflow of waters, the world might receive a purification; and he who had been preserved for the continuance of the race, being purified by water, might anew repair the world.

Chapter XIII.-Origin of Idolatry.

"But when all these things were done, men turned again to impiety; and on this account a law was given by God to instruct them in the manner of living. But in process of time, the worship of God and righteousness were corrupted by the unbelieving and the wicked, as we shall show more fully by and by. Moreover, perverse and erratic religions were introduced, to which the greater part of men gave themselves up, by occasion of holidays and solemnities, instituting drinkings and banquets, following pipes, and flutes, and harps, and diverse kinds of musical instruments, and indulging themselves in all kinds of drunkenness and luxury. Hence every kind of error took rise; hence they invented groves and altars, fillets and victims, and after drunkenness they were agitated as if with mad emotions. By this means power was given to the demons to enter into minds of this sort, so that they seemed to lead insane dances and to rave like Bacchanalians; hence were invented the gnashing of teeth, and bellowing from the depth of their bowels; hence a terrible countenance and a fierce aspect in men, so that he whom drunkenness had subverted and a demon had instigated, was believed by the deceived and the erring to be filled with the Deity.

Chapter XIV.-God Both Good and Righteous.

"Hence, since so many false and erratic religions have been introduced into the world, we have been sent, as good merchants, bringing unto you the worship of the true God, handed down from the fathers, and preserved; as the seeds of which we scatter these words amongst you, and place it in your choice to choose what seems to you to be right. For if you receive those things which we bring you, you shall not only be able yourselves to escape the incursions of the demon, but also to drive them away from others; and at the same time you shall obtain the rewards of eternal good things. But those who shall refuse to receive those things which are spoken by us, shall be subject in the present life to diverse demons and disorders of sicknesses, and their souls after their departure from the body shall be tormented for ever. For God is not only good, but also just; for if He were always good, and never just to render to every one according to his deeds, goodness would be found to be injustice. For it were injustice if the impious and the pious were treated by Him alike.

Chapter XV.-How Demons Get Power Over Men.

"Therefore demons, as we have just said, when once they have been able, by means of opportunities afforded them, to convey themselves through base and evil actions into the bodies of men, if they remain in them a long time through their own negligence, because they do not seek after what is profitable to their souls, they necessarily compel them for the future to fulfill the desires of the demons who dwell in them. But what is worst of all, at the end of the world, when that demon shall be consigned to eternal fire, of necessity the soul also which obeyed him, shall with him be tortured in eternal fires, together with its body which it hath polluted.

Chapter XVI.-Why They Wish to Possess Men.

"Now that the demons are desirous of occupying the bodies of men, this is the reason. They are spirits baring their purpose turned to wickedness. Therefore by immoderate eating and drinking, and lust, they urge men on to sin, but only those who entertain the purpose of sinning, who, while they seem simply desirous of satisfying the necessary cravings of nature, give opportunity to the demons to enter into them, because through excess they do not maintain moderation. For as long as the measure of nature is kept, and legitimate moderation is preserved, the mercy of God does not give them liberty to enter into men. But when either the mind falls into impiety, or the body is filled with immoderate meat or drink, then, as if invited by the will and purpose of those who thus neglect themselves, they receive power as against those who have broken the law imposed by God.

Chapter XVII.-The Gospel Gives Power Over Demons.

"You see, then, how important is the acknowledgment of God, and the observance of the divine religion, which not only protects those who believe from the assaults of the demon, but also gives them command over those who rule over others. And therefore it is necessary for you, who are of the Gentiles, to betake yourselves to God, and to keep yourselves from all uncleanness, that the demons may be expelled, and God may dwell in you And at the same time, by prayers, commit yourselves to God, and call for His aid against the impudence of the demons; for `whatever things ye ask, believing, ye shall receive.' But even the demons themselves, in proportion as they see faith grow in a man, in that proportion they depart from him, residing only in that part in which something of infidelity still remains; but from those who believe with full faith, they depart without any delay. For when a soul has come to the faith of God, it obtains the virtue of heavenly water, by which it extinguishes the demon like a spark of fire.

Chapter XVII.-This Power in Proportion to Faith.

"There is therefore a measure of faith, which, if it be perfect, drives the demon perfectly from the soul; but if it has any defect, something on the part of the demon still remains in the portion of infidelity; and it is the greatest difficulty for the soul to understand when or how, whether fully or less fully, the demon has been expelled from it. For if he remains in any quarter, when he gets an opportunity, he suggests thoughts to men's hearts; and they, not knowing whence they come, believe the suggestions of the demons, as if they were the perceptions of their own souls. Thus they suggest to some to follow pleasure by occasion of bodily necessity; they excuse the passionateness of others by excess of gall; they color over the madness of others by the vehemence of melancholy; and even extenuate the folly of some as the result of abundance of phlegm. But even if this were so, still none of these could be hurtful to the body, except from the excess of meats and drinks; because, when these are taken in excessive quantities, their abundance, which the natural warmth is not sufficient to digest, curdles into a sort of poison, and it, flowing through the bowels and all the veins like a common sewer, renders the motions of the body unhealthy and base. Wherefore moderation is to be attained in all things, that neither may place be given to demons, nor the soul, being possessed by them, be delivered along with them to be tormented in eternal fires.

Chapter XIX.-Demons Incite to Idolatry.

"There is also another error of the demons, which they suggest to the senses of men, that they should think that those things which they suffer, they suffer from such as are called gods, in order that thereby, offering sacrifices and gifts, as if to propitiate them, they may strengthen the worship of false religion, and avoid us who are interested in their salvation, that they may be freed from error; but this they do, as I have said, not knowing that these thing are suggested to them by demons, for fear they should be saved. It is therefore in the power of every one, since man has been made possessed of free-will, whether he shall hear us to life, or the demons to destruction. Also to some, the demons, appearing visibly under various figures, sometimes throw out threats, sometimes promise relief from sufferings, that they may instill into those whom they deceive the opinion of their being gods, and that it may not be known that they are demons. But they are not concealed from us, who know the mysteries of the creation, and for what reason it is permitted of the demons to do those things in the present world; how it is allowed them to transform themselves into what figures they please, and to suggest evil thoughts, and to convey themselves, by means of meats and of drink consecrated to them, into the minds or bodies of those who partake of it, and to concoct vain dreams to further the worship of some idol.

Chapter XX.-Folly of Idolatry.

"And yet who can be found so senseless as to be persuaded to worship an idol, whether it be made of gold or of any other metal? To whom is it not manifest that the metal is just that which the artificer pleased? How then can the divinity be thought to be in that which would not be at all unless the artificer had pleased? Or how can they hope that future things should be declared to them by that in which there is no perception of present things? For although they should divine something, they should not straightway be held to be gods; for divination is one thing, divinity is another. For the Pythons also seem to divine, yet they are not gods; and, in short, they are driven out of men by Christians. And how can that be God which is put to flight by a man? But perhaps you will say, What as to their effecting cures, and their showing how one can be cured? On this principle, physicians ought also to be worshipped as gods, for they cure many; and in proportion as any one is more skilful, the more he will cure.

Chapter XXI.-Heathen Oracles.

"Whence it is evident that they since they are demoniac spirits, know some things both more quickly and more perfectly *than men;* for they are not retarded in their learning by the heaviness of a body. And therefore they, as being spirits, know without delay and without difficulty what physicians attain after a long time and by much labor. It is not wonderful, therefore, if they know somewhat more than men do; but this is to be observed, that what they know they do not employ for the salvation of souls, but for the deception of them, that by means of it they may indoctrinate them in the worship of false religion. But God, that the error of so great deception might not be concealed, and that He Himself might not seem to be a cause of error in permitting them so great license to deceive men by divinations, and cures, and dreams, has of His mercy furnished men with a remedy, and has made the distinction of falsehood and truth patent to those who desire to know. This, there fore, is that distinction: what is spoken by the true God, whether by prophets or by diverse visions, is always true; but what is foretold by demons is not always true. It is therefore an evident sign that those things are not spoken by the true God, in which at any time there is falsehood; for in truth there is never falsehood. But in the case of those who speak falsehoods, there may occasionally be a slight mixture of truth, to give as it were seasoning to the falsehoods.

Chapter XXII.-Why They Sometimes Come True.

"But if any one say, What is the use of this, that they should be permitted even sometimes to speak truth, and thereby so much error be introduced amongst men? Let him take this for answer: If they had never been allowed to speak any truth, then they would not foretell anything at all; while if they did not foretell, they would not be known to be demons. But if demons were not known to be in this world, the cause of our struggle and contest would be concealed from us, and we should suffer openly what was done in secret, that is, if the power were granted to them of only acting against us, and not of speaking. But now, since they sometimes speak truth, and sometimes falsehood, we ought to acknowledge, as I have said, that their responses are of demons, and not of God, with whom there is never falsehood.

Chapter XXIII.-Evil Not in Substance.

"But if any one, proceeding more curiously, inquire: What then was the use of God's making these evil things, which should have so great a tendency to subvert the minds of men? To one proposing such a question, we answer that we must first of all inquire whether there is any evil in substance. And although it would be sufficient to say to him that it is not suitable that the creature judge the Creator, but that to judge the work of another belongs to him who is either of equal skill or equal power; yet, to come directly to the point, we say absolutely that there is no evil in substance. But if this be so, then the Creator of substance is vainly blamed.

Chapter XXIV.-Why God Permits Evil.

"But you will meet me by saying, Even if it has come to this through freedom of will, was the Creator ignorant that those whom He created would fall away into evil? He ought therefore not to have created those who, He foresaw, would deviate from the path of righteousness. Now we tell those who ask such questions, that the purpose of assertions of the sort made by us is to show why the wickedness of those who as yet were not, did not prevail over the goodness of the Creator. For if, wishing to fill up the number and measure of His creation, He had been afraid of the wickedness of those who were to be, and like one who could find no other way of remedy and cure, except only this, that He should refrain from His purpose of creating, lest the wickedness of those who were to be should be ascribed to Him; what else would this show but unworthy suffering and unseemly feebleness on the part of the Creator, who should so fear the actings of those who as yet were not, that He refrained from His purposed creation?

Chapter XXV.-Evil Beings Turned to Good Account.

"But, setting aside these things, let us consider this earnestly, that God the Creator of the universe, foreseeing the future differences of His creation, foresaw and provided diverse ranks and different offices to each of His creatures, according to the peculiar movements which were produced from freedom of will; so that while all men are of one substance in respect of the method of creation, there should yet be diversity in ranks and offices, according to the peculiar movements of minds, to be produced from liberty of will. Therefore He foresaw that there would be faults in

His creatures; and the method of His justice demanded that punishment should follow faults, for the sake of amendment. It behooved, therefore, that there should be ministers of punishment, and yet that freedom of will should draw them into that order. Moreover, those also must have enemies to conquer, who had undertaken the contests for the heavenly rewards. Thus, therefore, neither are those things destitute of utility which are thought to be evil, since the conquered unwillingly acquire eternal rewards for those by whom they are conquered. But let this suffice on these points, for in process of time even more secret things shall be disclosed.

Chapter XXVI.-Evil Angels Seducers.

"Now therefore, since you do not yet understand how great darkness of ignorance surrounds you, meantime I wish to explain to you whence the worship of idols began in this world. And by idols, I mean those lifeless images which you worship, whether made of wood, or earthenware, or stone, or brass, or any other metals: of these the beginning was in this wise. Certain angels, having left the course of their proper order, began to favor the vices of men, and in some measure to lend unworthy aid to their lust, in order that by these means they might indulge their own pleasures the more; and then, that they might not seem to be inclined of their own accord to unworthy services, taught men that demons could, by certain arts-that is, by magical invocations-be made to obey men; and so, as from a furnace and workshop of wickedness, they filled the whole world with the smoke of impiety, the light of piety being withdrawn.

Chapter XXVII.-Ham the First Magician.

"For these and some other causes, a flood was brought upon the world, as we have said already, and shall say again; and all who were upon the earth were destroyed, except the family of Noah, who survived, with his three sons and their wives. One of these, by name Ham, unhappily discovered the magical act, and handed down the instruction of it to one of his sons, who was called Mesraim, from whom the race of the Egyptians and Babylonians and Persians are descended. Him the nations who then existed called Zoroaster, admiring him as the first author of the magic art; trader whose name also many books on this subject exist. He therefore, being much and frequently intent upon the stars, and wishing to be esteemed a god among them, began to draw forth, as it were, certain sparks from the stars, and to show them to men, in order that the rude and ignorant might be astonished, as with a miracle; and desiring to increase this estimation of him, he attempted these things again and again, until he was set on fire, and consumed by the demon himself, whom he accosted with too great importunity.[1]

Chapter XXVIII.-Tower of Babel.

"But the foolish men who were then, whereas they ought to have abandoned the opinion which they had conceived of him, inasmuch as they had seen it confuted by his mortal punishment, extolled him the more. For raising a sepulcher to his honor, they went so far as to adore him as a friend of God, and one who had been removed to heaven in a chariot of lightning, and to worship him as if he were a living star. Hence also his name was called Zoroaster after his death-that is, *living star*-by those who, after one generation, had been taught to speak the Greek language. In fine, by this example, even now many worship those who have been struck with lightning, honoring them with sepulchers, and worshipping them as friends of God. But this man was born in the fourteenth generation, and died in the fifteenth, in which the tower was built, and the languages of men were divided into many.

---

[1] The state or quality of being demanding or persistent in solicitation. *Source: Dictionary.com Unabridged (v 1.1)*

Chapter XXIX.-Fire-Worship of the Persians.

"First among whom is named a certain king Nimrod, the magic art having been handed down to him as by a flash, whom the Greeks, also called Ninus, and from whom the city of Nineveh took its name. Thus, therefore, diverse and erratic superstitions took their beginning from the magic art. For, because it was difficult to draw away the human race from the love of God, and attach them to deaf and lifeless images, the magicians made use of higher efforts, that men might be turned to erratic worship, by signs among the stars, and motions brought down as it were from heaven, and by the will of God. And those who had been first deceived, collecting the ashes of Zoroaster,-who, as we have said, was burnt up by the indignation of the demon, to whom he had been too troublesome,-brought them to the Persians, that they might be preserved by them with perpetual watching, as divine fire fallen from heaven, and might be worshipped as a heavenly God.

Chapter XXX.-Hero-Worship.

"By a like example, other men in other places built temples, set up statues, instituted mysteries and ceremonies and sacrifices, to those whom they had admired, either for some arts or for virtue, or at least had held in very great affection; and rejoiced, by means of all things belonging to gods, to hand down their fame to posterity; and that especially, because, as we have already said, they hinted[1] to be supported by some phantasies of magic art, so that by invocation of demons something seemed to be done and moved by them towards the deception of men. To these they add also certain solemnities, and drunken banquets, in which men might with all freedom indulge; and demons, conveyed into them in the chariot of repletion, might be mixed with their very bowels, and holding a place there, might bind the acts and thoughts of men to their own will. Such errors, then, having been introduced from the

---

[1] Original word used in the text was: **scented**

beginning, and having been aided by lust and drunkenness, in which carnal men chiefly delight, the religion of God, which consisted in continence and sobriety, began to become rare amongst men, and to be nearly[1] abolished.

Chapter XXXI.-Idolatry Led to All Immorality.

"For whereas at first, men worshipping a righteous and all-seeing God, neither dared sin nor do injury to their neighbors, being persuaded that God sees the actions and movements of every one; when religious worship was directed to lifeless images, concerning which they were certain that they were incapable of hearing, or sight, or motion, they began to sin licentiously,[2] and to go forward to every crime, because they had no fear of suffering anything at the hands of those whom they worshipped as gods. Hence the madness of wars burst out; hence plunderings, rapines,[3] captivities, and liberty reduced to slavery; each one, as he could, satisfied his lust and his covetousness, although no power can satisfy covetousness. For as fire, the more fuel it gets, the more extensively kindled and strengthened, so also the madness of covetousness is made greater and more vehement by means of those things which it acquires.

Chapter XXXII.-Invitation.

"Wherefore begin now with better understanding to resist yourselves in those things which you do not rightly desire; if so be that you can in any way repair and restore in yourselves that purity of religion and innocence of life which at first were bestowed upon man by God, that thereby also the hope of immortal blessings may be restored to you. And give thanks to the bountiful Father of all, by Him whom He has constituted King of peace, and

---

[1] Original word used in the text was: **well-nigh**
[2] Lawless; immoral ; sexually unrestrained; lascivious; lewd.
[3] Forcible seizure of another's property.

Source: Dictionary.com Unabridged (v 1.1)

the treasury of unspeakable honors, that even at the present time your sins may be washed away[1] with the water of the fountain, or river, or even sea: the threefold name of blessedness being called over you, that by it not only evil spirits may be driven out, if any dwell in you, but also that, when you have forsaken your sins, and have with entire faith and entire purity of mind believed in God, you may drive out wicked spirits and demons from others also, and may be able to set others free from sufferings and sicknesses. For the demons themselves know and acknowledge those who have given themselves up to God, and sometimes they are driven out by the mere presence of such, as you saw a little while ago, how, when we had only addressed to you the word of salutation, straightway the demons, on account of their respect for our religion, began to cry out, and could not bear our presence even for a little.

Chapter XXXIII.-The Weakest Christian More Powerful Than the Strongest Demon.

"Is it, then, that we are of another and a superior nature, and that therefore the demons are afraid of us? Nay, we are of one and the same nature with you, but we differ in religion. But if you will also be *like us,* we do not grudge it, but rather we exhort you, and wish you to be assured, that when the same faith and religion and innocence of life shall be in you that is in us, you will have equal and the same power and virtue against demons, through God rewarding your faith. For as he who has soldiers under him, although he may be inferior, and they superior to him in strength, yet 'says to this one, Go, and he goeth; and to another, Come, and he cometh; and to another, Do this, and he doeth it; ' and this he is able to do, not by his own power, but by the fear of Caesar; so every faithful one commands the demons, although they seem to be much stronger than men, and that not by means of his own power, but by means of the power of God, who has put them in subjection. For even that which we have just spoken of, that Caesar is held

---

[1] Speaking here of Baptism.

in awe by all soldiers, and in every camp, and in his whole kingdom, though he is but one man, and perhaps feeble in respect of bodily strength, this is not effected but by the power of God, who inspires all with fear, that they may be subject to one.

Chapter XXXIV.-Temptation of Christ.

"This we would have you know assuredly, that a demon has no power against a man, unless one voluntarily submit himself to his desires. Whence even that one who is the prince of wickedness, approached Him who, as we have said, is appointed of God King of peace, tempting Him, and began to promise Him all the glory of the world; because he knew that when he had offered this to others, for the sake of deceiving them, they had worshipped him. Therefore, impious as he was, and unmindful of himself, which indeed is the special peculiarity of wickedness, he presumed that he should be worshipped by Him by whom he knew that he was to be destroyed. Therefore our Lord, confirming the worship of one God, answered him: `It is written, Thou shall worship the Lord thy God, and Him only shalt thou serve.' And he, terrified by this answer, and fearing lest the true religion of the one and true God should be restored, hastened straightway to send forth into this world false prophets, and false apostles, and false teachers, who should speak indeed in the name of Christ, but should accomplish the will of the demon.

Chapter XXXV.-False Apostles.

"Wherefore observe the greatest caution, that you believe no teacher, unless he bring from Jerusalem the testimonial of James the Lord's brother, or of whosoever may come after him. For no one, unless he has gone up thither, and there has been approved as a fit and faithful teacher for preaching the word of Christ,-unless, I say, he brings a testimonial thence, is by any means to be received. But let neither prophet nor apostle be looked for by you at this time, besides us. For there is one true Prophet, whose words we twelve apostles preach; for He is the accepted year of God, having us apostles as His twelve months. But for what reason the world itself was made, or what diversities have occurred in it, and why our Lord, coming for its restoration, has chosen and sent us twelve apostles, shall be explained more at length at another time. Meantime He has commanded us to go forth to preach, and to invite you to the supper of the heavenly King, which the Father hath prepared for the marriage of His Son, and that we should give you wedding garments, that is, the grace of baptism; which whosoever obtains, as a spotless robe with which he is to enter to the supper of the King, ought to beware that it be not in any part of it stained with sin, and so he be rejected as unworthy and reprobate.

Chapter XXXVI.-The Garments Unspotted.

"But the ways in which this garment may be spotted are these: If any one withdraw from God the Father and Creator of all, receiving another teacher besides Christ, who alone is the faithful and true Prophet, and who has sent us twelve apostles to preach the word; if any one think otherwise than worthily of the substance of the Godhead, which excels all things;-these are the things which even fatally pollute the garment of baptism. But the things which pollute it in actions are these: murders, adulteries, hatreds, avarice, evil ambition. And the things which pollute at once the soul and the body are these: to partake of the table of demons, that is, to taste things sacrificed, or blood, or a carcass which is strangled, and if there be aught else which has been offered to demons. Be this therefore the first step to you of three; which step brings forth thirty commands, and the second sixty, and the third a hundred, as we shall expound more fully to you at another time."

Chapter XXXVII.-The Congregation Dismissed.

When he had thus spoken, and had charged them to come to the same place in good time on the following day, he dismissed the crowds; and when they were unwilling to depart, Peter said to them: "Do me this favor on account of the fatigue of yesterday's journey; and now go away, and meet in good time to-morrow." And so they departed with joy. But Peter, commanding me to withdraw a little for the purpose of prayer, afterwards ordered the couches to be spread in the part of the garden which was covered with shade; and every one, according to custom, recognizing the place of his own rank, we took food. Then, as there was still some portion of the day left, he conversed with us concerning the Lord's miracles; and when evening was come, he entered his bed-chamber and went to sleep.

Book V.

Chapter I.-Peter's Salutation.

But on the following day, Peter rising a little earlier than usual, found us asleep; and when he saw it, he gave orders that silence should be kept for him, as though he himself wished to sleep longer, that we might not be disturbed in our rest. But when we rose refreshed with sleep, we found him, having finished his prayer, waiting for us in his bed-chamber. And as it was already dawn, he addressed us shortly, saluting us according to his custom, and forthwith proceeded to the usual place for the purpose of teaching; and when he saw that many had assembled there, having invoked peace upon them according to the first religious form, he began to speak as follows:-

Chapter II.-Suffering the Effect of Sin.

"God, the Creator of all, at the beginning made man after His own image, and gave him dominion over the earth and sea, and over the air; as the true Prophet has told us, and as the very reason of things instructs us: for man alone is rational, and it is fitting that reason should rule over the irrational. At first, therefore, while he was still righteous, he was superior to all disorders and all frailty; but when he sinned, as we taught you yesterday, and became the servant of sin, he became at the same time liable to frailty. This therefore is written, that men may know that, as by impiety they have been made liable to suffer, so by piety they may be made free from suffering; and not only free from suffering, but by even a little faith in God be able to cure the sufferings of others. For thus the true Prophet promised us, saying, 'Verily I say to you, that if ye have faith as a grain of mustard seed, ye shall say to this mountain, Remove hence, and it shall remove. Of this saying you have yourselves also had proofs; for you saw yesterday how at our presence the demons removed and were put to flight, with those sufferings which they had brought upon men.

Chapter III.-Faith and Unbelief.

"Whereas therefore some men suffer, and others cure those who suffer, it is necessary, to know the cause at once of the suffering and the cure; and this is proved to be naught else than unbelief on the part of the sufferers, and faith on the part of those who cure them. For unbelief, while it does not believe that there is to be a judgment by God, affords license to sin, and sin makes men liable to sufferings; but faith, believing that there is to be a judgment of God, restrains men from sin; and those who do not sin are not only free from demons and sufferings, but can also put to flight the demons and sufferings of others.

Chapter IV.-Ignorance the Mother of Evils.

"From all these things, therefore, it is concluded that all evil springs from ignorance; and ignorance herself, the mother of all evils, is sprung from carelessness and sloth, and is nourished, and increased, and rooted in the senses of men by negligence; and if any one teach that she is to be put to flight, she is with difficulty and indignantly torn away, as from an ancient and hereditary abode. And therefore we must labor for a little, that we may search out the presumptions of ignorance, and cut them off by means of knowledge, especially in those who are preoccupied with some erroneous opinions, by means of which ignorance is the more firmly rooted in them, as under the appearance of a certain kind of knowledge; for nothing is worse than for one to believe that he knows what he is ignorant of, and to maintain that to be true which is false. This is as if a drunk man should think himself to be sober, and should act indeed in all respects as a *drunk* man, and yet think himself to be sober, and should wish to be called so by others. Thus, therefore, are those also who do not know what is true, yet hold some appearance of knowledge, and do many evil things as if they were good, and hasten destruction as if it were to salvation.

Chapter V.-Advantages of Knowledge.

"Wherefore we must, above all things, hasten to the knowledge of the truth, that, as with a light kindled thereat, we may be able to dispel the darkness of errors: for ignorance, as we have said, is a great evil; but because it has no substance, it is easily dispelled by those who are: in earnest. For ignorance is nothing else than not knowing what is good for us; once know this, and ignorance perishes. Therefore the knowledge of truth ought to be eagerly sought after; and no one can confer it except the true Prophet. For this is the gate of life to those who will enter, and the road of good works to those going to the city of salvation.

Chapter VI.-Free-Will.

"Whether any one, truly hearing the word of the true Prophet; is willing or unwilling to receive it, and to embrace His burden, that is, the precepts of life, he has either in his power, for we are free in will. For if it were so, that those who hear had it not in their power to do otherwise than they had heard, there were some power of nature in virtue of which it were not free to him to pass over to another opinion. Or if, again, no one of the hearers could at all receive it, this also were a power of nature which should compel the doing of some one thing, and should leave no place for the other course. But now, since it is free for the mind to turn its judgment to which side it pleases, and to choose the way which it approves, it is clearly manifest that there is in men a liberty of choice.

Chapter VII.-Responsibility of Knowledge.

"Therefore, before any one hears what is good for him, it is certain that he is ignorant; and being ignorant, he wishes and desires to do what is not good for him; wherefore he is not judged for that. But when once he has heard the causes of his error, and has received the method of truth, then, if he remain in those errors with which he had been long ago preoccupied, he shall rightly be called into judgment, to suffer punishment, because he has spent in the sport of errors that portion of life which was given him to be spent in living well. But he who, hearing those things, willingly receives them, and is thankful that the teaching of good things has been brought to him, inquires more eagerly, and does not cease to learn, until he ascertains whether there be truly another world, in which rewards are prepared for the good. And when he is assured of this, he gives thanks to God because He has shown him the light of truth; and for the future directs his actions in all good works, for which he is assured that there is a reward prepared in the world to come; while he constantly wonders and is astonished at the errors of other men, and that no one sees the truth which is placed before his eyes. Yet he himself, rejoicing in the riches of wisdom which he hath found, desires insatiably to enjoy them, and is delighted with the practice of good works; hastening to attain, with a clean heart and a pure conscience, the world to come, when he shall be able even to see God, the king of all.

Chapter VIII.-Desires of the Flesh to Be Subdued.

"But the sole cause of our wanting and being deprived of all these things is ignorance. For while men do not know how much good there is in knowledge, they do not suffer the evil of ignorance to be removed from them; for they know not how great a difference is involved in the change of one of these things for the other. Wherefore I counsel every learner willingly to lend his ear to the word of God, and to hear with love of the truth what we say, that his mind, receiving the best seed, may bring forth joyful fruits by good deeds. For if, while I teach the things which pertain to salvation, any one refuses to receive them, and strives to resist them with a mind occupied by evil opinions, he shall have the cause of his perishing, not from us, but from himself. For it is his duty to examine with just judgment the things which we say, and to understand that we speak the words of truth, that, knowing how things are, and directing his life in good actions, he may be found a partaker of the kingdom of heaven, subjecting to himself the desires of the flesh, and becoming lord of them, that so at length he himself also may become the pleasant possession of the Ruler of all.

Chapter IX.-The Two Kingdoms.

"For he who persists in evil, and is the servant of evil, cannot be made a portion of good so long as he persists in evil, because from the beginning, as we have said, God instituted two kingdoms, and has given to each man the power of becoming a portion of that kingdom to which he shall yield himself to obey. And since it is decreed by God that no one man can be a servant of both kingdoms, therefore endeavor with all earnestness to betake yourselves to the covenant and laws of the good King. Wherefore also the true Prophet, when He was present with us, and saw some rich men negligent with respect to the worship of God, thus unfolded the truth of this matter: `No one, 'said He, `can serve two masters; ye cannot serve God and mammon; ` calling riches, in the language of His country, *mammon*.

Chapter X.-Jesus the True Prophet.

"He therefore is the true Prophet, who appeared to us, as you have heard, in Judea, who, standing in public places, by a simple command made the blind see, the deaf hear, cast out demons, restored health to the sick, and life to the dead; and since nothing was impossible to Him, He even perceived the thoughts of men, which is possible for none but God only. He proclaimed the kingdom of God; and we believed Him as a true Prophet in all that He spoke, deriving the confirmation of our faith not only from His words, but also from His works; and also because the sayings of the law, which many generations before had set forth His coming, were fulfilled in Him; and the figures of the doings of Moses, and of the patriarch Jacob before him, bore in all respects a type of Him. It is evident also that the time of His advent, that is, the very time at which He came, was foretold by them; and, above all, it was contained in the sacred writings, that He was to be waited for by the Gentiles. And all these things were equally fulfilled in Him.

Chapter XI.-The Expectation of the Gentiles.

"But that which a prophet of the Jews foretold, that He was to be waited for by the Gentiles, confirms above measure the faith of truth in Him. For if he had said that He was to be waited for by the Jews, he would not have seemed to prophesy anything extraordinary, that He whose coming had been promised for the salvation of the world should be the object of hope to the people of the same tribe with Himself, and to His own nation: for that this would take place, would seem rather to be a matter of natural inference than one requiring the grandeur of a prophetic utterance. But now, whereas the prophets say that all that hope which is set forth concerning the salvation of the world, and the newness of the kingdom which is to be established by Christ, and all things which are declared concerning Him are to be transferred to the Gentiles; the grandeur of the prophetic office is confirmed, not according to the sequence of things, but by an incredible fulfillment of the prophecy. For the Jews from the beginning had understood by a most certain tradition that this man should at some time come, by whom all things should be restored; and daily meditating and looking out for His coming, when they saw Him amongst them, and accomplishing the signs and miracles, as had been written of Him, being blinded with envy, they could not recognize Him when present, in the hope of whom they rejoiced while He was absent; yet the few of us who were chosen by Him understood it.

Chapter XII.-Call of the Gentiles.

"But this happened by the providence of God, that the knowledge of this good One should be handed over to the

Gentiles, and those who had never heard of Him, nor had learned from the prophets, should acknowledge Him, while those who had acknowledged Him in their daily meditations should not know Him. For, behold, by you who are now present, and desire to hear the doctrine of His faith, and to know what, and how, and of what sort is His coming, the prophetic truth is fulfilled. For this is what the prophets foretold, that He is to be sought for by you, who never heard of Him. And, therefore, seeing that the prophetic sayings are fulfilled even in yourselves, you rightly believe in Him alone, you rightly wait for Him, you rightly inquire concerning Him, that you not only may wait for Him, but also believing, you may obtain the inheritance of His kingdom; according to what Himself said, that every one is made the servant of him to whom he yields subjection.

Chapter XIII.-Invitation of the Gentiles.

"Wherefore awake, and take to yourselves our Lord and God, even that Lord who is Lord both of heaven and earth, and conform yourselves to His image and likeness, as the true Prophet Himself teaches, saying, `Be ye merciful, as also your heavenly Father is merciful, who makes His sun to rise upon the good and the evil, and rains upon the just and the unjust.' Imitate Him, therefore, and fear Him, as the commandment is given to men, `Thou shall worship the Lord thy God, and Him only shalt thou serve.' For it is profitable to you to serve this Lord alone, that through Him knowing the one God, ye may be freed from the many whom ye vainly feared. For he who fears not God the Creator of all, but fears those whom he himself with his own hands hath made, what does he do but make himself subject to a vain and senseless fear, and render himself more vile and abject than those very things, the fear of which he has conceived in his mind? But rather, by the goodness of Him who inviteth you, return to your former nobleness, and by good deeds show that you bear the image of your Creator, that by contemplation of His likeness ye may be believed to be even His sons.

Chapter XIV.-Idols Unprofitable.

"Begin, therefore, to cast out of your minds the vain ideas of idols, and your useless and empty fears, that at the same time you may also escape the condition of unrighteous bondage. For those have become your lords, who could not even have been profitable servants to you. For how should lifeless images seem fit even to serve you, when they can neither hear, nor see, nor feel anything? Yea, even the material of which they are made, whether it be gold or silver, or even brass or wood, though it might have profited you for necessary uses, you have rendered wholly inefficient and useless by fashioning gods out of it. We therefore declare to you the true worship of God, and at the same time warn and exhort the worshippers, that by good deeds they imitate Him whom they worship, and hasten to return to His image and likeness, as we said before.

Chapter XV.-Folly of Idolatry.

"But I should like if those who worship idols would tell me if they wish to become like those whom they worship? Does any one of you wish to see in such sort as they see? or to hear after the manner of their hearing? or to have such understanding as they have? Far be this from any of my hearers! For this were rather to be thought a curse and a reproach to a man, who bears in himself the image of God, although he has lost the likeness. What sort of gods, then, are they to be reckoned, the imitation of whom would be execrable to their worshippers, and to have whose likeness would be a reproach? What then? Melt your useless images, and make useful vessels. Melt the unserviceable and inactive metal, and make implements fit for the use of men. But, says one, human laws do not allow us. He says well; for it is human laws, and not their own power, that prevents it. What kind of gods, then, are those which are defended by human laws, and not by their own energies? And so also they are preserved from thieves by watch-dogs and the protection of bolts, at least if they be of silver, or gold, or even of brass; for those that are of stone and earthenware are protected by their own worthlessness, for no one will steal a stone or a crockery god. Hence those seem to be the more miserable whose more precious metal exposes them to the greater danger. Since, then, they can be stolen, since they must be guarded by men, since they can be melted, and weighed out, and forged with hammers, ought men possessed of understanding to hold them as gods?

Chapter XVI.-God Alone a Fit Object of Worship.

"Oh! into what wretched plight the understanding of men has fallen! For if it is reckoned the greatest folly to fear the dead, what shall we judge of those who fear something that is worse than the dead are? For those images are not even to be reckoned among the number of the dead, because they were never alive. Even the sepulchers of the dead are preferable to them, since, although they are now dead, yet they once had life; but those whom you worship never possessed even such base life as is in all, the life of frogs and owls. But why say more about them, since it is enough to say to him who adores them: Do you not see that he whom you adore sees not, hear that he whom you adore hears not, and understand that he understands not?-for he is the work of man's hand, and necessarily is void of understanding. You therefore worship a god without sense, whereas every one who has sense believes that not even those things are to be worshipped which have been made by God and have sense, such as the sun, moon, and stars, and all things that are in heaven and upon earth. For they think it reasonable, that not those things which have been made for the service of the world, but the Creator of those things themselves, and of the whole world, should be worshipped. For even these things rejoice when He is adored and worshipped, and do not take it well that the honor of the Creator should be bestowed on the creature. For the worship of God alone is acceptable *to them,* who alone is uncreated, and all things also are His creatures. For as it belongs to him who alone is uncreated to be God, so everything that has been created is not truly God

Chapter XVII.-Suggestions of the Old Serpent.

"Above all, therefore, you ought to understand the deception of the old serpent and his cunning suggestions, who deceives you as it were by prudence, and as by a sort of reason creeps through your senses; and beginning at the head, he glides through your inner marrow, accounting the deceiving of you a great gain. Therefore he insinuates into your minds opinions of gods of whatsoever kinds, only that he may withdraw you from the faith of one God knowing that your sin is his comfort. For he, for his wickedness, was condemned from the beginning to eat dust, for that he caused to be again resolved into dust him who had been taken from the dust, even till the time when your souls shall be restored, being brought through the fire; as we shall instruct you more fully at another time. From him, therefore, proceed all the errors and doubts, by which you are driven from the faith and belief of one God.

Chapter XVIII.-His First Suggestion.

"And first of all he suggests to men's thoughts not to hear the words of truth, by which they might put to flight the ignorance of those things which are evils. And this he does, as by the presentation of another knowledge, making a show of that opinion which very many hold, to think that they shall not be held guilty if they have been in ignorance, and that they shall not be called to account for what they have not heard; and thereby he persuades them to turn aside from hearing the word. But I tell you, in opposition to this, that ignorance is in itself a most deadly poison, which is sufficient to ruin the soul without any aid from without. And therefore there is no one who is ignorant who shall escape through his ignorance, but it is certain that he shall perish. For the power of sin naturally destroys the sinner. But since the judgment shall be according to reason, the cause and origin of ignorance shall be inquired into, as well as of every sin. For he who is unwilling to know how he may attain to life, and prefers to be in ignorance lest he thereby be made guilty, from this very fact is judged as if he knew and had knowledge. For he knew what it was that he was unwilling to hear; and the cunning obtained by the artifice of the serpent will avail him nothing for an excuse, for he will have to do with Him to whom the heart is open. But that you may know that ignorance of itself brings destruction, *I assure you that* when the soul departs from the body, if it leave it in ignorance of Him by whom it was created, and from whom in this world it obtained all things that were necessary for its uses, it is driven forth from the light of His kingdom as ungrateful and unfaithful.

Chapter XIX.-His Second Suggestion.

"Again, the wicked serpent suggests another opinion to men, which many of you are in the habit of bringing forward,-that there is, as we say, one God, who is Lord of all; but these also, they say, are gods. For as there is one Caesar, and he has under him many judges,-for example, prefects, consuls, tribunes, and other officers,-in like manner we think, that while there is one God greater than all, yet still that these gods are ordained in this world, after the likeness of those officers of whom we have spoken, subject indeed to that greater God, yet ruling us and the things that are in this world. In answer to this, I shall show you how, in those very things which you propose for deception, you are confuted by the reasons of truth. You say that God occupies the place of Caesar, and those who are called gods represent His judges and officers. Hold then, as you have adduced it, by the example of Caesar; and know that, as one of Caesar's judges or administrators, as prefects, proconsuls, generals, or tribunes, may lawfully take the name of Caesar,-or else both he who should take it and those who should confer it should be destroyed together,-so also in this case yon ought to observe, that if any one give the name of God to any but Himself, and he accept it, they shall partake one and the same destruction, by a much more terrible fate than the servants of Caesar. For he who offends against Caesar shall undergo temporal destruction; but he who offends against Him who is the sole and true God, shall suffer eternal punishment, and that deservedly, as having injured by a wrongful condition the name which is unique.

Chapter XX.-Egyptian Idolatry,

"Although this word God is pot the *name* of God, but meantime that word is employed by men as His name; and therefore, as I have said, when it is used reproachfully, the reproach is referred to the injury of the true name. In short, the ancient Egyptians, who thought that they had discovered the theory of the heavenly revolutions and the nature of the stars, nevertheless, through the demon's blocking up their senses, subjected the incommunicable name to all kinds of indignity. For some taught that their ox, which is called Apis, ought to be worshipped; others taught that the he-goat, others that cats, the ibis, a fish also, a serpent, onions, drains, crepitus ventris, ought to be regarded as deities, and innumerable other things, which I am ashamed even to mention."

Chapter XXI.-Egyptian Idolatry More Reasonable Than Others.

When Peter was speaking thus, all we who heard him laughed. Then said Peter: "You laugh at the absurdities of others, because through long custom you do not see your own. For indeed it is not without reason that you laugh at the folly of the Egyptians, who worship dumb animals, while they themselves are rational. But I will tell you how they also laugh at you; for they say, We worship living animals, though mortal; but you worship and adore things which never were alive at all. They add this also, that they are figures and allegories of certain powers by whose help the race of men is governed. Taking refuge in this for shame, they fabricate these and similar excuses, and so endeavor to screen their error. But this is not the time to answer the Egyptians, and leaving the care of those who are present to heal the disease of the absent. For it is a certain indication that you are held to be free from sickness of this sort, since you do not grieve over it as your own, but laugh at it as that of others.

Chapter XXII.-Second Suggestion Continued.

"But let us come back to you, whose opinion it is that God should be regarded as Caesar, and the gods as the ministers and deputies of Caesar. Follow me attentively, and I shall presently show you the lurking-places of the serpent, which lie in the crooked windings of this argument. It ought to be regarded by all as certain and beyond doubt, that no creature can be on a level with God, because He was made by none, but Himself made all things; nor indeed can any one be found so irrational, as to suppose that the thing made can be compared with the maker. If therefore the human mind, not only by reason, but even by a sort of natural instinct, rightly holds this opinion, that that is called God to which nothing can be compared or equaled, but which exceeds all and excels all; how can it be supposed that that name which is believed to be above all, is rightly given to those whom you think to be employed for the service and comfort of human life? But we shall add this also. This world was undoubtedly made, and is corruptible, as we shall show more fully by and by; meantime it is admitted both that it has been made and that it is corruptible. If therefore the world cannot be called God, and rightly so, because it is corruptible, how shall parts of the world take the name of God? For inasmuch as the whole world cannot be God, much more its parts cannot. Therefore, if we come back to the example of Caesar, you will see how far you are in error. It is not lawful for any one, though a man of the same nature with him, to be compared with Caesar: do you think, then, that any one ought to be compared with God, who excels all in this respect, that He was made by none, but Himself made all things? But, indeed, you dare not give the name of Caesar to any other, because he immediately punishes one who offends against him; you dare give that of God to others, because He delays the punishment of offenders against Him, in order to their repentance.

Chapter XXIII.-Third Suggestion.

"Through the mouths of others also that serpent is wont to speak in this wise: We adore visible images in honor of the invisible God. Now this is most certainly false. For if you really wished to worship the image of God, you would do good to man, and so worship the true image of God in him. For the image of God is in every man, though His likeness is not in all, but where the soul is benign and the mind pure. If, therefore, you wish truly to honor the image of God, we declare to you what is true, that you should do good to and pay honor and reverence to man, who is made in the image of God; that you minister food to the hungry, drink to the thirsty, clothing to the naked, hospitality to the stranger, and necessary things to the prisoner; and that is what will be regarded as truly bestowed upon God. And so far do these things go to the honor of God's image, that he who does not these things is regarded as casting reproach upon the divine image. What, then, is that honor of God which consists in running from one stone or wooden figure to another, in venerating empty and lifeless figures as deities, and despising men in whom the image of God is of a truth? Yea, rather be assured, that whoever commits murder or adultery, or anything that causes suffering or injury to men, in all these the image of God is violated. For to injure men is a great impiety towards God. Whenever, therefore, you do to another what you would not have another do to you, you defile the image of God with undeserved distresses. Understand, therefore, that that is the suggestion of the serpent lurking within you, which persuades you that you may seem to be pious when you worship insensible things, and may not seem impious when you injure sensible and rational beings.

Chapter XXIV.-Fourth Suggestion.

"But to these things the serpent answers us with another mouth, and says: If God did not wish these things to be, then they should not be. I am not telling you how it is that many contrary things are permitted to be in this world for the probation of every one's mind. But this is what is suitable to be said in the meantime: If, according to you, everything that was to be worshipped ought not to have been, there would have been almost nothing in this world. For what is there that you have left without worshipping it? The sun, the moon, the stars, the water, the earth, mountains, trees, stones, men; there is no one of these that ye have not worshipped. According to your saying, therefore, none of these ought to have been made by God, that you might not have anything that you could worship! Yea, He ought not even to have made men themselves to be the worshippers! But this is the very thing which that serpent which lurks within you desires: for he spares none of you; he would have no one of you escape from destruction. But it shall not be so. For I tell you, that not that which is worshipped is in fault, but he who worships. For with God is righteous judgment; and He judges in one way the sufferer, and in another way the doer, of wrong.

Chapter XXV.-Fifth Suggestion.

"But you say: Then those who adore what ought not to be adored, should be immediately destroyed by God, to prevent others doing the like. But are you wiser than God, that you should offer Him counsel? He knows what to do. For with all who are placed in ignorance He exercises patience, because He is merciful and gracious; and He foresees that many of the ungodly become godly, and that even some of those who worship impure statues and polluted images have been converted to God, and forsaking their sins and doing good works, attain to salvation. But it is said: We ought never to have come even to the thought of doing these things. You do not know what freedom of will is, and you forget that he is good who is so by his own intention; but, he who is retained in goodness by necessity cannot be called good, because it is not of himself that he is so. Because, therefore, there is in every one liberty to choose good or evil, he either acquires rewards, or brings destruction on himself. Nay it is said, God brings to our minds whatsoever we think. What mean ye, O then? Ye blaspheme. For if He brings all our thoughts into our minds, then it is He that suggests to us thoughts of adultery, and covetousness, and blasphemy, and every kind of effeminacy.[1] Cease, I entreat of you, these blasphemies, and understand what is the honor worthy of God. And say not, as some of you are wont to say, that God needs not honor from men. Indeed, He truly is in need of none; but you ought to know that the honor which you bestow upon God is profitable to yourselves. For what is so detestable,[2] as for a man not to render thanks to his Creator?

Chapter XXVI.-Sixth Suggestion.

"But it is said: We do better, who give thanks both to Himself, and to all with Him. In this you do not understand that there is the ruin of your salvation. For it is as if a sick man should call in for his cure at once a physician and poisoners; since these could indeed injure him, but not cure him; and the true physician would refuse to mix his remedies with their poisons, lest either the man's destruction should be ascribed to the good, or his recovery, to the injurious. But you say: Is God then indignant or envious, if, when He benefits us, our thanks be rendered to others? Even if He be not indignant, at all events He does not wish to be the author of error, that by means of His work credit should be given to a vain idol. And what is so impious, so ungrateful, as to obtain a benefit from God, and to render thanks to blocks of wood and stone? Wherefore arise, and understand your salvation. For God is in need of no one, nor does He require anything, nor is He hurt by anything; but we are either helped or hurt, in that we are grateful or ungrateful. For what does God gain from our praises, or what does He lose by our blasphemies? Only this we must remember, that God brings into proximity and friendship with Himself the soul that renders thanks to Him. But the wicked demon possesses the ungrateful soul.

---

[1] When a man exhibits traits, tastes, habits, traditionally considered feminine. *Source: Dictionary.com Unabridged (v 1.1)*
[2] Original word used in the text was: **execrable**

Chapter XXVII.-Creatures Take Vengeance on Sinners.

"But this also I would have you know, that upon such souls God does not take vengeance directly, but His whole creation rises up and inflicts punishments upon the impious; and although in the present world the goodness of God bestows the light of the world and the services of the earth alike upon the pious and the impious, yet not without grief does the sun afford his light, and the other elements perform their service, to the impious. And, in short, sometimes even in opposition to the goodness of the Creator, the elements are wearied out by the crimes of the wicked; and thence it is that either the fruit of the earth is blighted, or the composition of the air is vitiated, or the heat of the sun is increased beyond measure, or there is an excessive amount of rain or of cold. Thence pestilence, and famine, and death in various forms stalk forth, for the creature hastens to take vengeance on the wicked; yet the goodness of God restrains it, and bridles its indignation against the wicked, and compels it to be obedient to His mercy, rather than to be inflamed by the sins and the crimes of men. For the patience of God waiteth for the conversion of men, as long as they are in this body.

Chapter XXVIII.-Eternity of Punishments.

"But if any persist in impiety till the end of life, then as soon as the soul, which is immortal, departs, it shall pay the penalty of its persistence in impiety. For even the souls of the impious are immortal, though perhaps they themselves would wish them to end with their bodies. But it is not so; for they endure without end the torments of eternal fire, and to their destruction they have not the quality of mortality. But perhaps you will say to me, You terrify us, O Peter. And how shall we speak to you the things which are in reality? Can we declare to you the truth by keeping silence? We cannot state the things which are, otherwise than as they are. But if we were silent, we should make ourselves the cause of the ignorance that is ruinous to you, and should satisfy the serpent that lurks within you, and blocks up your senses, who cunningly suggests these things to you, that he may make you always the enemies of God. But we are sent for this end, that we may betray his disguises to you; and melting your enmities, may reconcile you to God, that you may be converted to Him, and may please Him by good works. For man is at enmity with God, and is in an unreasonable and impious state of mind and wicked disposition towards Him, especially when he thinks that he knows something, and is in ignorance. But when you lay aside these, and begin to be pleased and displeased with the same things which please and displease God, and to will what God willeth then ye shall truly be called His friends.

Chapter XXIX.-God's Care of Human Things.

"But perhaps some of you will say, God has no care of human things; and if we cannot even attain to the knowledge of Him, how shall we attain to His friendship? That God does concern Himself with the affairs of men, His government of the world bears witness: for the sun daily waits upon it, the showers minister to it; the fountains, rivers, winds, and all elements, attend upon it; and the more these things become known to men, the more do they indicate God's care over men. For unless by the power of the Most High, the more powerful would never minister to the inferior; and by this God is shown to have not only a care over men, but some great affection, since He has appointed[1] such noble elements to their service. But that men may also attain to the friendship of God, is proved to us by the example of those to whose prayers He has been so favorable, that He has withheld the heaven from rain when they wished, and has again opened it when they prayed. And many other things He has bestowed upon those who do His will, which could not be bestowed but upon His friends. But you will say, What harm is done to God if these things also are worshipped by us? If any one of you should pay to another the honor that is due to his father, from whom he has received innumerable benefits, and

---

[1] Original word used in the text was: **deputed**

should reverence a stranger and foreigner as his father, should you not think that he was undutiful towards his father, and most deserving to be disinherited?

Chapter XXX.-Religion of Fathers to Be Abandoned.

"Others say, It is wicked if we do not worship those *idols* which have come down to us from our fathers, and prove false to the religion bequeathed to us by our ancestors. On this principle, if any one's father was a robber or a base fellow, he ought not to change the manner of life handed down to him by his fathers, nor to be recalled from his father's errors to a better way; and it is reckoned impious if one do not sin with his parents, or does not persist in impiety with them. Others say, We ought not to be troublesome to God, and to be always burdening Him with complaints of our miseries, or with the urgency[1] of our petitions. How foolish and witless an answer! Do you think it is troublesome to God if you thank Him for His benefits, while you do not think it troublesome to Him if, for His gifts, you render thanks to stocks and stones? And how comes it, that when rain is withheld in a long drought, we all turn our eyes to heaven, and entreat the gift of rain from God Almighty, and all of us with our little ones pour out prayers on God and entreat His compassion? But truly ungrateful souls, when they obtain the blessing, quickly forget: for as soon as they have gathered in their harvest or their vintage, straightway they offer the first-fruits to deaf and dumb images, and pay vows in temples or groves for those things which God has bestowed upon them, and then offer sacrifices to demons; and having received a favor, deny the bestower of the favor.

Chapter XXXI.-Paganism, Its Enormities.

"But some say, These things are instituted for the sake of joy, and for refreshing our minds; and they have been devised for this end, that the human mind may be relaxed

---

[1] Original word used in the text was: **exigencies**

for a little from cares and sorrows. See now what a charge you yourselves bring upon the things which you practice. If these things have been invented for the purpose of lightening sorrow and affording enjoyment, how is it that the invocations of demons are performed in groves and woods? What is the meaning of the insane whirlings, and the slashing of limbs, and the cutting off of members? How is it that mad rage is produced in them? How is insanity produced? How is it that women are driven violently, raging with disheveled hair? Whence the shrieking and gnashing of teeth? Whence the bellowing of the heart and the bowels, and all those things which, whether they are pretended or are contrived by the ministration of demons, are exhibited to the terror of the foolish and ignorant? Are these things done for the sake of lightening the mind, or rather for the sake of oppressing it? Do ye not yet perceive nor understand, that these are the counsels of the serpent lurking within you, which draws you away from the apprehension of truth by irrational suggestions of errors, that he may hold you as slaves and servants of lust and concupiscence[1] and every disgraceful thing?

Chapter XXXII.-True Religion Calls to Sobriety and Modesty.

"But I protest to you with the clear voice of preaching, that, on the contrary, the religion of God calls you to sobriety and modesty; orders you to refrain from effeminacy and madness, and by patience and gentleness to prevent the inroads of anger; to be content with your own possessions, and with the virtue of frugality; not even when driven by poverty to plunder the goods of others, but in all things to observe justice; to withdraw yourselves wholly from the idol sacrifices: for by these things you invite demons to you, and of your own accord give them the power of entering into you; and so you admit that which is the cause either of madness or of unlawful love.

---

[1] Sexual desire; lust.
Source: Dictionary.com Unabridged (v 1.1)

Chapter XXXIII.-Origin of Impiety.

"Hence is the origin of all impiety; hence murders, adulteries, thefts; and a nursery is formed of all evils and wickedness, while you indulge in profane libations and odors, and give to wicked spirits an opportunity of ruling and obtaining some sort of authority over you. For when they invade your senses, what do they else than work the things which belong to lust and injustice and cruelty, and compel you to be obedient to all things that are pleasing to them? God, indeed, permits you to suffer this at their hands by a certain righteous judgment, that from the very disgrace of your doings and your feelings you may understand how unworthy it is to be subject to demons and not to God. Hence also, by the friendship of demons, men are brought to disgraceful and base deeds; hence, men proceed even to the destruction of life, either through the fire of lust, or through the madness of anger through excess of grief, so that, as is well known, some have even laid violent hands upon themselves. And this, as we have said, by a just sentence of God they are not prevented from doing, that they may both understand to whom they have yielded themselves in subjection, and know whom they have forsaken.

Chapter XXXIV.-Who are Worshippers of God?

"But some one will say, These passions sometimes befall even those who worship God. It is not true. For we say, that he is a worshipper of God, who does the will of God, and observes the precepts of His law. For in God's estimation he is not a Jew who is called a Jew among men (nor is he a Gentile that is called a Gentile), but he who, believing in God, fulfils His law and does His will, though he be not circumcised. He is the true worshipper of God, who not only is himself free from passions, but also sets others free from them; though they be so heavy that they are like mountains, he removes them by means of the faith with which he believes in God. Yea, by faith he truly removes mountains with their trees, if it be necessary. But he who seems to worship God, but is neither fortified by a full faith, nor by obedience to the commandments, but is a sinner, has given a place in himself, by reason of his sins, to passions, which are appointed of God for the punishment of those who sin, that they may exact from them the deserts of their sins by means of punishments inflicted, and may bring them purified to the general judgment of all, provided always that their faith do not fail them in their chastisement. For the chastisement of unbelievers in the present life is a judgment, by which they begin to be separated from future blessings; but the chastisement of those who worship God, while it is inflicted upon them for sins into which they have fallen, exacts from them the due of what they have done, that, preventing the judgment, they may pay the debt of their sin in the present life, and be freed, at least in half, from the eternal punishments which are there prepared.

Chapter XXXV.-Judgment to Come.

"But he does not receive these things as true who does not believe that there is to be a judgment of God, and therefore, being bound by the pleasures of the present life, is shut out from eternal good things; and therefore we do not neglect to proclaim to you what we know to be necessary for your salvation, and to show you what is the true worship of God, that, believing in God, you may be able, by means of good works, to be heirs with us of the world to come. But if you are not yet convinced that what we say is true, meantime, in the first instance, you ought not to take it amiss and to be hostile to us because we announce to you the things which we consider to be good, and because we do not grudge to bestow also upon you that which we believe brings salvation to ourselves, laboring, as I have said, with all eagerness, that we may have you as fellow-heirs of the blessings which we believe are to befall ourselves. But whether those things which we declare to you are certainly true, you shall not be able to know otherwise than by rendering obedience to the things which are commanded, that you may be taught by the issue of things, and the most certain end of blessedness.

Chapter XXXVI.-Conclusion of Discourse.

"And, therefore, although the serpent lurking within you occupies your senses with a thousand arts of corruption, and throws in your way a thousand obstacles, by which he may turn you away from the hearing of saving instruction, all the more ought you to resist him, and despising his suggestions, to come together the more frequently to hear the word and receive instruction from us, because nobody can learn anything who is not taught."

And when he had done speaking, he ordered those to be brought to him who were oppressed by sickness or demons, and laid his hands upon them with prayer; and so he dismissed the crowds, charging them to resort to the hearing of the word during the days that he was to remain there. Therefore, when the crowds had departed, Peter washed his body in the waters which ran through the garden, with as many of the others as chose to do so; and then ordered the couches to be spread on the ground under a very shady tree, and directed us to recline according to the order established at Caesarea. And thus, having taken food and given thanks to God after the manner of the Hebrews, as there was yet some portion of the day remaining, he ordered us to question him on any matters that we pleased. And although we were with him twenty in all, he explained to every one whatever he pleased to ask of him; the particulars of which I set down in books and sent to you some time ago. And when evening came we entered with him into the lodging, and went to sleep, each one in his own place.

Book VI.

Chapter I.-Book VI. Diligence in Study.

But as soon as day began to advance the dawn upon the retiring darkness, Peter having gone into the garden to pray, and returning thence and coming to us, by way of excuse for awaking and coming to us a little later than usual, said this: "Now that the spring-time has lengthened the day, of course the night is shorter; if, therefore, one desires to occupy some portion of the night in study, he must not keep the same hours for waking at all seasons, but should spend the same length of time in sleeping, whether the night be longer or shorter, and be exceedingly careful that he do not cut off from the period which he is wont to have for study, and so add to his sleep and lessen his time of keeping awake. And this also is to be observed, lest haply if sleep be interrupted while the food is still undigested, the undigested mass lead the mind, and by the exhalation of crude spirits render the inner sense confused and disturbed. It is right, therefore, that that part also be cherished with sufficient rest, so that, those things being sufficiently accomplished which are due to it, the body may be able in other things to render due service to the mind."

Chapter II.-Much to Be Done in a Little Time.

When he had said this, as very many had already assembled in the accustomed place of the garden to hear him, Peter went forth; and having saluted the crowds in his usual manner, began to speak as follows: "Since, indeed, as land neglected by the cultivator necessarily produces thorns and thistles, so your sense, by long neglect, has produced a plentiful crop of noxious opinions of things and dogmas of false science; there is need now of much care in cultivating the field of your mind, that the word of truth, which is the true and diligent husbandman of the heart, may cultivate it with continual instructions. It is therefore your part render obedience to it, and to lop off superfluous occupations and anxieties, lest a noxious growth choke the good seed of the word. For it may be that a short and earnest diligence may repair a long time's neglect; for the time of every one's life is uncertain, and therefore we must hasten to salvation, lest by chance[1] sudden death seize upon him who delays.

Chapter III.-Righteous Anger.

"And all the more eagerly must we strive on this account, that while there is time, the collected vices of evil custom may be cut off. And this you shall not be able to do otherwise, than by being angry with yourselves on account of your profitless and base doings. For this is righteous and necessary anger, by which every one is indignant with himself, and accuses himself for those things in which he has erred and done amiss; and by this indignation a certain fire is kindled in us, which, applied as it were to a barren field, consumes and burns up the roots of vile pleasure, and renders the soil of the heart more fertile for the good seed of the word of God. And I think that you have sufficiently worthy causes of anger, from which that most righteous fire may be kindled, if you consider into what errors the evil of ignorance has drawn you, and how it has caused you to fall and rush headlong into sin, from what good things it has withdrawn you, and into what evils it has driven you, and, what is of more importance than all the rest, how it has made you liable to eternal punishments in the world to come. Is not the fire of most righteous indignation kindled within you for all these things, now that the light of truth has shone upon you; and does not the flame of that anger which is pleasing to God rise within you, that every sprout may be burnt up and destroyed from the root, if by chance any shoot of evil desire[2] has budded within you?

Chapter IV.-Not Peace, But a Sword.

---

[1] Instead of 'by chance' the original word used in the text was: **haply** *From this point forward, wherever the word 'haply' originally appears in the text, it will be replaced with 'by chance' or 'perhaps'.*
[2] Original word used in the text was: **concupiscence**

Hence, also, He who hath sent us, when He had come, and had seen that all the world had fallen into wickedness, did not forthwith give peace to him who is in error, lest He should confirm him in evil; but set the knowledge of truth in opposition to the ruins of ignorance of it, that, if perhaps men would repent and look upon the light of truth, they might rightly grieve that they have been deceived and drawn away into the precipices of error, and might kindle the fire of salutary anger against the ignorance that had deceived, them. On this account, therefore, He said, `I have come to send fire on the earth; and how I wish that it were kindled!' There is therefore a certain fight, which is to be fought by us in this life; for the word of truth and knowledge necessarily separates men from error and ignorance, as we have often seen putrefied and dead flesh in the body separated by the cutting knife from its connection with the living members. Such is the effect produced by knowledge of the truth. For it is necessary that, for the sake of salvation, the son, for example, who has received the word of truth, be separated from his unbelieving parents; or again, that the father be separated from his son, or the daughter from her mother. And in this manner the battle of knowledge and ignorance, of truth and error, arises between believing and unbelieving kinsmen and relations. And therefore He who has sent us said again `I am not come to send peace on earth, but a sword.'

Chapter V.-How the Fight Begins.

"But if any one say, How does it seem right for men to be separated from their parents? I will tell you how. Because, if they remained with them in error, they would do no good to them, and they would themselves perish with them. It is therefore right, and very right, that he who will be saved be separated from him who will not. But observe this also, that this separation does not come from those who understand aright; for they wish to be with their relatives, and to do them good, and to teach them better things. But it is the vice peculiar to ignorance, that it will not bear to have near it the light of truth, which confutes it; and therefore that separation originates with them. For those who receive the knowledge of the truth, because it is full of goodness, desire, if it be possible, to share it with all, as given by the good God; yea, even with those who hate and persecute them: for they know that ignorance is the cause of their sin. Wherefore, in short, the Master Himself, when He was being led to the cross by those who knew Him not, prayed the Father for His murderers, and said, `Father, forgive their sin, for they know not what they do!' The disciples also, in imitation of the Master, even when themselves were suffering, in like manner prayed for their murderers. But if we are taught to pray even for our murderers and persecutors, how ought we not to bear the persecutions of parents and relations, and to pray for their conversion?

Chapter VI.-God to Be Loved More Than Parents.

"Then let us consider carefully, in the next place, what reason we have for loving our parents. For this cause, it is said, we love them, because they seem to be the authors of our life. But our parents are not authors of our life, but the means of it. For they do not bestow life, but afford the means of our entering into this life; while the one and sole author of life is God. If, therefore we would love the Author of our life, let us know that it is He that is to be loved. But then it is said, We cannot know Him; but them we know, and hold in affection. Be it so: you cannot know *what* God is, but you can very easily know what God is *not*. For how can any man fail to know that wood, or stone, or brass, or other such matter, is not God? But if you will not give your mind to consider the things which you might easily apprehend, it is certain that you are hindered in the knowledge of God, not by impossibility, but by indolence; for if you had wished it, even from these useless images you might have been set on the way of understanding.

Chapter VII.-The Earth Made for Men.

"For it is certain that these images are made with iron tools; but iron is wrought by fire, which fire is extinguished by water. But water is moved by spirit; and spirit has its beginning from God. For thus saith the prophet Moses: 'In the beginning God made the heaven and the earth. But the earth was invisible, and unarranged; and darkness was over the deep: and the Spirit of God was upon the waters.' Which Spirit, like the Creator's hand, by command of God separated light from darkness; and after that invisible heaven produced this visible one, that He might make the higher places a habitation for angels, and the lower for men. For your sake, therefore, by command of God, the water which was upon the face of the earth withdrew, that the earth might produce fruits for you; and into the earth also He inserted veins of moisture, that fountains and rivers might flow forth from it for you. For your sake it was commanded to bring forth living creatures, and all things which could serve for your use and pleasure. Is it not for you that the winds blow, that the earth, conceiving by them, may bring forth fruits? Is it not for you that the showers fall, and the seasons change? Is it not for you that the sun rises and sets, and the moon undergoes her changes? For you the sea offers its service, that all things may be subject to you, ungrateful as you are. For all these things shall there not be a righteous punishment of vengeance, because beyond all else you are ignorant of the bestower of all these things, whom you ought to acknowledge and reverence above all?

Chapter VIII.-Necessity of Baptism.

"But now I lead you to understanding by the same paths. For you see that all things are produced from waters. But water was made at first by the Only-begotten; and the Almighty God is the head of the Only-begotten, by whom we come to the Father in such order as we have stated above. But when you have come to the Father you will learn that this is His will, that you be born anew by means of waters, which were first created. For he who is regenerated by water, having filled up the measure of good works, is made heir of Him by whom he has been regenerated in incorruption. Wherefore, with prepared minds, approach as sons to a father, that your sins may be washed away, and it may be proved before God that ignorance was their sole cause. For if, after the learning of these things, you remain in unbelief, the cause of your destruction will be imputed to yourselves, and not to ignorance. And do you suppose that you can have hope towards God, even if you cultivate all piety and all righteousness, but do not receive baptism? Yea rather, he will be worthy of greater punishment, who does good works not well; for merit accrues to men from good works, but only if they be done as God commands. Now God has ordered every one who worships Him to be sealed by baptism; but if you refuse, and obey your own will rather than God's, you are doubtless contrary and hostile to His will.

Chapter IX.-Use of Baptism,

"But you will perhaps say, What does the baptism of water contribute towards the worship of God? In the first place, because that which hath pleased God is fulfilled. In the second place, because, when you are regenerated and born again of water and of God, the frailty of your former birth, which you have through men, is cut off, and so at length you shall be able to attain salvation; but otherwise it is impossible. For thus hath the true prophet testified to it with an oath: `Verily I say to you, That unless a man is born again of water, he shall not enter into the kingdom of heaven. Therefore make haste; for there is in these waters a certain power of mercy which was borne upon them at the beginning, and acknowledges those who are baptized under the name of the threefold sacrament, and rescues them from future punishments, presenting as a gift to God the souls that are consecrated by baptism. Betake yourselves there fore to these waters, for they alone can quench the violence of the future fire; and he who delays to approach to them, it is evident that the idol of unbelief remains in him, and by it he is prevented from hastening to the waters which confer salvation. For whether you be righteous or unrighteous, baptism is necessary for you in every respect: for the righteous, that perfection may be accomplished in him, and he may be born again to God; for the unrighteous, that pardon may he vouchsafed him of the sins which he has committed in ignorance. Therefore all should hasten to be horn again to God without delay, because the end of every one's life is uncertain.

Chapter X.-Necessity of Good Works.

"But when you have been regenerated by water, show by good works the likeness in you of that Father who hath begotten you. Now you know God, honor Him as a father; and His honor is that you live according to His will. And His will is, that you so live as to know nothing of murder or adultery, to flee from hatred and covetousness, to put away anger, pride, and boasting, to abhor envy, and to count all such things entirely unsuitable to you. There is truly a certain peculiar observance of our religion, which is not so much imposed upon men, as it is sought out by every worshipper of God by reason of its purity. By reason of chastity, I say, of which there are many kinds, but first, that every one be careful that he `come not near a menstruous woman; 'for this the law of God regards as detestable. But though the law had given no admonition concerning these things, should we willingly, like beetles, roll ourselves in filth? For we ought to have something more than the animals, as reasonable men, and capable of heavenly senses, whose chief study it ought to be to guard the conscience from every defilement of the heart.

Chapter XI.-Inward and Outward Cleansing.

"Moreover, it is good, and tends to purity, also to wash the body with water. I call it good, not as if it were that prime good of the purifying of the mind, but because this of the washing of the body is the sequel of that good. For so also our Master rebuked some of the Pharisees and scribes, who seemed to be better than others, and separated from the people, calling them hypocrites, because they purified only those things which were seen of men, but left defiled and sordid their hearts, which God alone sees. To some therefore of them-not to all-He said, 'Woe to you, scribes and Pharisees, hypocrites! because ye cleanse the outside of the cup and platter, but the inside is full of pollution. O blind Pharisees, first make clean what is within, and what is without shall be clean also.' For truly, if the mind be purified by the light of knowledge, when once it is clean and clear, then it necessarily takes care of that which is without a man, that is, his flesh, that it also may he purified. But when that which is without, the cleansing of the flesh, is neglected, it is certain that there is no care taken of the purity of the mind and the cleanness of the heart. Thus therefore it comes to pass, that he who is clean inwardly is without doubt cleansed outwardly also, but not always that he who is clean outwardly is also cleansed inwardly-to wit, when he does these things that he may please men.

Chapter XII.-Importance of Chastity.

"But this kind of chastity is also to be observed, that sexual intercourse must not take place heedlessly and for the sake of mere pleasure, but for the sake of begetting children. And since this observance is found even amongst some of the lower animals, it were a shame if it be not observed by men, reasonable, and worshipping God. But there is this further reason why chastity should be observed by those who hold the true worship of God, in those forms of it of which we have spoken, and others of like sort, that it is observed strictly even amongst those who are still held by the devil in error, for even amongst them there is in some degree the observance of chastity. What then? Will you not observe, now that you are reformed, what you observed when you were in error?

Chapter XIII.-Superiority of Christian Morality.

"But perhaps some one of you will say, Must we then observe all things which we did while we worshipped idols? Not all. But whatever things were done well, these you ought to observe even now; because, if anything is rightly done by those who are in error, it is certain that that is derived from the truth; whereas, if anything is not rightly done in the true religion, that is, without doubt, borrowed from error. For good is good, though it be done by those who are in error; and evil is evil, though it be done by those who follow the truth. Or shall we be so foolish, that if we see a worshipper of idols to be sober, we shall refuse to be sober, lest we should seem to do the same things which he does who worships idols? It is not so. But let this be our study, that if those who err do not commit murder, we should not even be angry; if they do not commit adultery, we should not even covet another's wife; if they love their neighbors, we should love even our enemies; if they lend to those who have the means of paying, we should give to those from whom we do not hope to receive anything. And in all things, we who hope for the inheritance of the eternal world ought to excel those who know only the present world; knowing that if their works, when compared with our works, be found like and equal in the day of judgment, there will be confusion to us, because we are found equal in our works to those who are condemned on account of ignorance, and had no hope of the world to come.

Chapter XIV.-Knowledge Enhances Responsibility.

"And truly confusion is our worthy portion, if we have done no more than those who are inferior to us in knowledge. But if it be confusion to us, to be found equal to them in works, what shall become of us if the examination that is to take place find us inferior and worse than them? Hear, therefore, how our true Prophet has taught us concerning these things; for, with respect to those who neglect to hear the words of wisdom, He speaks thus: `The queen of the south shall rise in judgment with this generation, and shall condemn it, because she came from the ends of the earth to hear the wisdom of Solomon; and, behold, a greater than Solomon is here, and they hear Him not.'" But with respect to those who refused to repent of their evil deeds, He spoke thus: `The men of Nineveh shall rise in the judgment with this generation, and shall condemn it; for they repented at the preaching of Jonas; and, behold, a greater than Jonas is here.' You see, therefore, how He condemned those who were instructed out of the law, by adducing[1] the example of those who came from Gentile ignorance, and showing that the former were not even equal to those who seemed to live in error. From all these things, then, the statement that He propounded is proved, that chastity, which is observed to a certain extent even by those who live in error, should be held much more purely and strictly, in all its forms, as we showed above, by us who follow the truth; and the rather because with us eternal rewards are assigned to its observance."

Chapter XV.-Bishops, Presbyters, Deacons, and Widows Ordained at Tripolis.

When he had said these things, and others to the same effect, he dismissed the crowds; and having, according to his custom, supped with his friends, he went to sleep. And while in this manner he was teaching the word of God for three whole months, and converting multitudes to the faith, at the last he ordered me to fast; and after the fast he conferred on me the baptism of ever-flowing water, in the fountains which adjoin the sea. And when, for the grace of regeneration divinely conferred upon me, we had joyfully kept holiday with our brethren, Peter ordered those who had been appointed to go before him, to proceed to Antioch, and there to wait three months more. And they having gone, he himself led down to the fountains, which, I have said, are near the sea, those who had fully received the faith of the Lord, and baptized them; and celebrating the Eucharist with them, he appointed, as bishop over them, Maro, who had entertained him in his house, and who was now perfect in all things; and with him he ordained twelve presbyters and deacons at the same time. He also instituted the order of widows, and arranged all the services of the Church; and charged them all to obey Maro their bishop in

---

[1] To bring forward in argument or as evidence.
Source: Dictionary.com Unabridged (v 1.1)

all things that he should command them. And thus all things being suitably arranged, when the three months were fulfilled, we bade farewell to those who were at Tripolis, and set out for Antioch.

Book VII.

Chapter I.-Journey from Tripolis.

At length leaving Tripolis, a city of Phoenicia, we made our first halt at Ortosias, not far from Tripolis; and there we remained the next day also, because almost all those that had believed in the Lord, unable to part from Peter, followed him thus far. Thence we came to Antharadus. But because there were many in our company, Peter said to Niceta and Aquila: "As there are immense crowds of brethren with as, and we bring upon ourselves no title envy as we enter into every city, it seems to me that we must take means, without doing so unpleasing a thing as to prevent their following us, to secure that the wicked one shall not stir up envy against us on account of any display! I wish, therefore, that you, Niceta and Aquila, would go before us with them, so that you may lead the multitude divided into two sections, that we may enter every city of the Gentiles traveling apart, rather than in one assemblage.

Chapter I.-Disciples Divided into Two Bands.

"But I know that you think it sad to be separated from me for the space of at least two days. Believe me, that in whatever degree you love me, my diction towards you is tenfold greater. But if, by reason of our mutual affection, we will not do the things that are right and honorable, such love will appear to be unreasonable. And therefore, without bating a little of our love, let us attend to those things which seem useful and necessary; especially since not a day can pass in which you may not be present at my discussions. For I purpose to pass through the most noted cities of the provinces one by one, as you also know, and to reside three months in each for the sake of teaching. Now, therefore, go before me to Laodicea, which is the nearest city, and I shall follow you after two or three days, so far as I purpose. But you shall wait for me at the inn nearest to the gate of the city; and thence again, when we have spent a few days there, you shall go before me to more distant cities. And this I wish you to do at every city, for the sake of avoiding envy as much as in us lies, and also that the brethren who are with us, finding lodgings prepared in the several cities by your foresight, may not seem to be vagabonds."

Chapter III.-Order of March.

When Peter thus spoke, they of course acquiesced, saying: "It does not greatly sadden us to do this, because we are ordered by you, who have been chosen by the foresight of Christ to do and to counsel well in all things; but also because, while it is a heavy loss not to see our lord Peter for one, or it may be two days, yet it is not intolerable. And we think of our twelve brethren who go before us, and who are deprived of the advantage of hearing and seeing you for a whole month out of the three that you stay in every city. Therefore we shall not delay doing as you order, because you order all things aright." And thus saying, they went forward, having received instructions that they should speak to the brethren who journeyed with them outside the city, and request them not to enter the cities in a crowd and with tumult, but apart, and divided

Chapter IV.-Clement's Joy at Remaining with Peter.

But when they were gone, I Clement rejoiced greatly because he had kept me with himself, and I said to him: "I give thanks to God that you have not sent me forward with the others, for I should have died through sadness." Then said Peter: "And what will happen if necessity shall demand that you be sent anywhere for the purpose of teaching? Would you die if you were separated from me for a good purpose? Would you not put a restraint upon yourself, to bear patiently what necessity has laid upon you? Or do you not know that friends are always together, and are joined in memory, though they be separated bodily;

as, on the other hand, some persons are near to one another in body, but are separate in mind?"

Chapter V.-Clement's Affection for Peter.

Then I answered: "Think not, my lord, that I suffer these things unreasonably; but there is a certain cause and reason of this affection of mine towards you. For I have you alone as the object of all my affections, instead of father and mother, and brethren; but above all this, is the fact that you alone are the cause of my salvation and knowledge of the truth. And also this I do not count of least moment, that my youthful age is subject to the snares of lusts; and I am afraid to be without you, by whose sole presence all effeminacy, however irrational it be, is put to shame; although I trust, by the mercy of God, that even my mind, from what it has conceived through your instruction, shall be unable to receive aught else into its thoughts. Besides, I remember your saying at Caesarea, `If any one wishes to accompany me, without violating dutifulness, let him accompany me.' And by this you meant that he should not make any one sad, to whom he ought according to God's appointment to cleave; for example, that he should not leave a faithful wife, or parents, or the like. Now from these I am entirely free, and so I am fit for following you; and I wish you would grant me that I might perform to you the service of a servant."

Chapter VI.-Peter's Simplicity of Life.

Then Peter, laughing. said: "And do you not think, Clement, that very necessity must make you my servant? For who else can spread my sheets, and arrange my beautiful coverlets? Who will be at hand to keep my rings, and prepare my robes, which I must be constantly changing? Who shall superintend my cooks, and provide various and choice meats to be prepared by most recondite[1] and various art; and all those things which are procured at

---

[1] Beyond ordinary knowledge or understanding.
Source: Dictionary.com Unabridged (v 1.1)

enormous expense, and are brought together for men of delicate up-bringing, yea rather, for their appetite, as for some enormous beast? But perhaps, although you live with me, you do not know my manner of life. I live on bread alone, with olives, and seldom even with pot-herbs; and my dress is what you see, a tunic with a pallium[1]: and having these, I require nothing more. This is sufficient for me, because my mind does not regard things present, but things eternal, and therefore no present and visible thing delights me. Whence I embrace and admire indeed your good mind towards me; and I commend you the more, because, though you have been accustomed to so great abundance, you have been able so soon to abandon it, and to accommodate yourself to this life of ours, which makes use of necessary things alone. For we-that is, I and my brother Andrew-have grown up from our childhood not only orphans, but also extremely poor, and through necessity have become used to labor, whence now also we easily bear the fatigues of our journeys. But rather, if you would consent and allow it, I, who am a working man, could more easily discharge the duty of a servant to you."

Chapter VII.-Peter's Humility.

But I trembled when I heard this, and my tears immediately gushed forth, because so great a man, who is worth more than the whole world, had addressed such a proposal to me. Then he, when he saw me weeping, inquired the reason; and I answered him: "How have I so sinned against you, that you should distress me with such a proposal? "Then Peter: "If it is evil that I said I should serve you, you were first in fault in saying the same thing to me." Then said I: "The cases are not alike: for it becomes me to do this to you; but it is grievous that you, who are sent as the herald of the Most High God to save the souls of men, should say it to me." Then said Peter: "I should agree with you, were it not that our Lord, who came for the salvation of the whole world, and who was nobler than any creature, submitted to

---

[1] A large, rectangular mantle worn by men in ancient Greece and Rome.   Source: Dictionary.com Unabridged (v 1.1)

be a servant, that He might persuade us not to be ashamed to perform the ministry of servants to our brethren." Then said I: "It were foolishness in me to suppose that I can prevail with you; nevertheless I give thanks to the providence of God, because I have merited to have you instead of parents."

Chapter VIII.-Clement's Family History.

Then said Peter: "Is there then no one of your family surviving? "I answered: "There are indeed many powerful men, coming of the stock of Caesar; for Caesar himself gave a wife to my father, as being his relative, and educated along with him, and of a suitably noble family. By her my father had twin sons, born before me, not very like one another, as my father told me; for I never knew them. But indeed I have not a distinct recollection even of my mother; but I cherish the remembrance of her face, as if I had seen it in a dream. My mother's name was Matthidia, my father's Faustinianus: my brothers', Faustinus and Faustus. Now, when I was barely five years old, my mother saw a vision-so I learned from my father-by which she was warned that, unless she speedily for the city with her twin sons, and was absent for ten years, she and her children should perish by a miserable fate.

Chapter IX.-Disappearance of His Mother and Brothers.

"Then my father, who tenderly loved his sons, put them on board a ship with their mother, and sent them to Athens to be educated, with slaves and maid-servants, and a sufficient supply of money; retaining me only to be a comfort to him, and thankful for this, that the vision had not commanded me also to go with my mother. And at the end of a year my father sent men to Athens with money for them, desiring also to know how they did; but those who were sent never returned. Again, in the third year, my sorrowful father sent other men with money, who returned in the fourth year, and related that they had seen neither my mother nor my brothers, that they had never reached Athens, and that no trace had been found of any one of those who had been with them.

Chapter X.-Disappearance of His Father.

"My father hearing this, and confounded with excessive sorrow, not knowing whither to go or where to seek, went down with me to the harbor, and began to ask of the sailors whether any of them had seen or heard of the bodies of a mother and two little children being cast ashore anywhere, four years ago; when one told one story and another another, but nothing definite was disclosed to us searching in this boundless sea. Yet my father, by reason of the great affection which he bore to his wife and children, was fed with vain hopes, until he thought of placing me under guardians and leaving me at Rome, as I was now twelve years old, and himself going in quest of them. Therefore he went down to the harbor weeping, and going on board a ship, took his departure; and from that time till now I have never received any letters from him, nor do I know whether he is alive or dead. But I rather suspect that he also has perished, either through a broken heart or by shipwreck; for twenty years have now elapsed since then, and no tidings of him have ever reached me."

Chapter XI.-Different Effects of Suffering on Heathens and Christians.

Peter, hearing this, shed tears of sympathy, and said to his friends who were present: "If any man who is a worshipper of God had endured what this man's father has endured, immediately men would assign his religion as the cause of his calamities; but when these things happen to miserable Gentiles, they charge their misfortunes upon fate. I call them miserable, because they are both vexed with errors here, and are deprived of future hope; whereas, when the worshippers of God suffer these things, their patient endurance of them contributes to their cleansing from sin."

211

Chapter XII.-Excursion to Aradus.

After this, one of those present began to ask Peter, that early next day we should go to a neighboring island called Aradus, which was not more than six furlongs off, to see a certain wonderful work that was in it, viz. vine-wood columns of immense size. To this Peter assented, as he was very complaisant; but he charged us that, when we left the ship, we should not rush all together to see it: "for," said he, "I do not wish you to be noticed by the crowd." When therefore, next day, we reached the island by ship in the course of an hour forthwith we hastened to the place where the wonderful columns were. They were placed in a certain temple, in which there were very magnificent works of Phidias,[1] on which every one of us gazed earnestly.

Chapter XIII.-The Beggar Woman.

But when Peter had admired only the columns, being no wise ravished with the grace of the painting, he went out, and saw before the gates a poor woman asking alms of those who went in; and looking earnestly at her, he said: "Tell me, O woman, what member of your body is wanting, that you subject yourself to the indignity of asking alms, and do not rather gain your bread by laboring with your hands which God has given you." But she, sighing, said: "Would that I had hands which could be moved; but now only the appearance of hands has been preserved, for they are lifeless, and have been rendered feeble and without feeling by my gnawing of them." Then Peter said: "What has been the cause of your inflicting so great an injury upon yourself?" "Want of courage," said she, "and nought else; for if I had had any bravery in me, I could either have thrown myself from a precipice, or cast myself into the depths of the sea, and so ended my grief."

---

[1] Greek sculptor (circa 500-432 BC) who supervised work on the Parthenon. His statue of Zeus at Olympia was one of the Seven Wonders of the World. *Source: The American Heritage® Dictionary of the English Language, Fourth Edition.*

Chapter XIV.-The Woman's Grief.

Then Peter said: "Do you think, O woman, that those who destroy themselves are set free from torments, and not rather that the souls of those who lay violent hands upon themselves are subjected to greater punishments? "Then said she: "I wish I were sure that souls live in the infernal regions, for I would gladly embrace the suffering of the penalty of suicide, only that I might see my darling children, if it were but for an hour." Then Peter: "What thing is it so great, that effects you with so heavy sadness? I should like to know. For if you informed me of the cause, I might be able both to show you clearly, O woman, that souls do live in the infernal regions; and instead of the precipice or the deep sea, I might give yon some remedy, that you may be able to end your life without torment."

Chapter XV.-The Woman's Story.

Then the woman, hearing this welcome promise, began to say: "It is neither easy of belief, nor do I think it necessary to tell, what is my extraction, or what is my country. It is enough only to explain the cause of my grief, why I have rendered my hands powerless by gnawing them. Being born of noble parents, and having become the wife of a suitably powerful man, I had two twin sons, and after them one other. But my husband's brother was vehemently enflamed with unlawful love towards me; and as I valued chastity above all things, and would neither consent to so great wickedness, nor wished to disclose to my husband the baseness of his brother, I considered whether in any way I could escape unpolluted, and yet not set brother against brother, and so bring the whole race of a noble family into disgrace. I made up my mind, therefore, to leave my country with my two twins, until the incestuous love should subside, which the sight of me was fostering and inflaming; and I thought that our other son should remain to comfort his father to some extent.

Chapter XVI.-The Woman's Story Continued.

"Now in order to carry out this plan, I pretended that I had had a dream, in which some deity stood by me in a vision, and told me that I should immediately depart from the city with my twins, and should be absent until he should command me to return; and that, if I did not do so, I should perish with all my children. And so it was done. For as soon as I told the dream to my husband, he was terrified; and sending with me my twin sons, and also slaves and maid-servants, and giving me plenty of money, he ordered me to sail to Athens, where I might educate my sons, and that I should stay there until he who commanded me to depart should give me leave to return. While I was sailing along with my sons, I was shipwrecked in the night by the violence of the winds, and, wretch that I am, was driven to this place; and when all had perished, a powerful wave caught me, and cast me upon a rock. And while I sat there with this only hope, that by chance I might be able to find my sons, I did not throw myself into the deep, although then my soul, disturbed and drunk with grief, had both the courage and the power to do it.

Chapter XVII.-The Woman's Story Continued.

"But when the day dawned, and I with shouting and howling was looking around, if I could even see the corpses of my unhappy sons anywhere washed ashore, some of those who saw me were moved with compassion, and searched, first over the sea, and then also along the shores, if they could find either of my children. But when neither of them was anywhere found, the women of the place, taking pity on me, began to comfort me, every one telling her own griefs, that I might take consolation from the likeness of their calamities to my own. But this saddened me all the more; for my disposition was not such that I could regard the misfortunes of others as comforts to me. And when many desired to receive me hospitably, a certain poor woman who dwells here constrained me to enter into her hut, saying that she had had a husband who was a sailor, and that he had died at sea while a young man, and that, although many afterwards asked her in marriage, she preferred widowhood through the love of her husband. `Therefore, 'said she. `we shall share whatever we can gain by the labor of our hands.'

Chapter XVIII.-The Woman's Story Continued.

"And, not to detain you with a long and profitless story, I willingly dwelt with her on account of the faithful affection which she retained for her husband. But not long after, my hands (unhappy woman that I was!), long torn with gnawing, became powerless, and she who had taken me in fell into palsy, and now lies at home in her bed; also the affection of those women who had formerly pitied me grew cold. We are both helpless. I, as you see, sit begging; and when I get anything, one meal serves two wretches. Behold, now you have heard enough of my affairs; why do you delay the fulfillment of your promise, to give me a remedy, by which both of us may end our miserable life without torment? "

Chapter XIX.-Peter's Reflections on the Story.

While she was speaking, Peter, being distracted with much thought, stood like one thunder-struck; and I Clement coming up, said: "I have been seeking you everywhere, and now what are we to do? "But he commanded me to go before him to the ship, and there to wait for him; and because he must not be gainsayed, I did as he commanded me. But he, as he afterwards told me the whole, being struck with a sort of suspicion, asked of the woman her family, and her country, and the names of her sons; "and straightway," he said, "if you tell me these things, I shall give you the remedy." But she, like one suffering violence, because she would not confess these things, and yet was desirous of the remedy, reigned one thing after another, saying that she was an Ephesian, and her husband a Sicilian, and giving false names to her sons. Then Peter, supposing that she had answered truly, said: "Alas! O woman, I thought that some great joy should spring up to us to-day; for I suspected that you were a certain woman, concerning whom I lately learned certain like things." But she adjured him, saying: "I entreat you to tell me what they are, that I may know if amongst women there be one more unfortunate than myself."

Chapter XX.-Peter's Statement to the Woman.

Then Peter, incapable of deception, and moved with compassion, began to say: "There is a certain young man among those who follow me for the sake of religion and sect, a Roman citizen, who told me that he had a father and two twin brothers, of whom not one is left to him. `My mother,' he said, `as I learned from my father, saw a vision, that she should depart from the Roman city for a time with her twin sons, else they should perish by a dreadful death; and when she had departed, she was nevermore seen.' And afterwards his father set out to search for his wife and sons, and was also lost."

Chapter XXI.-A Discovery.

When Peter had thus spoken, the woman, struck with astonishment, fainted. Then Peter began to hold her up, and to comfort her, and to ask what was the matter, or what she suffered. But she at length, with difficulty recovering her breath, and nerving herself up to the greatness of the joy which she hoped for, and at the same time wiping her face, said: "Is he here, the youth of whom you speak? "But Peter, when he understood the matter, said: "Tell me first, or else you shall not see him." Then she said: "I am the mother of the youth." Then says Peter: "What is his name? "And she answered: "Clement." Then said Peter: "It is himself; and he it was that spoke with me a little while ago, and whom I ordered to go before me to the ship." Then she fell down at Peter's feet and began to entreat him that he would hasten to the ship. Then Peter said: "Yes if you will promise me that you will do as I say." Then she said: "I will do anything; only show me my only son, for I think that in him

I shall see my twins also." Then Peter said: "When you have seen him, dissemble for a little time, until we leave the island." "I will do so," she said.

Chapter XXII.-A Happy Meeting.

Then Peter, holding her hand, led her to the ship. And when I saw him giving his hand to the woman, I began to laugh; yet, approaching to do him honor, I tried to substitute my hand for his, and to support the woman. But as soon as I touched her hand, she uttered a loud scream, and rushed into my embrace, and began to devour me with a mother's kisses. But I, being ignorant of the whole matter, pushed her off as a mad woman; and at the same time, though with reverence, I was somewhat angry with Peter.

Chapter XXIII.-A Miracle.

But he said: "Cease: what mean you, O Clement, my son? Do not push away your mother." But I as soon as I heard these words, immediately bathed in tears, fell upon my mother, who had fallen down, and began to kiss her, For as soon as I heard, by degrees I recalled her countenance to my memory; and the longer I gazed, the more familiar it grew to me. Mean time a great multitude assembled, hearing that the woman who used to sit and beg was recognized by her son, who was a good man. And when we wished to sail hastily away from the island, my mother said to me: "My darling son, it is right that I should bid farewell to the woman who took me in; for she is poor, and paralytic, and bedridden." When Peter and all who were present heard this, they admired the goodness and prudence of the woman; and immediately Peter ordered some to go and to bring the woman in her bed as she lay. And when she had been brought, and placed in the midst of the crowd, Peter said, in the presence of all: "If I am a preacher of truth, for confirming the faith of all those who stand by, that they may know and believe that there is one God, who made heaven and earth, in the name of Jesus Christ, His Son, let this woman rise." And as soon as he had said this, she arose whole, and fell down at Peter's feet; and greeting her friend and acquaintance with kisses asked of her was the meaning of it all. But she shortly related to her the whole proceeding of the Recognition, so that the crowds standing around wondered.

Chapter XXIV-Departure from Aradus.

Then Peter, so far as he could, and as time permitted, addressed the crowds on the faith of God, and the ordinances of religion; and then added, that if any one wished to know more accurately about these things, he should come to Antioch, "where," said he, "we have resolved to stay three months, and to teach fully the things which pertain to salvation. For if," said he, "men leave their country and their parents for commercial or military purposes, and do not fear to undertake long voyages, why should it be thought burdensome or difficult to leave home for three months for the sake of eternal life? "When he had said these things, and more to the same purpose, I presented a thousand drachmas to the woman who had entertained my mother, and who bad recovered her health by means of Peter, and in the presence of all committed her to the charge of a certain good man, the chief person in that town, who promised that he would gladly do what we demanded of him. I also distributed a little money among some others, and among those women who were said formerly to have comforted my mother in her miseries, to whom I also expressed my thanks. And after this we sailed, along with my mother, to Antaradus.

Chapter XXV.-Journeyings.

And when we had come to our lodging, my mother began to ask of me what had become of my father; and I told her that he had gone to seek her, and never returned. But she, hearing this, only sighed; for her great joy on my account lightened her other sorrows. And the next clay she journeyed with us, sitting with Peter's wife; and we came to Balaneae, where we stayed three days, and then went on to

Pathos, and afterwards to Gabala; and so we arrived at Laodicea, where Niceta and Aquila met us before the gates, and kissing us, conducted us to a lodging. But Peter, seeing that it was a large and splendid city, said that it was worthy that we should stay in it ten days, or even longer. Then Niceta and Aquila asked of me who was this unknown woman; and I answered: "It is my mother, whom God has given back to me by means of my lord Peter."

Chapter XXVI.-Recapitulation.

And when I had said this, Peter began to relate the whole matter to them in order, and said. "When we had come to Aradus, and I had ordered you to go on before us, the same day after you had gone, Clement was led in the course of conversation to tell me of his extraction and his family, and how he had been deprived of his parents, and had had twin brothers older than himself, and that, as his father told him, his mother once saw a vision, by which she was ordered to depart from the city of Rome with her twin sons, else she and they should suddenly perish. And when she had told his father the dream, he, loving his sons with tender affection, and afraid of any evil befalling them, put his wife and sons on board a ship with all necessaries, and sent them to Athens to be educated. Afterwards he sent once and again persons to inquire after them, but nowhere found even a trace of them. At last the father himself went on the search, and until now he is nowhere to be found. When Clement had given me this narrative, there came one to us, asking us to go to the neighboring island of Aradus, to see vine-wood columns of wonderful size. I consented; and when we came to the place, all the rest went into the interior of the temple; but I-for what reason I know not-had no mind to go farther.

Chapter XXVII.-Recapitulation Continued.

"But while I was waiting outside for them, I began to notice this woman, and to wonder in what part of her body she was disabled, that she did not seek her living by the labor of her hands, but submitted to the shame of beggary. I therefore asked of her the reason of it. She confessed that she was sprung of a noble race, and was married to a no less noble husband, `whose brother, 'said she, `being inflamed by unlawful love towards me, desired to defile his brother's bed. This I abhorring, and yet not daring to tell my husband of so great wickedness, lest I should stir up war between the brothers. and bring disgrace upon the family, judged it better to depart from my country with my two twin sons, leaving the younger boy to be a comfort to his father. And that this might be done with an honorable appearance, I thought good to feign a dream, and to tell my husband that there stood by me in a vision a certain deity, who told me to set out from the city immediately with my two twins, and remain until he should instruct me to return.' She told me that her husband, when he heard this, believed her, and sent her to Athens, with the twin children to be educated there; but that they were driven by a terrible tempest upon that island, where, when the ship had gone to pieces, she was lifted by a wave upon a rock, and delayed killing herself only for this, `until, 'said she, `I could embrace at least the dead limbs of my unfortunate sons, and commit them to burial. But when the day dawned, and crowds had assembled, they took pity upon me, and threw a garment over me. But I, miserable, entreated them with many tears, to search if they could find anywhere the bodies of my unfortunate sons. And I, tearing all my body with my teeth, with wailing and howling cried out constantly, Unhappy woman that I am, where is my Faustus? where my Faustinus? '"

Chapter XXVIII.-More Recognitions.

And when Peter said this, Niceta and Aquila suddenly started up, and being astonished, began to be greatly agitated, saying: "O Lord, Thou Ruler and God of all, are these things true, or are we in a dream? "Then Peter said: "Unless we be mad, these things are true." But they, after a short pause, and wiping their faces, said: "We are Faustinus and Faustus: and even at the first, when you began this narrative, we immediately fell into a suspicion that the matters that you spoke of might perhaps relate to us; yet again considering that many like things happen in men's lives, we kept silence, although our hearts were struck by some hope. Therefore we waited for the end of your story, that, if it were entirely manifest that it related to us, we might then confess it." And when they had thus spoken, they went in weeping to our mother. And when they found her asleep, and wished to embrace her, Peter prevented them, saying: "Permit me first to prepare your mother's mind, lest perhaps by the great and sudden joy she lose her reason, and her understanding he disturbed, especially as she is now stupefied with sleep."

Chapter XXIX.-"Nothing Common or Unclean."

Therefore, when our mother had risen from her sleep, Peter began to address her, saying: "I wish you to know, O woman an observance of our religion. We worship one God, who made the world, and we keep His law, in which He commands us first of all to worship Him, and to reverence His name, to honor our parents, and to preserve chastity and uprightness. But this also we observe, not to have a common table with Gentiles, unless when they believe, and on the reception of the truth are baptized, and consecrated by a certain threefold invocation of the blessed name; and then we eat with them. Otherwise, even if it were a father or a mother, or wife, or sons, or brothers, we cannot have a common table with them. Since, therefore, we do this for the special cause of religion, let it not seem hard to you that your son cannot eat with you, until you have the same judgment of the faith that he has."

Chapter XXX.-"Who Can Forbid Water? "

Then she, when she heard this, said: "And what hinders me to be baptized to-day? For even before I saw you I was wholly alienated from those whom they call gods because they were not able to do anything for me, although I frequently, and almost daily, sacrificed to them. And as to chastity, what shall I say, when neither in former times did pleasures deceive me, nor afterwards did poverty compel me to sin? But I think you know well enough how great was my love of chastity, when I pretended that dream that I might escape the snares of unhallowed love, and that I might go abroad with my two twins, and when I left this my son Clement alone to be a comfort to his father. For if two were scarcely enough for me, how much more it would have saddened their father, if he had had none at all? For he was wretched through his great affection towards our sons, so that even the authority of the dream could scarce prevail upon him to give up to me Faustinus and Faustus, the brothers of this Clement, and that himself should be content with Clement alone. "

Chapter XXXI.-Too Much Joy.

While she was yet speaking, my brothers could contain themselves no longer, but rushed into their mother's embrace with many tears, and kissed her. But she said: "What is the meaning of this "Then said Peter: "Be not disturbed, O woman; be firm. These are your sons Faustinus and Faustus, whom you supposed to have perished in the deep; but how they are alive, and how they escaped in that horrible night, and how the one of them is called Niceta and the other Aquila, they will be able to explain to you themselves, and we also shall hear it along with you." When Peter had said this, our mother fainted, being overcome with excess of joy; and after some time, being restored and come to herself, she said; "I beseech you, darling sons, tell me what has befallen you since that dismal and cruel night."

Chapter XXXII.-"He Bringeth Them Unto Their Desired Haven."

Then Niceta began to say: "On that night, O mother, when the ship was broken up, and we were being tossed upon the sea, supported on a fragment of the wreck, certain men, whose business it was to rob by sea, found us, and placed us in their boat, and overcoming the power of the waves by rowing, by various stretches brought us to Caesarea Stratonis. There they starved us, and beat us, and terrified us, that we might not disclose the truth; and having changed our names, they sold us to a certain widow, a very honorable women, named Justa. She, having bought us, treated us as sons, so that she carefully educated us in Greek literature and liberal arts. And when we grew up, we also attended to philosophic studies, that we night be able to confute the Gentiles, by supporting the doctrines of the divine religion by philosophic disputations.

Chapter XXXIII.-Another Wreck Prevented.

"But we adhered, for friendship's sake and boyish companionship, to one Simon, a magician, who was educated along with us, so that we were almost deceived by him. For there is mention made in our religion of a certain Prophet, whose coming was hoped for by all who observe that religion, through whom immortal and happy life is promised to be given to those who believe in Him. Now we thought that this Simon was he. But these things shall be explained to you, O mother, at a more convenient season. Meanwhile, when we were almost deceived by Simon, a certain colleague of my lord Peter, Zacchaeus by name, warned us that we should not be duped by the magician, but presented us to Peter on his arrival, that by him we might be taught the things which were sound and perfect. And this we hope will happen to you also, even as God has vouchsafed it to us, that we may be able to eat and have a common table with you. Thus therefore it was, O mother, that you believed that we were drowned in the sea, while we were stolen by pirates."

Chapter XXXIV.-Baptism Must Be Preceded by Fasting.

When Niceta had spoken thus, our mother fell down at Peter's feet, entreating and beseeching him that both herself and her hostess might be baptized without delay; "that," said she, "I may not even for a single clay suffer the loss of the company and society of my sons." In like manner, we her sons also entreated Peter. But he said: "What! Do you think that I alone am unpitiful, and that I do not wish you to enjoy your mother's society at meals? But she must fast at least one day first, and so be baptized; and this because I have heard from her a certain declaration, by which her faith has been made manifest to me, and which has given evidence of her belief; otherwise she must have been instructed and taught many days before she could have been baptized."

Chapter XXXV.-Desiring the Salvation of Others.

Then said I: "I pray you, my lord Peter, tell us what is that declaration which you say afforded you evidence of her faith? "Then Peter: "It is her asking that her hostess, whose kindnesses she wishes to requite, may be baptized along with her. Now she would not ask that this grace be bestowed upon her whom she loves, unless she believed that there is some great boon in baptism. Whence, also, I find fault with very many, who, when they are themselves baptized and believe, yet do nothing worthy of faith with those whom they love, such as wives, or children, or friends, whom they do not exhort to that which they themselves have attained, *as they would do* if indeed they believed that eternal life is thereby bestowed. In short, if they see them to be sick, or to be subject to any danger bodily, they grieve and mourn, because they are sure that in this destruction threatens them. So, then, if they were sure of this, that the punishment of eternal fire awaits those who do not worship God, when would they cease warning and exhorting? Or, if they refused, how would they not mourn and bewail them, being sure that eternal torments awaited them? Now, therefore, we shall send for that woman at once, and see if she loves the faith of our religion; and as we find, so shall we act. But since your mother has judged so faithfully concerning baptism, let her fast only one day before baptism."

Chapter XXXVI.-The Sons' Pleading.

But she declared with an oath, in presence of my lord Peter's wife, that from the time she recognized her son, she had been unable to take any food from excess of joy, excepting only that yesterday she drank a cup of water. Peter's wife also bore witness, saying that it was even so. Then Aquila said: "What, then, hinders her being baptized? "Then Peter, smiling, said: "But this is not the fast of baptism, for it was not done in order to baptism." Then Niceta said: "But perhaps God, wishing that our mother, on our recognition, should not be separated even for one day from participation of our table, pre-ordained this fasting. For as in her ignorance she preserved her chastity, that it might profit her in order to the grace of baptism; so she fasted before she knew the reason of fasting, that it might profit her in order to baptism, and that immediately, from the beginning of our acquaintance, she might enjoy communion of the table with us."

Chapter XXXVII.-Peter Inexorable.

Then said Peter: "Let not the wicked one prevail against us, taking occasion from a mother's love; but let you, and me with you, fast this day along with her, and to-morrow she shall be baptized: for it is not right that the precepts of truth be relaxed and weakened in favor of any person or friendship. Let us not shrink, then, from suffering along with her, for it is a sin to transgress any commandment. But let us teach our bodily senses, which are without us, to be in subjection to our inner senses; and not compel our inner senses, which savor the things that be of God, to follow the outer senses, which savor the things that be of the flesh. For to this end also the Lord commanded, saying: `Whosoever shall look upon a woman to lust after her, hath committed adultery with her already in his heart.' And to this He added: `If thy right eye offend thee, pluck it out, and cast it from thee: for it is profitable for thee that one of thy members perish, rather than thy whole body be cast into hell-fire.' He does not say, *has offended thee,* that you should then cast away the cause of sin after you have sinned; but *if it offend you,* that is, that before you sin you should cut off the cause of the sin that provokes and irritates you. But let none of you think, brethren, that the Lord commended the cutting off of the members. His meaning is, that the purpose should be cut off, not the members, and the causes which allure to sin, in order that our thought, borne up on the chariot of sight, may push towards the love of God, supported by the bodily senses; and not give loose reins to the eyes of the flesh as to wanton horses, eager to turn their running outside the way of the commandments, but may subject the bodily sight to the judgment of the mind, and not suffer those eyes of ours, which God intended to be viewers and witnesses of His work, to become panders of evil desire. And therefore let the bodily senses as well as the internal thought be subject to the law of God, and let them serve His will, whose work they acknowledge themselves to be."

Chapter XXXVIII.-Reward of Chastity.

Therefore, as the order and reason of the mystery demanded, on the following day she was baptized in the sea, and returning to the lodging, was initiated in all the mysteries of religion in their order. And we her sons, Niceta and Aquila, and I Clement, were present. And after this we dined with her, and glorified God with her, thankfully acknowledging the zeal and teaching of Peter, who showed us, by the example of our mother, that the good of chastity is not lost with God; "as, on the other hand," said he, "unchastity does not escape punishment, though it may not be punished immediately, but slowly. But so well pleasing," said he, "is chastity to God, that it confers some grace in the present life even upon those who are in error; for future blessedness is laid up for those only who preserve chastity and righteousness by the grace of baptism. In short, that which has befallen your mother is an example of this, for all this welfare has been restored to her in reward of her chastity, for the guarding and preserving of which continence alone is not sufficient; but when any one perceives that snares and deceptions are being prepared, he must straightway flee as from the violence of fire or the attack of a mad dog, and not trust that he can easily frustrate snares of this kind by philosophizing or by humoring them; but, as I have said, he must flee and withdraw to a distance, as your mother also did through her true and entire love of chastity. And on this account she has been preserved to you, and you to her; and in addition, she has been endowed with the knowledge of eternal life" When he had said this, and much more to the same effect, the evening having come, we went to sleep.

Book VIII.

Chapter I.-The Old Workman.

Now the next morning Peter took my brothers and me with him, and we went down to the harbor to bathe in the sea, and thereafter we retired to a certain secret place for prayer. But a certain poor old man, a workman, as he appeared by his dress, began to observe us eagerly, without our seeing him, that he might see what we were doing in secret. And when he saw us praying, he waited till we came out, and then saluted us, and said: "If you do not take it amiss, and regard me as an inquisitive and troublesome[1] person, I should wish to converse with you; for I take pity on you, and would not have you err under the appearance of truth, and be afraid of things that have no existence; or if you think that there is any truth in them, then declare it to me. If, therefore, you take it patiently, I can in a few words instruct you in what is right; but if it be unpleasant to you, I shall go on, and do my business." To him Peter answered: "Speak what you think good, and we will gladly hear, whether it be true or false; for you are to be welcomed, because, like a father anxious on behalf of his children, you wish to put us in possession of what you regard as good."

Chapter II.-Genesis.

Then the old man proceeded to say: "I saw you bathe in the sea, and afterwards retire into a secret place; wherefore observing, without your noticing me, what you were doing, I saw you praying. Therefore, pitying your error, I waited till you came out, that I might speak to you, and instruct you not to err in an observance of this sort; because there is neither any God, nor any worship, neither is there any providence in the world, but all things are done by

---

[1] Original word used in the text was: **importunate**

accidental[1] chance and *genesis*,[2] as I have discovered most clearly for thyself, being accomplished beyond others in the discipline of learning. Do not err, therefore: for whether you pray, or whether you do not pray, whatever your *genesis* contains, that shall befall you." Then I Clement was affected, I know not how, in my heart, recollecting many things in him that seemed familiar to me; for some one says well, that that which is sprung from any one, although it may be long absent, yet a spark of relationship is never extinguished. Therefore I began to ask of him who and whence he was, and how descended. But he, not wishing to answer these questions, said: "What has that to do with what I have told you? But first, if you please, let us converse of those matters which we have pro-pounded; and afterwards, if circumstances require, we can disclose to one another, as friends to friends, our names, and families, and country, and other things connected with these." Yet we all admired the eloquence of the man, and the gravity of his manners, and the calmness of his speech.

Chapter III.-A Friendly Conference.

But Peter, walking along leisurely while conversing, was looking out for a suitable place for a conference. And when he saw a quiet recess near the harbor, he made us sit down; and so he himself first began. Nor did he hold the old man in any contempt, nor did he look down upon him because his dress was poor and mean. He said, therefore: "Since you seem to me to be a learned man, and a compassionate, inasmuch as you have come to us, and wish that to be known to us which you consider to be good, we also wish to expound to you what things we believe to be good and right; and if you do not think them true, you will take in

---

[1] The original word used in the text was: **fortuitous**

[2] A theory that God, in the beginning, imposed a certain course and order upon all things, so that the life of man and everything in the world will play out according to its pre-ordained destiny.
Source: The American Heritage® Dictionary of the English Language, Fourth Edition.

good part our good intentions towards you, as we do yours towards us." While Peter was thus speaking, a great multitude assembled. Then said the old man: "Perhaps the presence of a multitude disconcerts you." Peter replied: "Not at all, except only on this account, that I am afraid lest perhaps, when the truth is made manifest in the course of our discussion, you be ashamed in presence of the multitude to yield and assent to the things which you may have understood to be spoken truly." To this the old man answered: "I am not such a fool in my old age, that, understanding what is true, I should deny it for the favor of the rabble.[1]"

Chapter IV.-The Question Stated.

Then Peter began to say: "Those who speak the word of truth, and who enlighten the souls of men, seem to me to be like the rays of the sun, which, when once they have come forth and appeared to the world, can no longer be concealed or hidden, while they are not so much seen by men, as they afford sight to all. There fore it was well said by One to the heralds of the truth, `Ye are the light of the world, and a city set upon a hill cannot be hid; neither do men light a candle and put it tinder a bushel, but upon a candlestick, that it may enlighten all who are in the house.' "Then said the old man: "He said well, whoever he is. But let one of you state what, according to his opinion, ought to be followed, that we may direct our speech to a definite aim. For, in order to find the truth, it is not sufficient to overthrow the things that are spoken on the other side, but also that one should himself bring forward what he who is on the other side may oppose. Therefore, in order that both parties may be on an equal footing, it seems to me to be right that each of us should first enunciate what opinion he holds. And, if you please, I shall begin first. I say, then, that the world is not governed according to the providence of God, because we see that many things in it are done

---

[1] A disorderly crowd; mob.
Source: Dictionary.com Unabridged (v 1.1)

unjustly and disorderly; but I say that it is *genesis* that does and regulates all things."

Chapter V.-Freedom of Discussion Allowed.

When Peter was about to reply to this, Niceta, anticipating him, said: "Would my lord Peter allow me to answer to this; and let it not be thought forward that I, a young man, should have an encounter with an old man, but rather let me converse as a son with a father." Then said the old man: "Not only do I wish, my son, that you should set forth your opinions; but also if any one of your associates, if any one even of the bystanders, thinks that he knows anything, let him unhesitatingly state it: we shall gladly hear it; for it is by the contribution of many that the things that are unknown are more easily found out." Then Niceta therefore answered: "Do not deem me to have done rashly, my father, because I have interrupted the speech of my lord Peter; but rather I meant to honor him by doing this. For he is a man of God, full of all knowledge, who is not ignorant even of Greek learning, because he is filled with the Spirit of God, to whom nothing is unknown. But because it is suitable to him to speak of heavenly things, I shall answer concerning those things which pertain to the babbling of the Greeks. But after we have disputed in the Grecian manner, and we have come to that point where no issue appears, then he himself, as filled with the knowledge of God, shall openly and clearly disclose to us the truth on all matters, so that not we only, but also all who are around us as hearers, shall learn the way of truth. And therefore now let him sit as umpire; and when either of us shall yield, then let him, taking up the matter, give an unquestionable judgment."

Chapter VI.-The Other Side of the Question Stated.

When Niceta had thus spoken, those who had assembled conversed among themselves: "Is this that Peter of whom we heard, the most approved disciple of Him who appeared in Judaea, and wrought many signs and miracles?" And they stood gazing upon him with great fear and veneration, as conferring upon the Lord the honor of His good servant. Which when Peter observed, he said to them: "Let us hear with all attention, holding an impartial judgment of what shall be said by each; and after their encounter we also shall add what may seem necessary." And when Peter had said this, the crowds rejoiced. Then Niceta began to speak as follows: "You have laid down, my father, that the world is not governed by the providence of God, but that all things are subject to *genesis*, whether the things which relate to the dispositions, or those which relate to the doings of every one. This I could answer immediately; but because it is right to observe order, we also lay down what we hold, as you yourself requested should be done. I say that the world is governed by the providence of God, at least in those things which need His government. For He it is alone who holds all things in His hand, who also made the world; the just God, who shall at some time render to every one according to his deeds. Now, then, you have our position; go on as you please, either overthrowing mine or establishing your own, that I may meet your statements. Or if you wish me to speak first, I shall not hesitate."

Chapter VII.-The Way Cleared.

Then the old man answered: "Whether it pleases you, my son, to speak first, or whether you prefer that I should speak, makes no difference, especially with those who discuss in a friendly spirit. However, speak you first, and I will gladly hear; and I wish you may be able even to follow out those things that are to be spoken by me, and to put in opposition to them those things that are contrary to them, and from the comparison of both to show the truth." Niceta answered: "If you wish it, I can even state your side of the argument, and then answer it." Then the old man: "Show me first how you can know what I have not yet spoken, and so I shall believe that you can follow out my side of the argument." Then Niceta: "Your sect is manifest, even by the proposition which you have laid down, to those who are skilled in doctrines of this sort; and its consequence is certain. And because I am not ignorant what are the propositions of the philosophers, I know what follows from those things which you have propounded; especially because I have frequented the schools of Epicurus in preference to the other philosophers. But my brother Aquila has attended more to the Pyrrhonists, and our other brother to the Platonists and Aristotelians; therefore you have to do with learned hearers." Then said the old man: "You have well and logically informed us how you perceived the things that follow from the statements which have been enunciated. But I professed something more than the tenet of Epicurus; for I introduced the *genesis*, and asserted that it is the cause of all the doings of men."

Chapter VIII-Instincts.

When the old man had said this, I Clement said to him: "Hear, my father: if my brother Niceta bring you to acknowledge that the world is not governed without the providence of God, I shall be able to answer you in that part which remains concerning the *genesis*; for I am well acquainted with this doctrine." And when I had thus spoken, my brother Aquila said: "What is the use of our calling him *father*, when we are commanded to call no man father upon earth?" Then, looking to the old man, he said, "Do not take it amiss, my father, that I have found fault with my brother for calling you father, for we have a precept not to call any one by that name." When Aquila said that, all the assembly of the bystanders, as well as the old man and Peter, laughed. And when Aquila asked the reason of their all laughing, I said to him: "Because you yourself do the very thing which you find fault with in another; for you called the old man *father*." But he denied it, saying: "I am not aware that I called him *father*." Meantime Peter was moved with certain suspicions, as he told us afterwards; and looking to Niceta, he said, "Go on with what you have proposed."

Chapter IX.-Simple and Compound.

Then Niceta began as follows: "Everything that is, is either simple or compound. That which is simple is without number, division, color, difference, roughness, smoothness, weight, lightness, quality, quantity, and therefore without end. But that which is compound is either compounded of two, or of three, or even of four *elements*, or at all events of several; and things which are compounded can also of necessity be divided." The old man, hearing this, said: "You speak most excellently and learnedly, my son." Then Niceta went on: "Therefore that which is simple, and which is without any of those things by which that which subsists can be dissolved, is without doubt incomprehensible and infinite, knowing neither beginning nor end, and therefore is one and alone, and subsisting without an author. But that which is compound is subject to number, and diversity, and division,-is necessarily compounded by some, author, and is a diversity collected into one species. That which is infinite is therefore, in respect of goodness, a Father; in respect of power, a Creator. Nor can the power of creating cease in the Infinite, nor the goodness be motionless[1]; but He is impelled by goodness to change existing things, and by power to arrange and strengthen them. Therefore some things, as we have said, are changed, and composed of two or three, some of four, others of more elements. But since our inquiry at present is concerning the method of the world and its substance, which, it is agreed, is compounded of four elements, to which all those ten differences belong which we have mentioned above, let us begin at these lower steps, and come to the higher. For a way is afforded us to intellectual and invisible things from those which we see and handle; as is contained in arithmetical[2] instructions, where, when inquiry is made concerning divine things, we rise from the lower to the higher numbers; but when the

---

[1] Original word used in the text was: **quiescent**

[2] The method or process of computation with figures: the most elementary branch of mathematics.
Source: Dictionary.com Unabridged (v 1.1)

method respecting present and visible things is expounded, the order is directed from the higher to the lower numbers. Is it not so? "

Chapter X.-Creation Implies Providence.

Then the old man said: "You are following it out exceedingly well." Then Niceta: "Now, then, we must inquire concerning the method of the world; of which the first inquiry is divided into two parts. For it is asked whether it has been made or not? And if it has not been made, itself must be that Unbegotten from which all things are. But if it has been made, concerning this again the question is divided into two parts, whether it was made by itself, or by another. And if indeed it was made by itself, then without doubt providence is excluded. If providence is not admitted, in vain is the mind incited to virtue, in vain justice is maintained, if there be no one to render to the just man according to his merits. But even the soul itself will not appear to be immortal, if there be no dispensation of providence to receive it after its escape from the body.

Chapter XI.-General or Special Providence.

"Now, if it be taught that there is a providence, and that the world was made by it, other questions meet us which must be discussed. For it will be asked, In what way providence acts, whether generally towards the whole, or specially towards the parts, or generally also towards the parts, or both generally towards the whole, and specially towards the parts? But by general providence we mean this: as if God, at first making the world, has given an order and appointed a course to things, and has ceased to take any further care of what is done. But special providence towards the parts is of this sort, that He exercises providence over some men or places, but not over others. But general over all, and at the same time special over the parts, is in this wise: if God made all things at first, and exercises providence over each individual even to the end, and renders to every one according to his deeds.

Chapter XII.-Prayer Inconsistent with Genesis.

"Therefore that first proposition, which declares that God made all things in the beginning, and having imposed a course and order upon things, takes no further account of them, affirms that all things are done according to, *genesis*. To this, therefore, we shall first reply; and especially to those who worship the gods and defend *genesis*. Assuredly, these men, when they sacrifice to the gods and pray to them, hope that they shall obtain something in opposition to *genesis*, and so they annul *genesis*. But when they laugh at those who incite to virtue and exhort to continence, and say that nobody can do or suffer anything unless what is decreed to him by fate, they assuredly cut up by the roots all worship of the Divinity. For why should you worship those from whom you can obtain nothing which the method of what is decreed does not allow? Let this suffice in the meantime, in opposition to these men. But I say that the world is made by God, and that it is at some time to be destroyed by Him, that that world may appear which is eternal, and which is made for this end, that it may be always, and that it may receive those who, in the judgment of God, are worthy of it. But that there is another and invisible world, which contains this visible world within itself,-after we have finished our discussion concerning the visible world, we shall come to it also.

Chapter XIII.-A Creator Necessary.

"Now, in the meantime, that this visible world has been made, very many wise men among the philosophers do testify. But that we may not seem to make use of assertions as witnesses, as though we needed them, let us inquire, if you please, concerning its principles. That this visible world is material, is sufficiently evident from the fact that it is visible. But every body receives *one of* two Differentiae[1]; for it is either compact and solid, or divided and separate.

---

[1] The character or attribute by which one entity is distinguished from another. *Source: Dictionary.com Unabridged (v 1.1)*

236

And if the body of which the world was made was compact and solid, and that body was parted and divided through diverse species and parts according to its differences, there must necessarily be understood to have been some one to separate the body which was compact and solid, and to draw it into many parts and diverse forms; or if all this mass of the world was compounded and compacted from diverse and dispersed parts of bodies, still there must be understood to have been some one to collect into one the dispersed parts, and to invest these things with their different species.

Chapter XIV.-Mode of Creation.

"And, indeed, I know that several of the philosophers were rather of this opinion, that God the Creator made divisions and distinctions from one body, which they call Matter, which yet consisted of four elements, mingled into one by a certain tempering of divine providence. For I think that what some have said is vain, that the body of the world is simple, that is, without any conjunction; since it is evident that what is simple can neither be a body, nor can be mixed, or propagated, or dissolved; all which, we see, happen to the bodies of the world. For how could it be dissolved if it were simple, and had not within it that from which it might be resolved and divided? But if bodies seem to be composed of two, or three, or even of four elements,-who that has even a small portion of sense does not perceive that there must have been some one who collected several into one, and preserving the measure of tempering, made a solid body out of diverse parts? This *some one,* therefore, we call God, the Creator of the world, and acknowledge Him as the author of the universe.

Chapter XV.-Theories of Creation.

"For the Greek philosophers, inquiring into the beginnings of the world, have gone, some in one way and some in another. In short, Pythagoras says that numbers are the elements of its beginnings; Callistratus, that qualities;

Alcmaeon, that contrarieties; Anaximander, that immensity; Anaxagoras, that equalities of parts; Epicurus, that atoms; Diodorus, that ☐μερ☐, that is, things in which there are no parts; Asclepius, that ☐γκοι, which we may call tumors or swellings; the geometricians, that ends; Democritus, that ideas; Thales, that water; Heraclitus, that fire; Diogenes, that air; Parmenides, that earth; Zeno, Empedocles, Plato, that fire, water, air, and earth. Aristotle also introduces a fifth element, which he called ☐κατον☐μαστον; that is, that which cannot be named; without doubt indicating Him who made the world, by joining the four elements into one. Whether, therefore, there be two, or three, or four, or more, or innumerable elements, of which the world consists, in every supposition there is shown to be a God, who collected many into one, and again drew them, when collected, into diverse species; and by this it is proved that the machine of the world could not have subsisted without a maker and a disposer.

Chapter XVI.-The World Made of Nothing by a Creator.

"But from this fact also, that in the conjunction of the elements, if one be deficient or in excess, the others are loosened and fall, is shown that they took their beginning from nothing. For if for example, moisture be wanting in any body, neither will the dry stand; for dry is fed by moisture, as also cold by heat; in which, as we have said, if one be defective, the whole are dissolved. And in this they give indications of their origin, that they were made out of nothing. Now if matter itself is proved to have been made, how shall its parts and its species, of which the world consists, be thought to be unmade? But about matter and its qualities this is not the time to speak: only let it suffice to have taught this, that God is the Creator of all things, because neither, if the body of which the world consists was solid and united, could it be separated and distinguished without a Creator; nor, if it was collected into one from diverse and separate parts, could it be collected and mixed without a Maker. Therefore, if God is so clearly shown to be the Creator of the world, what room is there for Epicurus to introduce atoms, and to assert that not only sensible bodies, but even intellectual and rational minds, are made of insensible corpuscles?

Chapter XVII.-Doctrine of Atoms Untenable.

"But you will say, according to the opinion of Epicurus, that successions of atoms coming in a ceaseless course, and mixing with one another, and conglomerating through unlimited and endless periods of time, are made solid bodies. I do not treat this opinion as a pure fiction, and that, too, a badly contrived one; but let us examine it, whatever be its character, and see if what is said can stand. For they say that those corpuscles,[1] which they call atoms, are of different qualities: that some are moist, and therefore heavy, and tending downwards; others dry and earthy, and therefore still heavy; but others fiery, and therefore always pushing upwards; others cold and inert, and always remaining in the middle. Since then some, as being fiery, always tend upward, and others, as being moist and dry, always downwards, and others keep a middle and unequal course, how could they meet together and form one body? For if any one throw down from a height small pieces of straw, for example, and pieces of lead of the same size, will the light straws be able to keep up with the pieces of lead, though they be equal in size? Nay; the heavier reach the bottom far more quickly. So also atoms, though they be equal in size, yet, being unequal in weight, the lighter will never be able to keep pace with the heavier; but if they cannot keep pace, certainly neither can they be mixed or form one body.

Chapter XVIII.-The Concourse of Atoms Could Not Make the World.

"Then, in the next place, if they are ceaselessly borne about, and always coming, and being added to things

---

[1] A discrete particle, such as a photon or an electron; a minute globular particle. *Source: Dictionary.com Unabridged (v 1.1)*

whose measure is already complete, how can the universe stand, when new weights are always being heaped upon so vast weights? And this also I ask: If this expanse of heaven which we see was constructed by the gradual concurrence of atoms, how did it not collapse while it was in construction, if indeed the yawning top of the structure was not propped and bound by any stays? For as those who build circular domes, unless they bind the fastening of the central top, the whole falls at once; so also the circle of the world, which we see to be brought together in so graceful a form, if it was not made at once, and under the influence of a single forth-putting of divine energy by the power of a Creator, but by atoms gradually concurring and constructing it, not as reason demanded, but as a chance[1] issue befell, how did it not fall down and crumble to pieces before it could be brought together and fastened? And further, I ask this: What is the pavement on which the foundations of such an immense mass are laid? And again, what you call the pavement, on what does it rest? And again that other, what supports it? And so I go on asking, until the answer comes to nothing and empty![2]

Chapter XIX.-More Difficulties of the Atomic Theory.

"But if any one say that atoms of a fiery quality, being joined together, formed a body, and because the quality of fire does not tend downwards, but upwards, that the nature of fire, always pushing upwards, supports the mass of the world placed upon it; to this we answer: How could atoms of a fiery quality, which always make for the highest place, descend to the lower, and be found in the lowest place of all, so as to form a foundation for all; whereas rather the heavier qualities, that is, the earthy or watery, always come before the lighter, as we have said; hence, also, they assert that the heaven, as the higher structure, is composed of fiery atoms, which are lighter, and always fly upwards? Therefore the world cannot have foundations of fire, or any other: nor can there be any association or compacting of the

---

[1] Original word used in the text was: **fortuitous**
[2] Original word used in the text was: **vacuity**

heavier atoms with the lighter, that is, of those which are always borne downwards, with those that always fly upwards. Thus it is sufficiently shown that the bodies of the world are consolidated by the union of atoms; and that insensible bodies, even if they could by any means concur and be united, could not give forms and measures to bodies, form limbs, or effect qualities, or express quantities; all which, therefore, by their exactness, attest the hand of a Maker, and show the operation of reason, which reason I call the Word, and God.

Chapter XX.-Plato's Testimony.

"But some one will say that these things are done by nature. Now, in this, the controversy is about a name. For while it is evident that it is a work of mind and reason, what you call nature, I call God the Creator. It is evident that neither the species of bodies, arranged with so necessary distinctions, nor the faculties of minds, could or can be made by irrational and senseless work. But if you regard the philosophers as fit witnesses, Plato testifies concerning these things in the *Timoeus*, where, in a discussion on the making of the world, he asks, whether it has existed always, or had a beginning, and decides that it was made. `For, 'says he, `it is visible and palpable, and corporeal; but it is evident that all things which are of this sort have been made; but what has been made has doubtless an author, by whom it was made. This Maker and Father of all, however, it is difficult to discover; and when discovered, it is impossible to declare Him to the vulgar.' Such is the declaration of Plato; but though he and the other Greek philosophers had chosen to be silent about the making of the world, would it not be manifest to all who have any understanding? For what man is there, having even a particle of sense, who, when he sees a house having all things necessary for useful purposes, its roof fashioned into the form of a globe, painted with various splendor and diverse figures, adorned with large and splendid lights; who is there, I say, that, seeing such a structure, would not immediately pronounce that it was constructed by a most wise and powerful artificer? And so, who can be found so foolish, as, when he gazes upon the fabric of the heaven, perceives the splendor of the sun and moon, sees the courses and beauty of the stars, and their paths assigned to them by fixed laws and periods, will not cry out that these things are made, not so much by a wise and rational artificer, as by wisdom and reason itself?

Chapter XXI.-Mechanical Theory.

"But if you would rather have the opinions of others of the Greek philosophers,-and you are acquainted with mechanical science,-you are of course familiar with what is their deliverance concerning the heavens. For they suppose a sphere, equally rounded in every direction, and looking indifferently to all points, and at equal distances in all directions from the center of the earth, and so stable buy its own symmetry, that its perfect equality does not permit it to fall off to any side; and so the sphere is sustained, although supported by no prop. Now if the fabric of the world really has this form, the divine work is evident in it. But if, as others think, the sphere is placed upon the waters, and is supported by them, or floating in them, even so the work of a great contriver is shown in it.

Chapter XXII.-Motions of the Stars.

"But lest the assertion may seem doubtful respecting things which are not manifest to all, let us come to those things of which nobody is ignorant. Who disposed the courses of the stars with so great reason, ordained their risings and settings, and appointed to each one to accomplish the circuit of the heavens in certain and regular times? Who assigned to some to be always approaching to the setting, and others to be returning to the rising? Who put a measure upon the courses of the sun, that he might mark out, by his diverse motions, hours, and days, and months, and changes of seasons?-that he might distinguish, by the sure measurement of his course, now winter, then spring, summer, and afterwards autumn, and always, by the same changes of the year, complete the circle with variety, without confusion? Who, I say, will not pronounce that the director of such order is the very wisdom of God? And these things we have spoken according to the relations given us by the Greeks respecting the science of the heavenly bodies.

Chapter XXIII.-Providence in Earthly Things.

"But what of those things also which we see on the earth, or in the sea? Are we not plainly taught, that not only the work, but also the providence, of God is in them? For whereas there are on the earth lofty mountains in certain places, *the object of this is,* that the air, being compressed and confined by them through the appointment of God, may be forced and pressed out into winds, by which fruits may germinate, and the summer heat may be moderated when the Pleiades glow, fired with the blaze of the sun. But you still say, Why that blaze of the sun, that moderating should be required? How, then, should fruits be ripened which are necessary for the uses of men? But observe this also, that at the meridian axis, where the heat is greatest, there is no great collection of clouds, nor an abundant fall of rain, lest disease should be produced among the inhabitants; for watery clouds, if they are acted on by rapid heat, render the air impure and pestilential. And the earth also, receiving the warm rain, does not afford nourishment to the crops, but destruction. In this who can doubt that there is the working of divine providence? In short, Egypt, which is scorched with the heat of Aethiopia, in its neighborhood, lest its air should be incurably vitiated by the effects of showers, its plains do not receive rain furnished to them from the clouds, but, as it were, an earthly shower from the overflow of the Nile.

Chapter XXIV.-Rivers and Seas.

"What shall we say of fountains and rivers, which flow with perpetual motion into the sea? And, by the divine providence, neither does their abundant supply fail, nor does the sea, though it receives so great quantities of water, experience any increase, but both those elements which contribute to it and those which are thus contributed remain in the same proportion. But you will say to me: The salt water naturally consumes the fresh water which is poured into it. Well, in this is manifest the work of providence, that it made that element salt into which it turned the courses of all the waters which it had provided for the use of men. So that through so great spaces of time the channel of the sea has not been filled, and produced a deluge destructive to the earth and to men. Nor will any one be so foolish as to think that this so great reason and so great providence has been arranged by irrational nature.

Chapter XXV.-Plants and Animals.

"But what shall I say of plants, and what of animals? Is it not providence that has ordained that plants, when they decay by old age, should be reproduced by the suckers or the seeds which they have themselves produced, and animals by propagation? And by a certain wonderful dispensation of providence, milk is prepared in the udders of the dams for the animals before they are born; and as soon as they are born, with no one to guide them, they seek out the store of nourishment provided for them. And not only males are produced, but females also, that by means of both the race may be perpetuated. But lest this should seem, as some think, to be done by a certain order of nature, and not by the appointment of the Creator, He has, as a proof and indication of His providence, ordained a few animals to preserve their stock on the earth in an exceptional way: for example, the crow conceives through the mouth, and the weasel brings forth through the ear; and some birds, such as hens, sometimes produce eggs conceived of wind or dust; other animals convert the male into the female, and change their sex every year, as hares and hyenas, which they call monsters; others spring from the earth, and get their bodies from it, as moles; others from ashes, as vipers; others from putrefying flesh, as wasps from horseflesh, bees from ox-flesh; others from cow-dung, as beetles; others from herbs, as the scorpion from the basil; and again, herbs from animals, as parsley and asparagus from the horn of the stag or the she goat.

Chapter XXVI.-Germination of Seeds.

"And what occasion is there to mention more instances in which divine providence has ordained the production of animals to be effected in various ways, that order being superseded which is thought to be assigned by nature, from which not an irrational course of things, but one arranged by his own reason, might be evinced?[1] And in this also is there not a full work of providence shown, when seeds sown are prepared by means of earth and water for the sustenance of men? For when these seeds are committed to the earth, the soil milks upon the seeds, as from its teats, the moisture which it has received into itself by the will of God. For there is in water a certain power of the spirit given by God from the beginning, by whose operation the structure of the body that is to be begins to be formed in the seed itself, and to be developed by means of the blade and the ear; for the grain of seed being swelled by the moisture, that power of the spirit which has been made to reside in water, running as an incorporeal substance through certain strait passages of veins, excites the seeds to growth, and forms the species of the growing plants. By means, therefore, of the moist element in which that vital spirit is contained and inborn, it is caused that not only is it revived, but also that an appearance and form in all respects like to the seeds that had been sown is reproduced. Now, who that has even a particle of sense will think that this method depends upon irrational nature, and not upon divine wisdom? Lastly, also these things are done in a resemblance of the birth of men; for the earth seems to take the place of the womb, into which the seed being east, is both formed and nourished by the power of water and spirit, as we have said above.

---

[1] To show clearly; make evident or manifest; prove.
Source: Dictionary.com Unabridged (v 1.1)

Chapter XXVII.-Power of Water.

"But in this also the divine providence is to be admired, that it permits us to see and know the things that are made, but has placed in secrecy and concealment the way and manner in which they are done, that they may not be competent to the knowledge of the unworthy, but may be laid open to the worthy and faithful, when they shall have deserved it. But to prove by facts and examples that nothing is imparted to seeds of the substance of the earth, but that all depends upon the element of water, and the power of the spirit which is in it,-suppose, for example, that a hundred talents' weight of earth are placed in a very large trough, and that there are sown in it several kinds of seeds, either of herbs or of shrubs, and that water enough is supplied for watering them, and that that care is taken for several years, and that the seeds which are gathered are stored up, for example of corn or barley and other sorts separately from year to year, until the seeds of each sort amount to a hundred talents' weight, then also let the stalks be pulled up by the roots and weighed; and after all these have been taken from the trough, let the earth be weighed, it will still give back its hundred talents' weight undiminished. Whence, then, shall we say that all that weight, and all the quantity of different seeds and stalks, has come? Does it not appear manifestly that it has come from the water? For the earth retains entire what is its own, but the water which has been poured in all through is nowhere, on account of the powerful virtue of the divine condition, which by the one species of water both prepares the substances of so many seeds and shrubs, and forms their species, and preserves the kind while multiplying the increase.

Chapter XXVIII.-The Human Body.

"From all these things I think it is sufficiently and abundantly evident that all things are produced; and the universe consists by a designing sense, and not by the irrational operation of nature. But let us come now, if you please, to our own substance, that is, the substance of man, who is a small world, *a microcosm,* in the great world; and let us consider with what reason it is compounded: and from this especially you will understand the wisdom of the Creator. For although man consists of different substances, one mortal and the other immortal, yet, by the skilful contrivance of the Creator, their diversity does not prevent their union, and that although the substances be diverse and alien the one from the other. For the one is taken from the earth and formed by the Creator, but the other is given from immortal substances; and yet the honor of its immortality is not violated by this union. Nor does it, as some think, consist of reason, and concupiscence, and passion, but rather such affections seem to be in it, by which it may be moved in each of these directions. For the body, which consists of bones and flesh, takes its beginning from the seed of a man, which is extracted from the marrow by warmth, and conveyed into the womb as into a soil, to which it adheres, and is gradually moistened from the fountain of the blood, and so is changed into flesh and bones, and is formed into the likeness of him who injected the seed.

Chapter XXIX.-Symmetry of the Body.

"And mark in this the work of the Designer, how He has inserted the bones like pillars, on which the flesh might be sustained and carried. Then, again, how an equal measure is preserved on either side, that is, the right and the left, so that foot answers to foot, hand to hand, and even finger to finger, so that each agrees in perfect equality with each; and also eye to eye, and ear to ear, which not only are suitable to and matched with each other, but also are formed fit for necessary uses. The hands, for instance, are so made as to be fit for work; the feet for walking; the eyes, protected with sentinel eyebrows, to serve the purpose of sight; the ears so formed for hearing, that, like a cymbal, they vibrate the sound of the word that falls upon them, and send it inward, and transmit it even in the understanding of the heart; whereas the tongue, striking against the teeth in speaking, performs the part of a fiddle-bow. The teeth also are formed, some for cutting and dividing the food, and handing it over to the inner ones; and these, in their turn, bruise and grind it like a mill, that it may be more conveniently digested when it is conveyed into the stomach; whence also they are called grinders.

Chapter XXX.-Breath and Blood.

"The nostrils also are made for the purpose of collecting, inspiring, and expiring air, that by the renewal of the breath, the natural heat which is in the heart may, by means of the lungs, be either warmed or cooled, as the occasion may require; while the lungs are made to abide in the breast, that by their softness they may soothe and cherish the vigor of the heart, in which the life seems to abide;-the life, I say, not the soul. And what shall I say of the substance of the blood, which, proceeding as a river from a fountain, and first borne along in one channel, and then spreading through innumerable veins, as through canals, irrigates the whole territory of the human body with vital streams, being supplied by the agency of the liver, which is placed in the right side, for effecting the digestion of food and turning it into blood? But in the left side is placed the spleen, which draws to itself, and in some way cleanses, the impurities of the blood.

Chapter XXXI.-The Intestines.

"What reason also is employed in the intestines, which are arranged in long circular windings, that they may gradually carry off the refuse of the food, so as neither to render places suddenly empty, and so as not to be hindered by the food that is taken afterwards! But they are made like a membrane, that the parts that are outside of them may gradually receive moisture, which if it were poured out suddenly would empty the internal parts; and not hindered by a thick skin, which would render the outside dry, and disturb the whole fabric of man with distressing thirst.

Chapter XXXII.-Generation.

"Moreover, the female form, and the cavity of the womb, most suitable for receiving, and cherishing, and vivifying the germ, who does not believe that it has been made as it is by reason and foresight?-because in that part alone of her body the female differs from the male, in which the fetus being placed, is kept and cherished. And again the male differs from the female only in that part of his body in which is the power of injecting seed and propagating mankind. And in this there is a great proof of providence, from the necessary difference of members; but more in this, where, under a likeness of form there is found to be diversity of use and variety of office. For males and females equally have teats, but only those of the female are filled with milk; that, as soon as they have brought forth, the infant may find nourishment suited to him. But if we see the members in man arranged with such method, that in all the rest there is seen to be similarity of form, and a difference only in those in which their use requires a difference, and we neither see anything superfluous nor anything wanting in man, nor in woman anything deficient or in excess, who will not, from all these things, acknowledge the operation of reason, and the wisdom of the Creator?

Chapter XXXIII.-Correspondences in Creation.

"With this agrees also the reasonable difference of other animals, and each one being suited to its own use and service. This also is testified by the variety of trees and the diversity of herbs, varying both in form and in juices. This also is asserted by the change of seasons, distinguished into four periods, and the circle closing the year with certain hours, days, months, and not deviating from the appointed reckoning by a single hour. Hence, in short, the age of the world itself is reckoned by a certain and fixed account, and a definite number of years.

Chapter XXXIV.-Time of Making the World.

"But you will say, When was the world made? And why so late? This you might have objected, though it had been made sooner. For you might say, Why not also before this? And so, going back through unmeasured ages, you might still ask, And why not sooner? But we are not now discussing this, why it was not made sooner; but whether it was made at all. For if it is manifest that it was made, it is necessarily the work of a powerful and supreme Artificer; and if this is evident, it must be left to the choice and judgment of the wise Artificer when He should please to make it; unless indeed you think that all this wisdom, which has constructed the immense fabric of the world, and has given to the several objects their forms and kinds, assigning to them a habit not only in accordance with beauty, but also most convenient and necessary for their future uses,-unless, I say, you think that this alone has escaped it, that it should choose a convenient season for so magnificent a work of creation. He has doubtless a certain reason and evident causes why, and when, and how He made the world; but it were not proper that these should be disclosed to those who are reluctant to inquire into and understand the things which are placed before their eyes, and which testify of His providence. For those things which are kept in secret, and are hidden within the senses of Wisdom, as in a royal treasury, are laid open to none but those who have learned of Him, with whom these things are sealed and laid up. It is God, therefore, who made all things, and Himself was made by none. But those who speak of nature instead of God, and declare that all things were made by nature, do not perceive the mistake of the name which they use. For if they think that nature is irrational, it is most foolish to suppose that a rational creature can proceed from an irrational creator. But if it is Reason-that is, Logos -by which it appears that all things were made, they change the name without purpose, when they make statements concerning the reason of the Creator. If you have anything to say to these things, my father, say on."

Chapter XXXV.-A Contest of Hospitality.

When Niceta had thus spoken, the old man answered: "You indeed, my son, have conducted your argument wisely and vigorously; so much so, that I do not think the subject of providence could be better treated. But as it is now late, I wish to say some things to-morrow in answer to what you have argued; and if on these you can satisfy me, I shall confess myself a debtor to your favor." And when the old man said this, Peter rose up. Then one of those present, a chief man of the Laodiceans, requested of Peter and us that he might give the old man other clothes instead of the mean and torn ones that he wore. This man Peter and we embraced; and praising him for his honorable and excellent intention, said: "We are not so foolish and impious as not to bestow the things which are necessary for bodily uses upon him to whom we have committed so precious words; and we hope that he will willingly receive them, as a father from his sons, and also we trust that he will share with us our house and our living." While we said this, and that chief man of the city strove to take the old man away from us with the greatest urgency and with many blandishments,[1] while we the more eagerly strove to keep him with us, all the people cried out that it should rather be done as the old man himself pleased; and when silence was obtained, the old man, with an oath, said: "To-day I shall stay with no one, nor take anything from any one, lest the choice of the one should prove the sorrow of the other; afterwards these things may be, if so it seem right."

Chapter XXXVI.-Arrangements for To-Morrow.

And when the old man had said this, Peter said to the chief man of the city: "Since you have shown your good-will in our presence, it is not right that you should go away sorrowful; but we will accept from you favor for favor. Show us your house, and make it ready, so that the discussion which is to be to-morrow may be held there, and

---

[1] Something, as an action or speech, that tends to flatter, coax, or entice. *Source: Dictionary.com Unabridged (v 1.1*

that any who wish to be present to hear it may be admitted." When the chief man of the city heard this, he rejoiced greatly; and all the people also heard it gladly. And when the crowds had dispersed, he pointed out his house; and the old man also was preparing to depart. But I commanded one of my attendants to follow the old man secretly, and find out where he stayed. And when we returned to our lodging, we told our brethren all our dealings with the old man; and so, as usual, we supped and went to sleep.

Chapter XXXVII.-"The Form of Sound Words, Which Ye Have Heard of Me."

But on the following day Peter arose early and called us, and we went together to the secret place in which we had been on the previous day, for the purpose of prayer. And when, after prayer, we were coming thence to the appointed place, he exhorted us by the way, saying: "Hear me, most beloved fellow-servants: It is good that every one of you, according to his ability, contribute to the advantage of those who are approaching to the faith of our religion; and therefore do not shrink from instructing the ignorant, and teaching according to the wisdom which has been bestowed upon you by the providence of God, yet so that you only join the eloquence of your discourse with those things which you have heard from me, and which have been committed to you. But do not speak anything which is your own, and which has not been committed to you, though it may seem to yourselves to be true; but hold forth those things, as I have said, which I myself have received from the true Prophet, and have delivered to you, although they may seem to be less full of authority. For thus it often happens that men turn away from the truth, while they believe that they have found out, by their own thoughts, a form of truth more true and powerful."

Chapter XXXVLII.-The Chief Man's House.

To these counsels of Peter we willingly assented, saying to him that we should do nothing but what was pleasing to him. Then said he: "That you may therefore be exercised without danger, each of you conduct the discussion in my presence, one succeeding another, and each one clarifying[1] his own questions. Now, then, as Niceta discoursed sufficiently yesterday, let Aquila conduct the discussion to-day; and after Aquila, Clement; and then I, if the case shall require it, will add something." Meantime, while we were talking in this way, we came to the house; and the master of the house welcomed us, and led us to a certain apartment, arranged after the manner of a theatre, and beautifully built. There we found great crowds waiting for us, who had come during the night, and amongst them the old man who had argued with us yesterday. Therefore we entered, having Peter in the midst of us, looking about if we could see the old man anywhere; and when Peter saw him hiding in the midst of the crowd, he called him to him, saying: "Since you possess a soul more enlightened than most, why do you hide yourself, and conceal yourself in modesty? Rather come hither, and propound your sentiments."

Chapter XXXIX.-Recapitulation of Yesterday's Argument.

When Peter had thus spoken, immediately the crowd began to make room for the old man. And when he had come forward, he thus began: "Although I do not remember the words of the discourse which the young man delivered yesterday, yet I recollect the purport and the order of it; and therefore I think it necessary, for the sake of those who were not present yesterday, to call up what was said, and to repeat everything shortly, that, although something may have escaped me, I may be reminded of it by him who delivered the discourse, who is now present. This, then, was the purport of yesterday's discussion: that all things that we see, inasmuch as they consist in a certain

---

[1] Original word used in the text was: **elucidating**

proportion, and art, and form, and species, must be believed to have been made by intelligent power; but if it be mind and reason that has formed them, it follows that the world is governed by the providence of the same reason, although the things which are done in the world may seem to us to be not quite rightly done. But it follows, that if God and mind is the creator of all things, He must also be just; but if He is just, He necessarily judges. If He judges, it is of necessity that men be judged with respect to their doings; and if every one is judged in respect of his doings, there shall at some time be a righteous separation between righteous men and sinners. This, I think, was the substance of the whole discourse.

Chapter XL.-Genesis.

"If, therefore, it can be shown that mind and reason created all things, it follows that those things which come after are also managed by reason and providence. But if unintelligent and blind nature produces all things, the reason of judgment is undoubtedly overthrown; and there is no ground to expect either punishment of sin or reward of well-doing where there is no judge. Since, then, the whole matter depends upon this, and hangs by this head, do not take it amiss, if I wish this to be discussed and handled somewhat more fully. For in this the first gate, as it were, is shut towards all things which are propounded, and therefore I wish first of all to have it opened to me. Now therefore hear what my doctrine is; and if any one of you pleases, let him reply to me: for I shall not be ashamed to learn, if I hear that which is true, and to assent to him who speaks rightly. The discourse, then, which you delivered yesterday, which asserted that all things consist by art, and measure, and reason, does not fully persuade me that it is mind and reason that has made the world; for I have many things which I can show to consist by competent measure, and form, and species, and which yet were not made by mind and reason. Then, besides, I see that many things are done in the world without arrangement, consequence, or justice, and that nothing can be done without the course of *genesis*. This I shall in the sequel prove most clearly from my own case."

Chapter XLI.-The Rainbow.

When the old man had thus spoken, Aquila answered: "As you yourself proposed that any one who pleased should have an opportunity of answering to what you might say, my brother Niceta permits me to conduct the argument today." Then the old man: "Go on, my son, as you please." And Aquila answered: "You promised that you would show that there are many things in the world which have a form and species arranged by equal reason, which yet it is evident were not effected by God as their Creator. Now, then, as you have promised, point out these things." Then said the old man: "Behold, we see the bow in the heaven assume a circular shape, completed in all proportion, and have an appearance of reality, which perhaps neither mind could have constructed nor reason described; and yet it is not made by any mind. Behold, I have set forth the whole in a word: now answer me."

Chapter XLII.-Types and Forms.

Then said Aquila: "If anything is expressed from a type and form, it is at once understood that it is from reason, and that it could not be made without mind; since the type itself, which expresses figures and forms, was not made without mind. For example, if wax be applied to an engraved ring, it takes the stamp and figure from the ring, which undoubtedly is without sense; but then the ring, which expresses the figure, was engraved by the hand of a workman, and it was mind and reason that gave the type to the ring. So then the bow also is expressed in the air; for the sun, impressing its rays on the clouds in the process of rarefaction, and affixing the type of its circularity to the cloudy moisture, as it were to soft wax, produces the appearance of a bow; and this, as I have said, is effected by the reflection of the sun's brightness upon the clouds, and reproducing the brightness of its circle from them. Now this does not always take place, but only when the opportunity is presented by the rarefaction of moistened clouds. And consequently, when the clouds again are condensed and unite, the form of the bow is dissolved and vanishes. Finally, the bow never is seen without sun and clouds, just as the image is not produced, unless there be the type, and wax, or some other material. Nor is it wonderful if God the Creator in the beginning made types, from which forms and species may now be expressed. But this is similar to that, that in the beginning God created insensible elements, which He might use for forming and developing all other things. But even those who form statues first make a mould of clay or wax, and from it the figure of the statue is produced. And then afterwards a shadow is also produced from the statue, which shadow always bears the form and likeness of the statue. What shall we say then? That the insensible statue forms a shadow finished with as diligent care as the statue itself? Or shall the finishing of the shadow be unhesitatingly ascribed to him who has also fashioned the statue?

Chapter XLIII.-Things Apparently Useless and Vile Made by God.

"If, then, it seems to you that this is so, and what has been said on this subject is enough, let us come to inquire into other matters; or if you think that something is still wanting, let us go over it again." And the old man said: "I wish you would go over this again, since there are many other things which I see to be made in like manner: for both the fruits of trees are produced in like manner, beautifully formed and wonderfully rounded; and the appearance of the leaves is formed with immense gracefulness, and the green membrane is woven with exquisite art: then, moreover, fleas, mice, lizards, and such like, shall we say that these are made by God? Hence, from these vile objects a conjecture is derived concerning the superior, that they are by no means formed by the art of mind." "You infer well," said Aquila, "concerning the texture of leaves, and concerning small animals, that from these belief is withdrawn from the superior creatures; but let not these things deceive you, that you should think that God, working as it were only with two hands, could not complete all things that are made; but remember how my brother Niceta answered you yesterday, and truly disclosed the mystery before the time, as a son speaking with his father, and explained why and how things are made which seem to be useless."

Chapter XLIV.-Ordinate and Inordinate.

Then the old man: "I should like to hear from you why those useless things are made by the will of that supreme mind?" "If," said he, "it is fully manifest to you that there is in them the work of mind and reason, then you will not hesitate to say also why they were made, and to declare that they have been rightly made." To this the old man answered: "I am not able, my son, to say that those things which seem formed by art are made by mind, by reason of other things which we see to be done unjustly and disorderly in the world." "If," says Aquila, "those things which are done disorderly do not allow you to say that they are done by the providence of God, why do not those things which are done orderly compel you to say that they are done by God, and that irrational nature cannot produce a rational work? For it is certain, nor do we at all deny, that in this world some things are done orderly, and some disorderly. Those things, therefore, that are done rationally, believe that they are done by providence; but those that are done irrationally and inordinately, that they befall naturally, and happen accidentally. But I wonder that men do not perceive that where there is sense things may be done ordinately and inordinately, but where there is no sense neither the one nor the other can be done; for reason makes order, and the course of order necessarily produces something inordinate, if anything contrary happen to disturb order." Then the old man: "This very thing I wish you to show me."

Chapter XLV.-Motions of the Sun and Moon.

Says Aquila: "I shall do so without delay. Two visible signs are shown in heaven-one of the sun, the other of the moon; and these are followed by five other stars, each describing its own separate orbit. These, therefore, God has placed in the heaven, by which the temperature of the air may be regulated according to the seasons, and the order of vicissitudes[1] and alternations may be kept. But by means of the very same *signs*, if at any time plague and corruption is sent upon the earth for the sins of men, the air is disturbed, pestilence is brought upon animals, blight upon crops, and a destructive year in every way upon men; and thus it is that by one and the same means order is both kept and destroyed. For it is manifest even to the unbelieving and unskillful, that the course of the sun, which is useful and necessary to the world, and which is assigned by providence, is always kept orderly; but the courses of the moon, in comparison of the course of the sun, seem to the unskillful to be inordinate and unsettled in her waxings and wanings. For the sun moves in fixed and orderly periods: for from him are hours, from him the day when he rises, from him also the night when he sets; from him months and years are reckoned, from him the variations of seasons are produced; while, rising to the higher regions, he tempers the spring; but when he reaches the top of the heaven, he kindles the summer's heats: again, sinking, he produces the temper of autumn; and when he returns to his lowest circle, he bequeaths to us the rigor of winter's cold from the icy binding of heaven.

Chapter XLVI.-Sun and Moon Ministers Both of Good and Evil.

"But we shall discourse at greater length on these subjects at another time. Now, meantime, *we remark that* though he is that good servant for regulating the changes of the seasons, yet, when chastisement is inflicted upon men

---

[1] A change or variation occurring in the course of something.
Source: Dictionary.com Unabridged (v 1.1)

according to the will of God, he glows more fiercely, and burns up the world with more vehement fires. In like manner also the course of the moon, and that changing which seems to the unskillful to be disorderly, is adapted to the growth of crops, and cattle, and all living creatures; for by her waxings and wanings, by a certain wonderful contrivance of providence, everything that is born is nourished and grows; concerning which we could speak more at length and unfold the matter in detail, but that the method of the question proposed recalls us. Yet, by the very same appliances by which they are produced, all things are nourished and increased; but when, from any just cause, the regulation of the appointed order is changed, corruption and distemper arise, so that chastisement may come upon men by the will of God, as we have said above.

Chapter XLVII.-Chastisements on the Righteous and the Wicked.

"But perhaps you will say, What of the fact that, in that common chastisement, like things befall the pious and the impious? It is true, and we confess it; but the chastisement turns to the advantage of the pious, that, being afflicted in the present life, they may come more purified to the future, in which perpetual rest is prepared for them, and that at the same time even the impious may somewhat profit from their chastisement, or else that the just sentence of the future judgment may be passed upon them; since in the same chastisements the righteous give thanks to God, while the unrighteous blaspheme. Therefore, since the opinion of things is divided into two parts, that some things are done by order and others against order, it ought, from those things which are done according to order, to be believed that there is a providence; but with respect to those things which are done against order, we should inquire their causes from those who have learned them by prophetic teaching: for those who have become acquainted with prophetic discourse know when, and for what reason, blight, hail, and pestilence, and such like, have occurred in every generation, and for what sins these have been sent as a punishment; whence causes of sadness, lamentations, and grief have befallen the human race; whence also trembling sickness has ensued, and that this has been from the beginning the punishment of parricide.

Chapter XLVIII.-Chastisements for Sins.

"For in the beginning of the world there were none of these evils, but they took their rise from the impiety of men; and thence, with the constant increase of iniquities, the number of evils has also increased. But for this reason divine providence has decreed a judgment with respect to all men, because the present life was not such that every one could be dealt with according to his deserving. Those things, therefore, which were well and orderly appointed from the beginning, when no causes of evil existed, are not to be judged of from the evils which have befallen the world by reason of the sins of men. In short, as an indication of the things which were from the beginning, some nations are found which are strangers to these evils. For the Seres[1], because they live chastely, are kept free from them all; for with them it is unlawful to come at a woman after she has conceived, or while she is being purified. No one there eats unclean flesh, no one knows aught of sacrifices; all are judges to themselves according to justice. For this reason they are not chastened with those plagues which we have spoken of; they live to extreme old age, and die without sickness. But we, miserable as we are, dwelling as it were with deadly serpents -I mean with wicked men-necessarily suffer with them the plagues of afflictions in this world, but we cherish hope from the comfort of good things to come."

---

[1] The ancient Greek and Roman name for the northwestern part of China and its inhabitants. It meant "of silk," The people were said to be of mild, just, and frugal temper, eschewing collisions with their neighbors, and shy of close contact, but not averse to trade with other people. They were rumored to have long life, some to exceed 200 years.

Source: The American Heritage® Dictionary of the English Language, Fourth Edition.

Chapter XLIX.-God's Precepts Despised.

"If," said the old man, "even the righteous are tormented on account of the iniquities of others, God ought, as foreseeing this, to have commanded men not to do those things from which it should be necessary that the righteous be afflicted with the unrighteous; or if they did them, He ought to have applied some correction or purification to the world." "God," said Aquila, "did so command, and gave precepts by the prophets how men ought to live; but even these precepts they despised: yea, if any desired to observe them, them they afflicted with various injuries, until they drove them from their purposed observance, and turned them to the rabble of infidelity, and made them like unto themselves.

Chapter L.-The Flood.

"Wherefore, in short, at the first, when all the earth had been stained with sins, God brought a flood upon the world, which you say happened under Deucalion[1]; and at that time He saved a certain righteous man, with his sons, in an ark, and with him the race of all plants and animals. And yet even those who sprang from them, after a time, again did deeds like to those of their predecessors; for those things that had befallen them were forgotten, so that their descendants did not even believe that the flood had taken place. Wherefore God also decreed that there should not be another flood in the present world, else there should have been one in every generation, according to the account of their sins by reason of their unbelief; but He rather granted that certain angels who delight in evil should bear sway over the several nations-and to them was given power over individual men, yet only on this condition, if any one first

---

[1] Greek mythology: a son of Prometheus who survived the flood to regenerate the human race.

Source: The American Heritage® Dictionary of the English Language, Fourth Edition.

had made himself subject to them by sinning-until He should come who delights in good, and by Him the number of the righteous should be completed, and by the increase of the number of pious men all over the world impiety should be in some measure repressed, and it should be known to all that all that is good is done by God.

Chapter LI.-Evils Brought in by Sin.

"But by the freedom of the will, every man, while he is unbelieving in regard to things to come, by evil deeds runs into evils. And these are the things in the world which seem to be done contrary to order, which owe their existence to unbelief. Therefore the dispensation of divine providence is withal to be admired, which granted to those men in the beginning, walking in the good way of life, to enjoy incorruptible good things; but when they sinned, they gave birth to evil by sin. And to every good thing evil is joined as by a certain covenant of alliance on the part of sin, since indeed the earth has been polluted with human blood, and altars have been lighted to demons, and they have polluted the very air by the filthy smoke of sacrifices; and so at length the elements, being first corrupted, have handed over to men the fault of their corruption, as roots *communicate their qualities* to the branches and the fruit.

Chapter LII.-"No Rose Without Its Thorn."

"Observe therefore in this, as I have said, how justly divine providence comes to the help of things vitiated; that, inasmuch as evils which had derived their origin from sin were associated with the good things of God, He should assign two chiefs to these two departments. And *accordingly*, to Him who rejoices in good He has appointed the ordering of good things, that He might bring those who believe *in Him* to the faith of His providence; but to him who rejoices in evil, He has given over those things which are done without order and uselessly, from which of course the faith of His providence comes into doubt; and thus a just division has been made by a just God. Hence therefore it is, that whereas the orderly course of the stars produces faith that the world was made by the hand of a designer, on the other hand, the disturbance of the air, the pestilent breeze, the uncontrolled fire of the lightning, cast doubt upon the work of providence. For, as we have said, every good thing has its corresponding contrary evil thing joined with it; as hail is opposite to the fertilizing showers, the corruption of mildew is associated with the gentle dew, the whirlwinds of storms are joined with the soft winds, unfruitful trees with fruitful, noxious herbs with useful, wild and destructive animals with gentle ones. But all these things are arranged by God, because that the choice of men's will has departed from the purpose of good, and fallen away to evil.

Chapter LIII.-Everything Has Its Corresponding Contrary.

"Therefore this division holds in all the things of the world; and as there are pious men, so there are also impious; as there are prophets, so also there are false prophets; and amongst the Gentiles there are philosophers and false philosophers. Also the Arabian nations, and many others, have imitated the circumcision of the Jews for the service of their impiety. So also the worship of demons is contrary to the divine worship, baptism to baptism, laws to the law, false apostles to apostles, and false teachers to teachers. And hence it is that among the philosophers some assert providence, others deny it; some maintain that there is one God, others that there are more than one: in short, the matter has come to this, that whereas demons are expelled by the word of God, by which it is declared that there is a providence, the magical art, for the confirmation of infidelity, has found out ways of imitating this by contraries. Thus has been discovered the method of counteracting the poison of serpents by incantations, and the effecting of cures contrary to the word and power of God. The magic art has also found out ministries contrary to the angels of God, placing the calling up of souls and the figments of demons in opposition to these. And, not to prolong the discourse by a further enumeration, there is nothing whatever that makes for the belief of providence, which has not something, on the other hand, prepared for unbelief; and therefore they who do not know that division of things, think that there is no providence, by reason of those things in the world which are discordant from themselves. But do you, my father, as a wise man, choose from that division the part which preserves order and makes for the belief of providence, and do not only follow that part which runs against order and neutralizes the belief of providence."

Chapter LIV.-An Illustration.

To this the old man answered: "Show me a way, my son, by which I may establish in my mind one or other of these two orders, the one of which asserts, and the other denies, providence." "To one having a right judgment," says Aquila, "the decision is easy. For this very thing that you say, order and disorder, may be produced by a contriver, but not by insensible nature. For let us suppose, by way of illustration, that a great mass were torn from a high rock, and cast down headlong, and when clashed upon the ground were broken into many pieces, could it in any way happen that, amongst that multitude of fragments, there should be found even one which should have any perfect figure and shape? "The old man answered: "`It is impossible." "But," said Aquila, "if there be present a statuary, he can by his skilful hand and reasonable mind form the stone cut from the mountain into whatever figure he pleases." The old man said: "That is true." "Therefore," says Aquila, "when there is not a rational mind, no figure can be formed out of the mass; but when there is a designing mind, there may be both form and deformity: for example, if a workman cuts from the mountain a block to which he wishes to give a form, he must first cut it out unformed and rough; then, by degrees hammering and hewing it by the rule of his art, he expresses the form which he has conceived in his mind. Thus, therefore, from informity or deformity, by the hand of the workman form is attained, and both proceed from the workman. In like manner, therefore, the things which are done in the world are accomplished by the providence of a contriver, although they may seem not quite orderly. And therefore, because these two ways have been made known to you, and you have heard the divisions of them, flee from the way of unbelief, lest perhaps it lead you to that prince who delights in evils; but follow the way of faith, that you may come to that King who delighteth in good men."

Chapter LV.-The Two Kingdoms.

To this the old man answered: "But why was that prince made who delights in evil? And from what was he made? Or was he not made? "Aquila said: "The treatment of that subject belongs to another time; but that you may not go away altogether without an answer to this, I shall give a few hints on this subject also. God, foreseeing all things before the creation of the world, knowing that the men who were to be would some of them indeed incline to good, but others to the opposite, assigned those who should choose the good to His own government and His own cure, and called them His peculiar inheritance; but He gave over the government of those who should turn to evil to those angels who, not by their substance, but by opposition, were unwilling to remain with God, being corrupted by the vice of envy and pride. Those, therefore, he made worthy princes of worthy subjects; yet he so delivered them over to those angels, that they have not the power of doing what they will against them, unless they transgress the bounds assigned to them from the beginning. And this is the bound assigned, that unless one first do the will of the demons, the demons have no power over him."

Chapter LVI.-Origin of Evil.

Then the old man said: "You have stated it excellently, my son. It now remains only that you tell me whence is the substance of evil: for if it was made by God, the evil fruit shows that the root is in fault; for it appears that it also is of an evil nature. But if this substance was co-eternal with

God, how can that which was equally unproduced and co-eternal be subject to the other?" "It was not always," said Aquila; "but neither does it necessarily follow, if it was made by God, that its Creator should be thought to be such as is that which has been made by Him. For indeed God made the substance of all things; but if a reasonable mind, which has been made by God, do not acquiesce in the laws of its Creator, and go beyond the bounds of the temperance prescribed to it, how does this reflect on the Creator? Or if there is any reason higher than this, we do not know it; for we cannot know anything perfectly, and especially concerning those things for our ignorance of which we are not to be judged. But those things for which we are to be judged are most easy to be understood, and are dispatched almost in a word. For almost the whole rule of our actions is summed up in this, that what we are unwilling to suffer we should not do to others. For as you would not be killed, you must beware of killing another; and as you would not have your own marriage violated, you must not defile another's bed; you would not be stolen from, neither must you steal; and every matter of men's actions is comprehended within this rule."

Chapter LVII.-The Old Man Unconvinced.

Then the old man: "Do not take amiss, my son, what I am going to say. Though your words are powerful, yet they cannot lead me to believe that anything can be done apart from *genesis*. For I know that all things have happened to me by the necessity of *genesis*, and therefore I cannot be persuaded that either to do well or to do ill is in our power; and if we have not our actions in our power, it cannot be believed that there is a judgment to come, by which either punishments may be inflicted on the evil, or rewards bestowed on the good. In short, since I see that you are initiated in this sort of learning, I shall lay before you a few things from the art itself." "If," says Aquila, "you wish to add anything from that science, my brother Clement will answer you with all care, since he has attended more fully to the science of mathematics. For I can maintain in other ways that our actions are in our own power; but I ought not to presume upon those things which I have not learned."

Chapter LVIII.-Sitting in Judgment Upon God.

When Aquila had thus spoken, then I Clement said: "To-morrow, my father, you shall speak as you please, and we will gladly hear you; for I suppose it will also be gratifying to you that you have to do with those who are not ignorant of the science which you profess." When, therefore, it had been settled between the old man and me, that on the following day we should hold a discussion on the subject of *genesis*-whether all things are done under its influence, or there be anything in us which is not done by *genesis*, but by the judgment of the mind-Peter rose up, and began to speak to the following effect: "To me it is exceedingly wonderful, that things which can easily be found out men make difficult by recondite[1] thoughts and words; and those especially who think themselves wise, and who, wishing to comprehend the will of God, treat God as if He were a man, yea, as if He were something less than a man: for no one can know the purpose or mind of a man unless he himself reveal his thoughts; and neither can any one learn a profession unless he be for a long time instructed by a master. How much more must it be, that no one can know the mind or the work of the invisible and incomprehensible God, unless He Himself send a prophet to declare His purpose, and expound the way of His creation, so far as it is lawful for men to learn it! Hence I think it ridiculous when men judge of the power of God in natural ways, and think that this is possible and that impossible to Him, or this greater and that less, while they are ignorant of everything; who, being unrighteous men, judge the righteous God; unskilled, judge the contriver; corrupt, judge the incorruptible; creatures, judge the Creator.

---

[1] Dealing with very profound, difficult, esoteric, or abstruse subject matter.   *Source: Dictionary.com Unabridged (v 1.1)*

Chapter LIX.-The True Prophet.

But I would not have you think, that in saying this I take away the power of judging concerning things; but I give counsel that no one walk through devious places, and rush into errors without end. And therefore I advise not only wise men, but indeed all men who have a desire of knowing what is advantageous to them, that they seek after the true Prophet; for it is He alone who knoweth all things, and who knoweth what and how every man is seeking. For He is within the mind of every one of us, but in those who have no desire of the knowledge of God and His righteousness, He is inoperative; but He works in those who seek after that which is profitable to their souls, and kindles in them the light of knowledge. Wherefore seek Him first of all; and if you do not find Him, expect not that you shall learn anything from any other. But He is soon found by those who diligently seek Him through love of the truth, and whose souls are not taken possession of by wickedness. For He is present with those who desire Him in the innocence of their spirits, who bear patiently, and draw sighs from the bottom of their hearts through love of the truth; but He deserts malevolent minds, because as a prophet He knows the thoughts of every one. And therefore let no one think that he can find Him by his own wisdom, unless, as we have said, he empty his mind of all wickedness, and conceive a pure and faithful desire to know Him. For when any one has so prepared himself, He Himself as a prophet, seeing a mind prepared for Him, of His own accord offers Himself to his knowledge.

Chapter LX.-His Deliverances Not to Be Questioned.

"Therefore, if any one wishes to learn all things, *he cannot do it by* discussing them one by one; for, being mortal, he shall not be able to trace the counsel of God, and to scan immensity itself. But if, as we have said, he desires to learn all things, let him seek after the true Prophet; and when he has found Him, let him not treat with Him by questions and disputations and arguments; but if He has given any response, or pronounced any judgment, it cannot be doubted that this is certain. And therefore, before all things, let the true Prophet be sought, and His words be laid hold of. In respect to these this only should be discussed by every one, that he may satisfy himself if they are truly His prophetic words; that is, if they contain undoubted faith of things to come, if they mark out definite times, if they preserve the order of things, if they do not relate as last those things which are first, nor as first those things which were done last, if they contain nothing subtle, nothing composed by magic art to deceive, or if they have not transferred to themselves things which were revealed to others, and have mixed them with falsehoods. And when, all these things having been discussed by right judgment, it is established that they are prophetic words, so they ought to be at once believed concerning all things on which they have spoken and answered.

Chapter LXI.-Ignorance of the Philosophers.

"For let us consider carefully the work of divine providence. For whereas the philosophers have introduced certain subtle and difficult words, so that not even the terms that they use in their discourses can be known and understood by all, God has shown that those who thought themselves word-framers are altogether unskillful as respects the knowledge of the truth. For the knowledge of things which is imparted by the true Prophet is simple, and plain, and brief; which those men walking through devious places, and through the stony difficulties of words, are wholly ignorant of. Therefore, to modest and simple minds, when they see things come to pass which have been foretold, it is enough, and more than enough, that they may receive most certain knowledge from most certain prescience[1]; and for the rest may be at peace, having received evident knowledge of the truth. For all other things are treated by opinion, in which there can be nothing

---

[1] Knowledge of things before they exist or happen; foreknowledge; foresight. *Source: Dictionary.com Unabridged (v 1.1)*

firm. For what speech is there which may not be contradicted? And what argument is there that may not be overthrown by another argument? And hence it is, that by disputation of this sort men can never come to any end of knowledge and learning, but find the end of their life sooner than the end of their questions.

Chapter LXII.-End of the Conference.

"And, therefore, since amongst these *philosophers* are things uncertain, we must come to the true Prophet. Him God the Father wished to be loved by all, and accordingly He has been pleased wholly to extinguish those opinions which have originated with men, and in regard to which there is nothing like certainty-that He *the true Prophet* might be the more sought after, and that He whom they had obscured should show to men the way of truth. For on this account also God made the world, and by Him the world is filled; whence also He is everywhere near to them who seek Him, though He be sought in the remotest ends of the earth. But if any one seek Him not purely, nor holily, nor faithfully, He is indeed within him, because He is everywhere, and is found within the minds of all men; but, as we have said before, He is dormant to the unbelieving, and is held to be absent from those by whom His existence is not believed." And when Peter had said this, and more to the same effect, concerning the true Prophet, he dismissed the crowds; and when he very earnestly entreated the old man to remain with us, he could prevail nothing; but he also departed, to return next day, as had been agreed upon. And after this, we also, with Peter, went to our lodging, and enjoyed our accustomed food and rest.

Book IX.

Chapter I.-An Explanation.

On the following day, Peter, along with us, hastened early to the place in which the discussion had been held the day before; and when he saw that great crowds had assembled there to hear, and saw the old man with them, he said to him: "Old man, it was agreed yesterday that you should confer to-day with Clement; and that you should either show that nothing takes place apart from *genesis*, or that Clement should prove that there is no such thing as *genesis*, but that what we do is in our own power." To this the old man answered: "I both remember what was agreed upon, and I keep in memory the words which you spoke after the agreement was made, in which you taught that it is impossible for man to know any thing, unless he learn from the true Prophet." Then Peter said: "You do not know what I meant; but I shall now explain to you. I spoke of the will and purpose of God, which He had before the world was, and by which purpose He made the world, appointed times, gave the law, promised a world to come to the righteous for the rewarding of their good deeds, and decreed punishments to the unjust according to a judicial sentence. I said that this counsel and this will of God cannot be found out by men, because no man can gather the mind of God from conjectures and opinion, unless a prophet sent by Him declare it. I did not therefore speak of any doctrines or studies, that they cannot be found out or known without a prophet; for I know that both arts and sciences can be known and practiced by men, which they have learned, not from the true Prophet, but from human instructors.

Chapter II.-Preliminaries.

"Since, therefore, you profess to be conversant with the position of the stars and the courses of the heavenly bodies, and that from these you can convince Clement that all things are subject to *genesis*, or that you will learn from him that all things are governed by providence, and that we have something in our own power, it is now time for you two to set about this." To this the old man answered: "Now indeed it was not necessary to raise questions of this kind, if it were possible for us to learn from the true Prophet, and to hear in a definite proposition, that anything depends on is and on the freedom of our will; for your yesterday's discourse affected me greatly, in which you disputed concerning the prophetic power. Whence also I assent to and confirm your judgment, that nothing can be known by man with certainty, and without doubt, seeing that he has but a short period of life, and a brief and slender breath, by which he seems to be kept in life. However, since I am understood to have promised to Clement, before I heard anything of the prophetic power, that I should show that all things are subject to *genesis*, or that I should learn from him that there is something in ourselves, let him do me this favor, that he first begin, and propound and explain what may be objected: for I, ever since I heard from you a few words concerning the power of prophecy, have, I confess, been confounded, considering the greatness of prescience; nor do I think that anything ought to be received which is collected from conjectures and opinion."

Chapter III.-Beginning of the Discussion.

When the old man had said this, I Clement began to speak as follows: "God by His Son created the world as a double house, separated by the interposition of this firmament, which is called heaven; and appointed angelic powers to dwell in the higher, and a multitude of men to be born in this visible world, from amongst whom He might choose friends for His Son, with whom He might rejoice, and who might be prepared for Him as a beloved bride for a bridegroom. But even till the time of the marriage, which is the manifestation of the world to come, He has appointed a certain power, to choose out and watch over the good ones of those who are born in this world, and to preserve them for His Son, set apart in a certain place of the world, which is without sin; in which there are already some, who are there being prepared, as I said, as a bride adorned for the coming of the bridegroom. For the prince of this world and of the present age is like an adulterer, who corrupts and violates the minds of men, and, seducing them from the love of the true bride groom, allures them to strange lovers.

Chapter IV.-Why the Evil Prince Was Made.

But some one will say, How then was it necessary that that prince should be made, who was to turn away the minds of men from the true prince? Because God, who, as I have said, wished to prepare friends for His Son, did not wish them to be such as by necessity of nature could not be aught else, but such as should desire of their own choice and will to be good; because neither is that praiseworthy which is not desirable, nor is that judged to be good which is not sought for with purpose. For there is no credit in being that from which the necessity of your nature does not admit of your changing. Therefore the providence of God has willed that a multitude of men should be born in this world, that those who should choose a good life might be selected from many. And because He foresaw that the present world could not consist except by variety and inequality, He gave to each mind freedom of motions, according to the diversities of present things, and appointed this prince, through his suggestion of those things which run contrary, that the choice of better things might depend upon the exercise of virtue.

Chapter V.-Necessity of Inequality.

"But to make our meaning plainer, we shall explain it by particulars. Was it proper, for example, that all men in this world should be kings, or princes, or lords, or teachers, or lawyers, or geometers, or goldsmiths, or bakers, or smiths, or grammarians, or rich men, or farmers, or perfumers, or fishermen, or poor men? It is certain that all could not be these. Yet all these professions, and many more, the life of men requires, and without these it cannot be passed;

therefore inequality is necessary in this world. For there cannot be a king, unless he has subjects over whom he may rule and reign; nor can there be a master, unless he has one over whom he may bear sway; and in like manner of the rest.

Chapter VI.-Arrangements of the World for the Exercise of Virtue.

"Therefore the Creator, knowing that no one would come to the contest of his own accord, while labor is shunned,-that is, to the practice of those professions which we have mentioned, by means of which either the justice or the mercy of every one can be manifested,-made for men a body susceptible of hunger, and thirst, and cold, in order that men, being compelled for the sake of supporting their bodies, might come down to all the professions which we have mentioned, by the necessity of livelihood. For we are taught to cultivate every one of these arts, for the sake of food, and drink, and clothing. And in this the purpose of each one's mind is shown, whether he will supply the demands of hunger and cold by means of thefts, and murders, and perjuries, and other crimes of that sort; or whether, keeping justice and mercy and continence, he will fulfill the service of imminent necessity by the practice of a profession and the labor of his hands. For if he supply his bodily wants with justice, and piety, and mercy, he comes forth as a victor in the contest set before him, and is chosen as a friend of the Son of God. But if he serve carnal lusts, by frauds, iniquities, and crimes, he becomes a friend of the prince of this world, and of all demons; by whom he is also taught this, to ascribe to the courses of the stars the errors of his own evil doings, although he chose them of purpose, and willingly. For arts are learned and practiced, as we have said, under the compulsion of the desire of food and drink; which desire, when the knowledge of the truth comes to any one, becomes weaker, and frugality takes its place. For what expense have those who use water and bread, and only expect it from God?

Chapter VII.-The Old and the New Birth.

"There is therefore, as we have said, a certain necessary inequality in the dispensation of the world. Since indeed all men cannot know all things, and accomplish all works, yet all need the use and service of almost all. And on this account it is necessary that one work, and another pay him for his work; that one be servant, and another be master; that one be subject, another be king. But this inequality, which is a necessary provision for the life of men, divine providence has turned into an occasion of justice, mercy, and humanity: that while these things are transacted between man and man, every one may have an opportunity of acting justly with him to whom he has to pay wages for his work; and of acting mercifully, to him who, perhaps through sickness or poverty, cannot pay his debt; and of acting humanely towards those who by their creation seem to be subject to him; also of maintaining gentleness towards subjects, and of doing all things according to the law of God. For He has given a law, thereby aiding the minds of men, that they may the more easily perceive how they ought to act with respect to everything, in what way they may escape evil, and in what way tend to future blessings; and how, being regenerate in water, they may by good works extinguish the fire of their old birth. For our first birth descends through the fire of lust, and therefore, by the divine appointment, this second birth is introduced by water, which may extinguish the nature of fire; and that the soul, enlightened by the heavenly Spirit, may cast away the fear of the first birth: provided, however, it so live for the time to come, that it do not at all seek after any of the pleasures of this world, but be, as it were, a pilgrim and a stranger, and a citizen of another city.

Chapter VIII.-Uses of Evils.

"But perhaps you will say, that in those things indeed in which the necessity of nature demands the service of arts and works, any one may have it in his power to maintain justice, and to put what restraint he pleases either upon his desires or his actions; but what shall we say of the sicknesses and infirmities which befall men, and of some being harassed with demons, and fevers, and cold fits, and some being attacked with madness, or losing their reason, and all those things which overwhelm the race of man with innumerable misfortunes? To this we say, that if any one consider the reason of the whole mystery, he will pronounce these things to be more just than those that we have already explained. For God has given a nature to men, by which they may be taught concerning what is good, and to resist evil; that is, they may learn arts, and to resist pleasures, and to set the law of God before them in all things. And for this end He has permitted certain contrary powers to wander up and down in the world, and to strive against us, for the reasons which have been stated before, that by striving with them the palm of victory and the merit of rewards may accrue to the righteous.

Chapter IX.-"Conceived in Sin."

"From this, therefore, it sometimes happens, that if any persons have acted incontinently, and have been willing not so much to resist as to yield, and to give harbor to these *demons* in themselves, by their noxious breath an intemperate, ill-conditioned, and diseased progeny is begotten. For while lust is wholly gratified, and no care is taken in the copulation, undoubtedly a weak generation is affected with the defects and frailties of those demons by whose instigation these things are done. And therefore parents are responsible for their children's defects of this sort, because they have not observed the law of intercourse. Though there are also more secret causes, by which souls are made subject to these evils, which it is not to our present purpose to state, yet it behooves every one to acknowledge the law of God, that he may learn from it the observance of generation, and avoid causes of impurity, that that which is begotten may be pure. For it is not right, while in the planting of shrubs and the sowing of crops a suitable season is sought for, and the land is cleaned, and all things are suitably prepared, lest haply the seed which is sown be injured and perish, that in the case of man only, who is over all these things, there should be no attention or caution in sowing his seed.

Chapter X.-Tow Smeared with Pitch.

"But what, it is said, of the fact that some who in their childhood are free from any bodily defect, yet in process of time fall into those evils, so that some are even violently hurried on to death? Concerning these also the account is at hand, and is almost the same: for those powers which we have said to be contrary to the human race, are in some way invited into the heart of every one by many and diverse lusts, and find a way of entrance; and they have in them such influence and power as can only encourage and incite, but cannot compel or accomplish. If, therefore, any one consents to them, so as to do those things which he wickedly desires, his consent and deed shall find the reward of destruction and the worst kind of death. But if, thinking of the future judgment, he be checked by fear, and reclaim himself, so that he do not accomplish in action what he has conceived in his evil thought, he shall not only escape present destruction, but also future punishments. For every cause of sin seems to be like tow[1] smeared over with pitch, which immediately breaks into flame as soon as it receives the heat of fire; and the kindling of this fire is understood to be the work of demons. If, therefore, any one be found smeared with sins and lusts as with pitch, the fire easily gets the mastery of him. But if the tow be not steeped in the pitch of sin, but in the water of purification and regeneration, the fire of the demons shall not be able to be kindled in it.

Chapter XI.-Fear.

"But some one will say, And what shall we do now, whom it has already happened to us to be smeared with sins as

---

[1] The fiber of flax, hemp, or jute prepared for spinning by scutching. *Source: Dictionary.com Unabridged (v 1.1)*

with pitch? I answer: Nothing; but hasten to be washed, that the fuel of the fire may be cleansed out of you by the invocation of the holy name, and that for the future you may bridle your lusts by fear of the judgment to come, and with all constancy beat back the hostile powers whenever they approach your senses. But you say, If any one fall into love, how shall he be able to contain himself, though he see before his eyes even that river of fire which they call Pyriphlegethon?[1] This is the excuse of those who will not be converted to repentance. But now I would not have you talk of Pyriphlegethon. Place before you human punishments, and see what influence fear has. When any one is brought to punishment for the crime of love, and is bound to the stake to be burned, can he at that time conceive any desire of her whom he loved, or place her image before his eyes? By no means, you will say. You see, then, that present fear cuts off unrighteous desires. But if those who believe in God, and who confess the judgment to come, and the penalty of eternal fire,-if they do not refrain from sin, it is certain that they do not believe with full faith: for if faith is certain, fear also becomes certain; but if there be any detect in faith, fear also is weakened, and then the contrary powers find opportunity of entering. And when they have consented to their persuasions, they necessarily become subject also to their power, and by their instigation are driven to the precipices of sin.

Chapter XII.-Astrologers.

"Therefore the astrologers, being ignorant of such mysteries, think that these things happen by the courses of the heavenly bodies: hence also, in their answers to those who go to them to consult them as to future things, they are deceived in very many instances. Nor is it to be wondered at, for they are not prophets; but, by long practice, the authors of errors find a sort of refuge in those things by

---

[1] Greek Mythology: A river of fire, one of the five rivers of Hades.
Source: The American Heritage® Dictionary of the English Language, Fourth Edition.

which they were deceived, and introduce certain Climacteric[1] Periods, that they may pretend a knowledge of uncertain things. For they represent these Climacterics as times of danger, in which one sometimes is destroyed, sometimes is not destroyed, not knowing that it is not the course of the stars, but the operation of demons, that regulates these things; and those demons, being anxious to confirm the error of astrology, deceive men to sin by mathematical calculations, so that when they suffer the punishment of sin, either by the permission of God or by legal sentence, the astrologer may seem to have spoken truth. And yet they are deceived even in this; for if men be quickly turned to repentance, and remember and fear the future judgment, the punishment of death is remitted to those who are converted to God by the grace of baptism.

Chapter XIII.-Retribution Here or Hereafter.

"But some one will say, Many have committed even murder, and adultery, and other crimes, and have suffered no evil. This indeed rarely happens to men, but to those who know not the counsel of God it frequently seems to happen. But God, who knows all things, knows how and why he who sins does sin, and what cause leads each one to sin. This, however, is in general to be noticed, that if any are evil, not so much in their mind as in their doings, and are not borne to sin under the incitement of purpose, upon them punishment is inflicted more speedily, and more in the present life; for everywhere and always God renders to every one according to his deeds, as He judges to be expedient. But those who practice wickedness of purpose, so that they sometimes even rage against those from whom they have received benefits, and who take no thought for repentance-their punishment He defers to the future. For these men do not, like those of whom we spoke before, deserve to end the punishment of their crimes in the present

---

[1] A year in which important changes in health, fortune, etc., are held by some theories to occur. *Source: Dictionary.com Unabridged (v 1.1)*

life; but it is allowed them to occupy the present time as they will, because their correction is not such as to need temporal chastisements, but such as to demand the punishment of eternal fire in heir; and there their souls shall seek repentance, where they shall not be able to find it.

Chapter XIV.-Knowledge Deadens Lusts.

"But if, while in this life, they had placed before their eyes the punishments which they shall then suffer, they would certainly have bridled their lusts, and would in nowise have fallen into sin. For the understanding in the soul has much power for cutting off all its desires, especially when it has acquired the knowledge of heavenly things, by means of which, having received the light of truth, it will turn away from all darkness of evil actions. For as the sun obscures and conceals all the stars by the brightness of his shining, so also the mind, by the light of knowledge, renders all the lusts of the soul ineffective and inactive, sending out upon them the thought of the judgment to come as its rays, so that they can no longer appear in the soul.

Chapter XV.-Fear of Men and of God.

"But as a proof that the fear of God has much efficacy for the repressing of lusts, take the example of human fear. Who is there among men that does not covet his neighbor's goods? And yet they are restrained, and act honestly, through fear of the punishment which is prescribed by the laws. Through fear, nations are subject to their kings, and armies obey with arms in their hands. Slaves, although they are stronger than their masters, yet through fear submit to their masters' rule. Even wild beasts are tamed by fear; the strongest bulls submit their necks to the yoke, and huge elephants obey their masters, through fear. But why do we use human examples, when even divine are not wanting? Does not the earth itself remain under the fear of precept, which it testifies by its motion and quaking? The sea keeps its prescribed bounds; the angels maintain peace; the stars keep their order, and the rivers their channels: it is certain also that demons are put to flight by fear. And not to lengthen the discourse by too many particulars, see how the fear of God, restraining everything, keeps all things in proper harmony, and in their fixed order. How much more, then, may you be sure that the lusts of demons which arise in your hearts may be extinguished and wholly abolished by the admonition of the fear of God, when even the inciters of lust are themselves put to flight by the influence of fear? You know that these things are so; but if you have anything to answer, proceed."

Chapter XVI.-Imperfect Conviction.

Then said the old man: "My son Clement has wisely framed his argument, so that he has left us nothing to say to these things; but all his discourse which he has delivered on the nature of men has this bearing, that along with the fact that freedom of will is in man, there is also some cause of evil without him, whereby men are indeed incited by various lusts, yet are not compelled to sin; and that for this reason, he said, because fear is much more powerful than they, and it resists and checks the violence of desires, so that, although natural emotions may arise, yet sin may not be committed, those demons being put to flight who incite and inflame these emotions. But these things do not convince me; for I am conscious of certain things from which I know well, that by the arrangement of the heavenly bodies men become murderers or adulterers, and perpetrate other evils; and in like manner honorable and modest women are compelled to act well.

Chapter XVII.-Astrological Lore.

"In short, when Mars, holding the centre in his house, regards Saturn quarterly, with Mercury towards the centre, the full moon coming upon him, in the daily *genesis*, he produces murderers, and those who are to fall by the sword, bloody, drunken, lustful, devilish men, inquirers into secrets, malefactors, sacrilegious persons, and such like; especially when there was no one of the good stars looking on. But again Mars himself, having a quarterly position with respect to Venus, in a direction toward the centre, while no good star looks on, produces adulterers and incestuous persons. Venus with the Moon, in the borders and houses of Saturn, if she was with Saturn, and Mars looking on, produces women that are viragos,[1] ready for agriculture, building, and every manly work, to commit adultery with whom they please, and not to be convicted by their husbands, to use no delicacy, no ointments, nor feminine robes and shoes, but to live after the fashion of men. But the unpropitious Venus makes men to be as women, and not to act in any respect as men, if she is with Mars in Aries; on the contrary, she produces women if she is in Capricorn or Aquarius."

Chapter XVIII.-The Reply.

And when the old man had pursued this subject at great length, and had enumerated every kind of mathematical figure, and also the position of the heavenly bodies, wishing thereby to show that fear is not sufficient to restrain lusts, I answered again: "Truly, my father, you have argued most learnedly and skillfully; and reason herself invites me to say something in answer to your discourse, since indeed I am acquainted with the science of mathematics, and gladly hold a conference with so learned a man. Listen therefore, while I reply to what you have said that you may learn distinctly that *genesis* is not at all from the stars, and that it is possible for those to resist the assault of demons who have recourse to God; and, as I said before, that not only by the fear of God can natural lusts be restrained, but even by the fear of men, as we shall now instruct you.

Chapter XIX.-Refutation of Astrology.

---

[1] A woman regarded as loud-voiced, ill-tempered, scolding or domineering. *Source: Dictionary.com Unabridged (v 1.1)*

"There are, in every country or kingdom, laws imposed by men, enduring either by writing or simply through custom, which no one easily transgresses. In short, the first Seres, who dwell at the beginning of the world, have a law not to know murder, nor adultery, nor whoredom, and not to commit theft, and not to worship idols; and in all that country, which is very large, there is neither temple, nor image, nor harlot, nor adulteress, nor is any thief brought to trial. But neither is any man ever slain there; and no man's liberty of will is compelled, according to your doctrine, by the fiery star of Mars, to use the sword for the murder of man; nor does Venus in conjunction with Mars compel to adultery, although of course with them Mars occupies the middle circle of heaven every day. But amongst the Seres the fear of laws is more powerful than the configuration of *genesis*.

Chapter XX.-Brahmans.

"There are likewise amongst the Bactrians[1], in the Indian countries, immense multitudes of Brahmans[2], who also themselves, from the tradition of their ancestors, and peaceful customs and laws, neither commit murder nor adultery, nor worship idols, nor have the practice of eating animal food, are never drunk, never do anything maliciously, but always fear God. And these things indeed they do, though the rest of the Indians commit both murders and adulteries, and worship idols, and are drunken, and practice other wickedness of this sort. Yea, in the western parts of India itself there is a certain country, where strangers, when they enter it, are taken and slaughtered and eaten; and neither have good stars prevented these men from such wickedness and from

---

[1] An Indo-European people originally of Bactria, situated in what is now modern northern Afghanistan, Tajikistan, and southern Uzbekistan.
[2] A people who lived in India.

Source: The American Heritage® Dictionary of the English Language, Fourth Edition.

accursed food, nor have malign stars compelled the Brahmans to do any evil. Again, there is a custom among the Persians to marry mothers, and sisters, and daughters. In all that district the Persians contract incestuous marriages.

Chapter XXI.-Districts of Heaven.

"And that those who study mathematics may not have it in their power to use that subterfuge by which they say that there are certain districts of heaven to which it is granted to have some things peculiar to themselves, some of that nation of Persians have gone to foreign countries, who are called Magusaei, of whom there are some to this day in Media, others in Parthia, some also in Egypt, and a considerable number in Galatia and Phrygia, all of whom maintain the form of this incestuous tradition without variation, and hand it down to their posterity to be observed, even although they have changed their district of heaven; nor has Venus with the Moon in the confines and houses of Saturn, with Saturn also and Mars looking on, compelled them to have a *genesis* among other men.

Chapter XXII.-Customs of the Gelones.

"Amongst the Geli also there is a custom, that women cultivate the fields, build, and do every manly work; and they are also allowed to have intercourse with whom they please, and are not found fault with by their husbands, or called adulteresses: for they have promiscuous intercourse everywhere, and especially with strangers; they do not use ointments; they do not wear dyed garments, nor shoes. On the other hand, the men of the Gelones are adorned, combed, clothed in soft and various-colored garments, decked with gold, and besmeared with ointments, and that not through lack of manliness, for they are most warlike, and most keen hunters. Yet the whole women of the Gelones had not at their birth the unfavorable Venus in Capricornus or Aquarius; nor had all their men Venus placed with Mars in Aries, by which configuration the

Chaldean science asserts that men are born effeminate and dissolute.

Chapter XXIII.-Manners of the Susidae.

"But, further, in Susae[1] the women use ointments, and indeed of the best sort, being decked with ornaments and precious stones; also they go abroad supported by the aid of their maidservants, with much greater ambition than the men. They do not, however, cultivate modesty, but have intercourse indifferently with whomsoever they please, with slaves and guests, such liberty being allowed them by their husbands; and not only are they not blamed for this, but they also rule over their husbands. And yet the *genesis* of all the Susian women has not Venus, with Jupiter and Mars in the middle of the heaven in the houses of Jupiter. In the remoter parts of the East, if a boy be treated unnaturally, when it is discovered, he is killed by his brothers, or his parents, or any of his relations, and is left unburied. And again, among the Gauls[2], an old law allows boys to be thus treated publicly; and no disgrace is thought to attach to it. And is it possible, that all those who are so basely treated among the Gauls, have had Lucifer with Mercury in the houses of Saturn and the confines of Mars?

Chapter XXIV.-Different Customs of Different Countries.

"In the regions of Britain several men have one wife; in Parthia many women have one husband; and each part of the world adheres to its own manners and institutions. None of the Amazons have husbands, but, like animals, they go out from their own territories once a year about the vernal

---

[1] Susa, ancient city, capital of Elam. The site is 15 mi (23 km) SW of modern Dizful, Iran.

[2] Gaul was the name given, in ancient times, to the region of Western Europe comprising present-day northern Italy, France, Belgium, Switzerland, the Netherlands and Germany.

Source: The American Heritage® Dictionary of the English Language, Fourth Edition.

equinox, and live with the men of the neighboring nation, observing a sort of solemnity the while, and when they have conceived by them they return; and if they bring forth a male child, they cast him away, and rear only females. Now, since the birth of all is at one season, it is absurd to suppose that in the case of males Mars is at the time in equal portions with Saturn, but never in the *genesis* of females; and that they have not Mercury placed with Venus in his own houses, so as to produce either painters, or sculptors, or money-changers; or in the houses of Venus, so that perfumers, or singers, or poets might be produced. Among the Saracens, and Upper Libyans, and Moors, and the dwellers about the mouths of the ocean, and also in the remote districts of Germany, and among the Sarmatians and Scythians, and all the nations who dwell in the regions of the Pontic shore, and in the island Chrysea, there is never found a money-changer, nor a sculptor, nor a painter, nor an architect, nor a geometrician, nor a tragedian, nor a poet. Therefore the influence of Mercury and Venus must be wanting among them.

Chapter XXV.-Not Genesis, But Free-Will.

"The Medes alone in all the world, with the greatest care, throw men still breathing to be devoured by dogs; yet they have not Mars with the Moon placed in Cancer all through their daily *genesis*. The Indians burn their dead, and the wives of the dead voluntarily offer themselves, and are burned with them. But all the Indian women who are burned alive have not the Sun under the earth in nightly *genesis*, with Mars in the regions of Mars. Very many of the Germans end their lives by the halter; but all have not therefore the Moon with Hora encompassed[1] by Saturn and Mars. From all this it appears that the fear of the laws bears sway in every country, and the freedom of will which is implanted in man by the Spirit complies with the laws; and *genesis* can neither compel the Seres to commit murder, nor the Brahmans to eat flesh, nor the Persians to shun incest,

---

[1] Original word used in the text was: **begirt**

nor the Indians to refrain from burning, nor the Medes from being devoured by dogs, nor the Parthians from having many wives, nor the women of Mesopotamia from preserving their chastity, nor the Greeks from athletic exercises, nor the Gallic boys from being abused; nor can it compel the barbarous nations to be instructed in the studies of the Greeks; but, as we have said, each nation observes its own laws according to free-will, and annuls the decrees of *genesis* by the strictness of laws.

Chapter XXVI-Climates.

"But some one skilled in the science of mathematics will say that *genesis* is divided into seven parts, which they call climates, and that over each climate one of the seven heavenly bodies bears rule; and that those diverse laws to which we have referred are not given by men, but by those dominant stars according to their will, and that that which pleases the star is observed by men as a law. To this we shall answer, in the first place, that the world is not divided into seven parts; and in the second place, that if it were so, we find many different laws in one part and one country; and therefore there are neither seven *laws* according to the number of the heavenly bodies, nor twelve according to the number of the signs, nor thirty-six according to that of the divisions of ten degrees; but they are innumerable.

Chapter XXVII.-Doctrine of "Climates" Untenable.

"Moreover, we ought to remember the things which have been mentioned, that in the one country of India there are both persons who feed on human flesh, and persons who abstain even from the flesh of sheep, and birds, and all living creatures; and that the Magusaei marry their mothers and daughters not only in Persia, but that in every nation where they dwell they keep up their incestuous customs. Then, besides, we have mentioned also innumerable nations, which are wholly ignorant of the studies of literature, and also some wise men have changed the laws themselves in several places; and some laws have been voluntarily abandoned, on account of the impossibility of observing them, or on account of their baseness. Assuredly we can easily ascertain how many rulers have changed the laws and customs of nations which they have conquered, and subjected them to their own laws. This is manifestly done by the Romans, who have brought under the Roman law and the civil decrees almost the whole world, and all nations who formerly lived under various laws and customs of their own. It follows, therefore, that the stars of the nations which have been conquered by the Romans have lost their climates and their portions.

Chapter XXVII.-Jewish Customs.

"I shall add another thing which may satisfy even the most incredulous. All the Jews who live under the law of Moses circumcise their sons on the eighth day without fail, and shed the blood of the tender infant. But no one of the Gentiles has ever submitted to this on the eighth day; and, on the other hand, no one of the Jews has ever omitted it. How then shall the account of *genesis* stand with this, since Jews live in all parts of the world, mixed with Gentiles, and on the eighth day suffer the cutting of a member? And no one of the Gentiles, but only they themselves, as I have said, do this, induced to it not by the compulsion of any star, nor by the perfusion of blood, but by the law of their religion; and in whatever part of the world they are, this sign is familiar to them. But also the fact that one name is among them all, wheresoever they are, does this also come through *genesis*? And also that no child born among them is ever exposed, and that on every seventh day they all rest, wherever they may be, and do not go upon a journey, and do not use fire? Why is it, then, that no one of the Jews is compelled by *genesis* to go on a journey, or to build, or to sell or buy anything on that day?

Chapter XXIX.-The Gospel More Powerful Than "Genesis."

"But I shall give a still stronger proof of the matters in hand. For, behold, scarcely seven years have yet passed since the advent of the righteous and true Prophet; and in the course of these, inert of all nations coming to Judaea, and moved both by the signs and miracles which they saw, and by the grandeur of His doctrine, received His faith; and then going back to their own countries, they rejected the lawless rites of the Gentiles, and their incestuous marriages. In short, among the Parthians-as Thomas, who is preaching the Gospel amongst them, has written to us-not many now are addicted to polygamy; nor among the Medes do many throw their dead to dogs; nor are the Persians pleased with intercourse with their mothers, or incestuous marriages with their daughters; nor do the Susian women practice the adulteries that were allowed them; nor has *genesis* been able to force those into crimes whom the teaching of religion restrained.

Chapter XXX.-"Genesis" Inconsistent with God's Justice.

"Behold, from the very matter in which we are now engaged draw an inference, and from the circumstances in which we are now placed deduce a conclusion, how, through a rumor only reaching the ears of men that a Prophet had appeared in Judaea to teach men with signs and miracles to worship one God, all were expecting with prepared and eager minds, even before the coming of my lord Peter, that some one would announce to them what He taught who had appeared. But lest I should seem to carry the enumeration too far, I shall tell you what conclusion ought to be drawn from the whole. Since God is righteous, and since He Himself made the nature of men, how could it be that He should place *genesis* in opposition to us, which should compel us to sin, and then that He should punish us when we do sin? Whence it is certain that God punishes no sinner either in the present life or in that to come, except because He knows that he could have conquered, but neglected victory. For even in the present world He takes vengeance upon men, as He did upon those who perished in the deluge, who were all destroyed in one day, yea, in one hour, although it is certain that they were not all born in one hour according to the order of *genesis*. But it is most absurd to say that it befalls us by nature to suffer evils, if sins had not gone before.

Chapter XXXI.-Value of Knowledge.

"And therefore, if we desire salvation, we ought above all to seek after knowledge, being sure that if our mind remain in ignorance, we shall endure not only the evils of *genesis*, but also whatever other evils from without the demons may please, unless fear of laws and of the judgment to come resist all our desires, and check the violence of sinning. For even human fear does much good, and also much evil, unknown to *genesis*, as we have shown above. Therefore our mind is subject to errors in a threefold manner: from those things which come to us through evil custom; or from those lusts which the body naturally stirs up in us; or from those which hostile powers compel us to. But the mind has it in its own nature to oppose and fight against these, when the knowledge of truth shines upon it, by which knowledge is imparted fear of the judgment to come, which is a fit governor of the mind, and which can recall it from the precipices of lusts. That these things, therefore, are in our power, has been sufficiently stated.

Chapter XXXII.-Stubborn Facts.

"Now, old man, if you have any thing to say in answer to these things, say on." Then said the old man: "You have most fully argued, my son; but I, as I said at first, am prevented by my own consciousness from according assent to all this incomparable statement of yours. For I know both my own *genesis* and that of my wife, and I know that those things have happened which our *genesis* prescribed to each of us; and I cannot now be withdrawn by words from those things which I have ascertained by facts and deeds. In short, since I perceive that you are excellently skilled in this sort of learning, hear the horoscope of my wife, and you shall find the configuration whose issue has occurred. For she had Mars with Venus above the centre, and the Moon setting in the houses of Mars and the confines of Saturn. Now this configuration leads women to be adulteresses, and to love their own slaves, and to end their days in foreign travel and in waters. And this has so come to pass. For she fell in love with her slave, and fearing at once danger and reproach, she fled with him, and going abroad, where she satisfied her love, she perished in the sea."

Chapter XXXIII.-An Approaching Recognition.

Then I answered: "How know you that she cohabited with her slave abroad, and died in his society?" Then the old man said: "I know it with perfect certainty; not indeed that she was married to the slave, as indeed I had not even discovered that she loved him. But after she was gone, my brother gave me the whole story, telling me that first she had loved himself; but he, being honorable as a brother, would not pollute his brother's bed with the stain of incest. But she, being both afraid of me, and unable to bear the unhappy reproaches (and yet she should not be blamed for that to which her *genesis* compelled her), pretended a dream, and said to me: `Some one stood by me in a vision, who ordered me to leave the city without delay with my two twins.' When I heard this, being anxious for her safety and that of my sons, I immediately sent away her and the children, retaining with myself one who was younger. For this she said that he had permitted who had given her warning in her sleep."

Chapter XXXIV.-The Other Side of the Story.

Then I Clement, understanding that he perchance was my father, was drowned in tears, and my brothers also were ready to rush forward and to disclose the matter; but Peter restrained them, saying: "Be quiet, until I give you permission." Therefore Peter, answering, said to the old man: "What was the name of your younger son?" And he said: "Clement." Then Peter: "If I shall this day restore to you your most chaste wife and your three sons, will you believe that a modest mind can overcome unreasonable impulses, and that all things that have been spoken by us are true, and that *genesis* is nothing? "Then said the old man: "As it is impossible for you to perform what you have promised, so it is impossible that anything can take place apart from *genesis*." Then says Peter: "I wish to have all who are here present as witnesses that I shall this day hand over to you your wife, who is living most chastely, with your three sons. And now take a token of these things from this, that I know the whole story much more accurately than you do; and I shall relate the whole occurrences in order, both that you may know them, and that those who are present may learn."

Chapter XXXV.-Revelations.

When he had said this, he turned to the crowds, and thus began: "This person whom you see, O men, in this poor garb, is a citizen of the city Rome, descended of the stock of Caesar himself. His name is Faustinianus. He obtained as his wife a woman of the highest rank, Matthidia by name. By her he had three sons, two of whom were twins; and the one who was the younger, whose name was Clement, is this man!" When he said this, he pointed to me with his finger. "And his twin sons are these men, Niceta and Aquila, the one of whom was formerly called Faustinus and the other Faustus." But as soon as Peter pronounced our names, all the old man's limbs were weakened, and he fell down in a swoon. But we his sons rushed to him, and embraced and kissed him, fearing that we might not be able to recall his spirit. And while these things were going on, the people were confounded with very wonder.

Chapter XXXVI.-New Revelations.

But Peter ordered us to rise from embracing our father, lest we should kill him; and he himself, laying hold of his hand, and lifting him up as from a deep sleep, and gradually reviving him, began to set forth to him the whole transactions as they had really happened: how his brother had fallen in love with Matthidia, and how she, being very modest, had been unwilling to inform her husband of his brother's lawless love, lest she should stir up hostility between the brothers, and bring disgrace upon the family; and how she had wisely pretended a dream, by which she was ordered to depart from the city with her twin sons, leaving the younger one with his father; and how on their voyage they had suffered shipwreck through the violence of a storm; and how, when they were cast upon an island called Antaradus, Matthidia was thrown by a wave upon a rock, but her twin children were seized by pirates and carried to Caesarea, and there sold to a pious woman, who treated them as sons, and brought them up, and caused them to be educated as gentlemen; and how the pirates had changed their names, and called the one Niceta and the other Aquila; and how afterwards, through common studies and acquaintanceship, they had adhered to Simon; and how they had turned away from him when they saw him to be a magician and a deceiver, and had come to Zacchaeus; and how subsequently they had been associated with himself; and how Clement also, setting out from the city for the sake of learning the truth, had, through his acquaintance with Barnabas, come to Caesarea. and had become known to him, and had adhered to him, and how he had been taught by him the faith of his religion; and also how he had found and recognized his mother begging at Antaradus, and how the whole island rejoiced at his recognition of her; and also concerning her sojourn with her most chaste hostess, and the cure that he bad wrought upon her, and concerning t he liberality of Clement to those who bad been kind to his mother; and how afterwards, when Niceta and Aquila asked who the strange woman was, and had heard the whole story from Clement, they cried out that they were her twin sons

Faustinus and Faustus; and how they had unfolded the whole history of what had befallen them; and how afterwards, by the persuasion of Peter himself, they were presented to their mother with caution, lost she should be cut off by the sudden joy.

Chapter XXXVII.-Another Recognition.

But while Peter was detailing these things in the hearing of the old man, in a narrative which was most pleasing to the crowd, so that the hearers wept through wonder at the events, and through compassion for sufferings incident to humanity, my mother, hearing (I know not how) of the recognition of my father, rushed into the middle of us in breathless haste, crying out, and saying: "Where is my husband, my lord Faustinianus, who has been so long afflicted, wandering from city to city in search of me?" While she shouted thus like one demented, and gazed around, the old man, running up, began to embrace and hug her with many tears. And while these things were going on, Peter requested the crowds to disperse, saying that it was unseemly to remain longer; but that opportunity must be afforded them of seeing one another more privately. "But to-morrow," said he, "if any of you wish it, let them assemble to hear the word."

Chapter XXXVIII.-"Angels Unawares."

When Peter had said this, the crowds dispersed; and when we also were intending to go to our lodging, the master of the house said to us: "It is base and wicked that such and so great men should stay in a hostelry, when I have almost my whole house empty, and very many beds spread, and all necessary things provided." But when Peter refused, the wife of the householder prostrated herself before him with her children, and besought him, saying, "I entreat yon, stay with us." But not even so did Peter consent, until the daughter of those people who asked him, who had been for a long time vexed with an unclean spirit, and bound with chains, who had been shut up in a closet, having had the demon expelled from her, and the door of the closet opened, came with her chains and fell down at Peter's feet, saying: "It is right, my lord, that you keep my deliverance-feast here to-day, and not sadden me or my parents." But when Peter asked what was the meaning of her chains and of her words, her parents, gladdened beyond hope by the recovery of their daughter, were, as it were, thunderstruck with astonishment, and could not speak; but the servants who were in attendance said: "This girl has been possessed of a demon from her seventh year, and used to cut, and bite, and even to tear in pieces, all who attempted to approach her, and this she has never ceased to do for twenty years till the present time. Nor could any one cure her, or even approach her, for she rendered many helpless, and even destroyed some; for she was stronger than any man, being doubtless strengthened by the power of the demon. But now, as you see, the demon has fled from your presence, and the doors which were shut with the greatest strength have been opened, and she herself stands before you in her sound mind, asking of you to make the clay of her recovery gladsome both to herself and her parents, and to remain with them." When one of the servants had made this statement, and the chains of their own accord were loosened from her hands and feet, Peter, being sure that it was by his means that soundness was restored to the girl, consented to remain with them. And he ordered those also who had remained in the lodging, with his wife, to come over; and every one of us having got a separate bed-chamber, we remained; and having taken food in the usual manner, and given praises to God, we went to sleep in our several apartments.

Book X.

Chapter I.-Probation.

But in the morning, after sunrise, I Clement, and Niceta and Aquila, along with Peter, came to the apartment in which my father and mother were sleeping; and finding them still asleep, we sat down before the door, when Peter addressed us in such terms as these: "Listen to me, most beloved fellow-servants: I know that you have a great affection for your father; therefore I am afraid that you will urge him too soon to take upon himself the yoke of religion, while he is not yet prepared for it; and to this he may perhaps consent, through his affection for you. But this is not to be depended on; for what is done for the sake of men is not worthy of approbation, and soon falls to pieces. Therefore it seems to me, that you should permit him to live for a year according to his own judgment; and during that time he may travel with us, and while we are instructing others he may hear with simplicity; and as he hears, if he has any right purpose of acknowledging the truth, he will himself request that he may take up the yoke of religion; or if he do not please to take it, he may remain a friend. For those who do not take it up heartily, when they begin not to be able to bear it, not only cast off that which they had taken up, but by way of excuse, as it were, for their weakness, they begin to speak evil of the way of religion, and to malign those whom they have not been able to follow or to imitate."

Chapter II.-A Difficulty.

To this Niceta answered: "My lord Peter, I say nothing against your right and good counsels; but I wish to say one thing, that thereby I may learn something that I do not know. What if my father should die within the year during which you recommend that he should be put off? He will go down to hell helpless, and so be tormented for ever." Then said Peter: "I embrace your kindly purpose towards your father, and I forgive you in respect of things of which you are ignorant. For do you suppose that, if any one is thought to have lived righteously, he shall forthwith be saved? Do you not think that he must be examined by Him who knows the secrets of men, as to how he has lived righteously, whether perchance according to the rule of the Gentiles, obeying their institutions and laws; or for the sake of the friendship of men; or merely from custom, or any other cause; or from necessity, and not on account of righteousness itself, and for the sake of God? For those who have lived righteously, for the sake of God alone and His righteousness, they shall come to eternal rest, and shall receive the perpetuity of the heavenly kingdom. For salvation is not attained by force, but by liberty; and not through the favor of men, but by the faith of God. Then, besides, you ought to consider that God is prescient, and knows whether this man is one of His. But if He knows that he is not, what shall we do with respect to those things which have been determined by Him from the beginning? But wherein I can, I give counsel: when he is awake, and we sit down together, then do you, as if you wished to learn something, ask a question about those matters which it is fitting for him to learn; and while we speak to one another, he will gain instruction. But yet wait first to see if he himself ask anything; for if he do so, the occasion of discourse will be the fitter. But if he do not ask anything, let us by turns put questions to one another, wishing to learn something, as I have said. Such is my judgment, state what is yours."

Chapter III.-A Suggestion.

And when we had commended his right counsel, I Clement said: "In all things, the end for the most part looks back upon the beginning, and the issue of things is similar to their commencement. I hope, therefore, with respect to our father also, since God by your means has given a good beginning, that He will bestow also an ending suitable to the beginning, and worthy of Himself. However, I make this suggestion, that if, as you have said, we begin to speak, in presence of my father, as if for the purpose of discussing some subject, or learning something from one another, you, my lord Peter, ought not to occupy the place of one who has anything to learn; for if he see this, he will rather be offended. For he is convinced that you fully know all things, as indeed you do. How then will it be, if he see you pretending ignorance? This, as I have said, will rather hurt him, being ignorant of your design. But if we brothers, while we converse among ourselves, are in any doubt, let a fitting solution be given by you to our inquiry. For if he see even you hesitating and doubting, then truly he will think that no one has knowledge of the truth."

Chapter IV.-Free Inquiry.

To this Peter answered: "Let us not concern ourselves about this; and if indeed it is fitting that he enter the gate of life, God will afford a fitting opportunity; and there shall be a beginning from God, and not from man. And therefore, as I have said, let him journey with us, and hear our discussions; but because I saw you in haste, therefore I said that opportunity must be sought; and when God shall give it, do you comply with my advice in what I shall say." While we were thus talking, a boy came to tell us that our father was now awake; and when we were intending to go in to him, he himself came to us, and saluting us with a kiss, after we had sat down again, he said: "Is it permitted to one to ask a question, if he wishes it; or is silence enforced, after the manner of the Pythagoreans?" Then said Peter: "We do not compel those who come to us either to keep silence continually, or to ask questions; but we leave them free to do as they will knowing that he who is anxious about his salvation, if he feels pain in any part of his soul, does not suffer it to be silent. But he who neglects his salvation, no advantage its conferred upon him if he is compelled to ask, excepting this only, that he may seem to be earnest and diligent. Wherefore, if you wish to get any information, ask on."

Chapter V.-Good and Evil.

Then the old man said: "There is a saying very prevalent among the Greek philosophers, to the effect that there is in reality neither good nor evil in the life of man; but that men call things good or evil as they appear to them, prejudiced by the use and custom of life. For not even murder is really an evil, because it sets the soul free from the bonds of the flesh. Further, they say that even just judges put to death those who commit crimes; but if they knew homicide to be an evil, just men would not do that. Neither do they say that adultery is an evil; for if the husband does not know, or does not care, there is, they say, no evil in it. But neither, say they is theft an evil; for it takes away what one does not possess from another who has it. And, indeed, it ought to be taken freely and openly; but in that it is done secretly, that is rather a reproof of his inhumanity from whom it is secretly taken. For all men ought to have the common use of all things that are in this world; but through injustice one says that this is his, and another that that is his, and so division is caused among men. In short, a certain man, the wisest among the Greeks, knowing that these things are so, says that friends should have all things common. Now, in *all things* unquestionably wives are included. He says also that, as the air and the sunshine cannot be divided, so neither ought other things to be divided, which are given in this world to all to be possessed in common, but should be so possessed. But I wished to say this, because I am desirous to turn to well-doing, and I cannot act well unless I first learn what is good; and if I can understand that, I shall thereby perceive what is evil, that is, opposite to good.

Chapter VI.-Peter's Authority.

"But I should like that one of you, and not Peter, should answer what I have said; for it is not fitting to take words and instruction at his hand, with questions; but when he gives a deliverance on any subject, that should be held without answering again. And therefore let us keep him as an umpire; so that if at any time our discussion does not come to an issue, he may declare what seems good to him, and so give an undoubted end to doubtful matters. And now therefore I could believe, content with his sole opinion, if he expressed any opinion; and this is what I shall do at last. Yet I wish first to see if it is possible by discussion to find what is sought. My wish therefore is, that Clement should begin first, and should show if there is any good or evil in substance or in actions."

Chapter VII.-Clement's Argument.

To this I answered: "Since indeed you wish to learn from me if there is any good or evil in nature or in act, or whether it is not rather that men, prejudiced by custom, think some things to be good, and others to be evil, forasmuch as; they have made a division among themselves of common things, which ought, as you say, to be as common as the air and the sunshine; I think that I ought not to bring before you any statements from any other quarter than from those studies in which you are well versed, and which you support, so that what I say you will receive without hesitation. You assign certain boundaries of all the elements and the heavenly bodies, and these, you say, meet in some without hurt, as in marriages; but in others they are hurtfully united, as in adulteries. And you say that some things are general to all, but other things do not belong to all, and are not general. But not to make a long discussion, I shall speak briefly of the matter. The earth which is dry is in need of the addition and admixture of water, that it may be able to produce fruits, without which man cannot live: this is therefore a legitimate conjunction. On the contrary if the cold of hoar-frost be mixed with the earth, or heat with the water, a conjunction of this sort produces corruption; and this, in such things, is adultery."

Chapter VIII.-Admitted Evils.

Then my father answered: "But as the harmfulness of an inharmonious conjunction of elements or stars is immediately betrayed, so ought also adultery to be immediately shown that it is an evil." Then I: "First tell me this, whether, as you yourself have confessed, evils are produced from incongruous and inharmonious mixture; and then after that we shall inquire into the other matter." Then my father said: "The nature of things is as you say, my son." Then I answered: "Since, then, you wish to learn of these things, see how many things there are which no one doubts to be evils. Do you think that a fever, a fire, sedition, the fall of a house, murder, holds, racks, pains, mournings, and such like, are evils? "Then said my father: "It is true, my son, that these things are evil, and very evil; or, at all events, whoever denies that they are evil, let him suffer them!"

Chapter IX.-Existence of Evil on Astrological Principles.

Then I answered: "Since, therefore, I have to deal with one who is skilled in astrological science, I shall treat the matter with you according to that science, that, taking my method from those things with which you are familiar, you may the more readily acquiesce. Listen now, therefore: you confess that those things which we have mentioned are evils, such as fevers, conflagrations, and such like. Now these, according to you, are said to be produced by malignant stars, such as the humid Saturn and the hot Mars; but things contrary to these are produced by benignant stars, such as the temperate Jupiter and the humid Venus. Is it not so? "My father answered: "It is so, my son; and it cannot be otherwise." Then said I: "Since you say, therefore, that good things are produced by good stars-by Jupiter and Venus, for example-let us see what is the product where any one of the evil stars is mixed with the good, and let us understand that that is evil. For you lay it down that Venus makes marriages, and if she have Jupiter in her configuration she makes the marriages chaste; but if Jupiter he not regarding, and Mars be present, then you pronounce that the marriages are corrupted by adultery." Then said my father: "It is even so." Then I answered: "Therefore adultery is an evil, seeing that it is committed through the admixture of evil stars; and, to state it in a word all things that you say that the good stars suffer from the mixture of evil stars, are undoubtedly to be pronounced to be evil. Those stars, therefore, by whose admixture we have said that fevers, configurations, and other such like evils are produced,-those, according to you, work also murders, adulteries, thefts, and also produce haughty and stolid men."

Chapter X.-How to Make Progress.

Then my father said: "Truly you have shown briefly and incomparably that there are evils in actions; but still I should wish to learn this how God justly judges those who sin, as you say, if *genesis* compels them to sin?" Then I answered: "I am afraid to speak anything to you, my father, because it becomes me to hold you in all honor, else I have an answer to give you, if it were becoming." Then says my father: "Speak what occurs to you, my son; for it is not you, but the method of inquiry, that does the wrong, as a modest woman to an incontinent man, if she is indignant for her safety and her honor." Then I answered "If we do not hold by the principles that we have acknowledged and confessed, but if those things which have been defined are always loosened by forgetfulness, we shall seem to be weaving Penelope's web[1], undoing what we have done. And therefore we ought either not to acquiesce too easily,

---

[1] Penelope, in Greek mythology, wife of Odysseus and the mother of Telemachus. In Homer's *Odyssey* she is pictured as a chaste and faithful wife. When Odysseus was away, she was surrounded by suitors who tried to persuade her that he would never return. She agreed to choose another husband when she finished weaving her father-in-law's shroud, but this was never done, for she unraveled by night what she wove by day. At last her stratagem was discovered, and the suitors were enraged. She promised to marry the man who could bend her husband's great bow. None of the suitors could do this but Odysseus, who had returned disguised as a beggar. With the aid of the strung bow, Odysseus slaughtered the suitors and then revealed himself to Penelope.

Taken from the Columbia Electronic Encyclopedia*. Retrieved May 24, 2007, from Reference.com website:*
http://www.reference.com/browse/columbia/Penelope

before we have diligently examined the doctrine propounded; or if we have once acquiesced, and the proposition has been agreed to, then we ought to keep by what has been once determined, that we may go on with our inquiries respecting other matters." And my father said: "You say well, my son; and I know why you say this: it is because in the discussion yesterday on natural causes, you showed that some malignant power, transferring itself into the order of the stars, excites the lusts of men, provoking them in various ways to sin, yet not compelling or producing sins." To this I answered: "It is well that you remember it; and yet, though you remember it, you have fallen into error." Then said my father: "Pardon me, my son; for I have not yet much practice in these things: for indeed your discourses yesterday, by their truth, shut me up to agree with you; yet in my consciousness there are, as it were, some remains of fevers, which for a little hold me back from faith, as from health. For I am distracted, because I know that many things, yea, almost all things, have befallen me according to *genesis*."

Chapter XI.-Test of Astrology.

Then I answered: "I shall therefore tell you, my father, what is the nature of mathematics, and do you act according to what I tell you. Go to a mathematician, and tell him first that such and such evils have befallen you at such a time, and that you wish to learn of him whence, or how, or through what stars they have befallen you. He will no doubt answer you that a malignant Mars or Saturn has ruled your times, or that some one of them has been periodic; or that some one has regarded you diametrically, or in conjunction, or centrally; or some such answer will he give, adding that in all these some one was not in harmony with the malignant one, or was invisible, or was in the figure, or was beyond the division, or was eclipsed, or was not in contact, or was among the dark stars; and many other like things will he answer, according to his own reasons, and will condescend upon particulars. After him go to another mathematician, and tell him the opposite, that such and such good happened to you at that time, mentioning to him the same time, and ask him from what parts of your *genesis* this good has come to you, and take care, as I said, that the times are the same with those about which you asked concerning evils. And when you have deceived him concerning the times, see what figures he will invent for you, by which to show that good things ought to have befallen you at those very times. For it is impossible for those treating of the *genesis* of men not to find in every quarter, as they call it, of the heavenly bodies, some stars favorably placed, and some unfavorably; for the circle is equally complete in every part, according to mathematics, admitting of diverse and various causes, from which they can take occasion of saying whatever they please.

Chapter XII.-Astrology Baffled by Free-Will.

"For, as usually happens when men see unfavorable dreams, and can make nothing certain out of them, when any event occurs, then they adapt what they saw in the dream to what has occurred; so also is mathematics. For before anything happens, nothing is declared with certainty; but after something has happened, they gather the causes of the event. And thus often, when they have been at fault, and the thing has fallen out otherwise, they take the blame to themselves, saying that it was such and such a star which opposed, and that they did not see it; not knowing that their error does not proceed from their unskillfulness in their art, but from the inconsistency of the whole system. For they do not know what those things are which we indeed desire to do, but in regard to which we do not indulge our desires. But we who have learned the reason of this mystery know the cause, since, having freedoms of will, we sometimes oppose our desires, and sometimes yield to them. And therefore the issue of human doings is uncertain, because it depends upon freedom of will. For a mathematician can indeed indicate the desire which a malignant power produces; but whether the acting or the issue of this desire shall be fulfilled or not, no one can know before the accomplishment of the thing, because it depends upon freedom of will. And this is why ignorant astrologers have invented to themselves the talk about climacterics as their refuge in uncertainties, as we showed fully yesterday.

Chapter XIII.-People Admitted.

"If you have anything that you wish to say to this, say on." Then my father: "Nothing can be more true, my son, than what you have stated." And while we were thus speaking among ourselves, some one informed us that a great multitude of people were standing outside, having assembled for the purpose of hearing. Then Peter ordered them to be admitted, for the place was large and convenient. And when they had come in, Peter said to us: "If any one of you wishes, let him address the people, and discourse concerning idolatry." To whom I Clement answered: "Your great benignity and gentleness and patience towards all encourages us, so that we dare speak in your presence, and ask what we please; and therefore, as I said, the gentleness of your disposition invites and encourages all to undertake the precepts of saving doctrine. This I never saw before in any one else, but in you only, with whom there is neither envy nor indignation. Or what do you think?

Chapter XIV.-No Man Has Universal Knowledge.

Then Peter said: "These things come not only from envy or indignation; but sometimes there is a bashfulness in some persons, lest by chance they may not be able to answer fully the questions that may be proposed, and so they avoid the discovery of their want of skill. But no one ought to be ashamed of this, because there is no man who ought to profess that he knows all things; for there is only One who knows all things, even He who also made all things. For if our Master declared that He knew not the day and the hour whose signs even He foretold, and referred the whole to the Father, how shall we account it disgraceful to confess that we are ignorant of some things, since in this we have the example of our Master? But this only we profess, that we know those things which we have learned from the true Prophet; and that those things have been delivered to us by the true Prophet, which He judged to be sufficient for human knowledge."

Chapter XV.-Clement's Disclosure.

Then I Clement went on to speak thus: "At Tripolis, when you were disputing against the Gentiles, my lord Peter, I greatly wondered at you, that although you were instructed by your father according to the fashion of the Hebrews and in observances of your own law, and were never polluted by the studies of Greek learning, you argued so magnificently and so incomparably; and that you even touched upon some things concerning the histories of the gods, which are usually declaimed in the theatres. But as I perceived that their fables and blasphemies are not so well known to you, I shall discourse upon these in your hearing, repeating them from the very beginning, if it please you." Then says Peter: Say on; you do well to assist my preaching." Then said I: "I shall speak, therefore, because you order me, not by way of teaching you, but of making public what foolish opinions the Gentiles entertain of the gods."

Chapter XVI.-World that All God's People Were Prophets."

But when I was about to speak, Niceta, biting his lip, beckoned to me to be silent. And when Peter saw him, he said: "Why would you repress his liberal disposition and noble nature, that you would have him be silent for my honor, which is nothing? Or do you not know, that if all nations, after they have heard from me the preaching of the truth, and have believed, would betake themselves to teaching, they would gain the greater glory for me, if indeed you think me desirous of glory? For what so glorious as to prepare disciples for Christ, not who shall be silent, and shall be saved alone, but who shall speak what they have learned, and shall do good to others? I wish indeed that both you, Niceta, and you, beloved Aquila, would aid me in preaching the word of God, and the rather because those things in which the Gentiles err are well known to you; and not you only, but all who hear me, I wish, as I have said, so to hear and to learn, that they may be able also to teach: for the world needs many helpers, by whom men may be recalled from error." When he had spoken thus, he said to me: "Go on then, Clement, with what you have begun."

Chapter XVII.-Gentile Cosmogony.

And I immediately rejoined: "Seeing that when you were disputing at Tripolis, as I said, you discoursed much concerning the gods of the Gentiles profitably and convincingly, I desire to set forth in your presence the ridiculous legends concerning their origin, both that you may not be unacquainted with the falsehood of this vain superstition, and that the hearers who are present may know the disgraceful character of their error. The wise men, then, who are among the Gentiles, say that first of all things was chaos; that this, through a long time solidifying its outer parts, made bounds to itself and a sort of foundation, being gathered, as it were, into the manner and form of a huge egg, within which, in the course of a long time, as within the shell of the egg, there was cherished and vivified a certain animal; and that afterwards, that huge globe being broken, there came forth a certain kind of man of double sex, which they call masculo-feminine. This they called Phanetas, from appearing, because when it appeared, they say, then also light shone forth. And from this, they say that there were produced substance, prudence, motion, and coition[1], and from these the heavens and the earth were made. From the heaven they say that six males were produced, whom they call Titans; and in like manner, from the earth six females, whom they called Titanides. And these are the names of the males who sprang from the heaven: Oceanus, Coeus, Crios, Hyperion, Iapetus,

---

[1] The act of sexual procreation between a man and a woman.
Source: Dictionary.com Unabridged (v 1.1)

Chronos, who amongst us is called Saturn. In like manner, the names of the females who sprang from the earth are these: Theia, Rhea, Themis, Mnemosyne, Tethys, Hebe.

Chapter XVIII.-Family of Saturn.

"Of all these, the first-born of the heaven took to wife the first-born of earth; the second the second, and in like manner all the rest. The first male, therefore, who had married the first female, was on her account drawn downwards; but the second female rose upwards, by reason of him to whom she was married; and so each doing in their order, remained in those places which fell to their share by the nuptial lot. From their intercourse they assert that innumerable others sprang. But of these six males, the one who is called Saturn received in marriage Rhea, and having been warned by a certain oracle that he who should be born of her should be more powerful than himself, and should drive him from his kingdom, he determined to devour all the sons that should be born to him. First, then, there is born to him a son called Aides, who amongst us is called Orcus; and him, for the reason we have just stated, he took and devoured. After him he begot a second son, called Neptune; and him he devoured in like manner. Last of all, he begot him whom they call Jupiter; but him his mother Rhea pitying, by stratagem withdrew from his father when he was about to devour him. And first, indeed, that the crying of the child might not be noticed, she made certain Corybantes[1] strike cymbals and drums, that by the deafening sound the crying of the infant might not be heard.

Chapter XIX.-Their Destinies.

"But when he understood from the lessening of her belly that her child was born, he demanded it, that he might devour it; then Rhea presented him with a large stone, and

---

[1] Classical Mythology. any of the spirits or secondary divinities attending Cybele with wild music and dancing.
Reference: Dictionary.com Unabridged (v 1.1).

told him that that was what she had brought forth. And he took it, and swallowed it; and the stone, when it was devoured, pushed and drove forth those sons whom he had formerly swallowed. Therefore Orcus, coming forth first, descended, and occupies the lower, that is, the infernal regions. The second, being above him-he whom they call Neptune-is thrust forth upon the waters. The third, who survived by the artifice of his mother Rhea, she put upon a she-goat and sent into heaven.

Chapter XX.-Doings of Jupiter.

"But enough of the old wife's fables and genealogy of the Gentiles; for it were endless if I should set forth all the generations of those whom they call gods, and their wicked doings. But by way of example, omitting the rest, I shall detail the wicked deeds of him only whom they hold to be the greatest and the chief, and whom they call Jupiter. For they say that he possesses heaven, as being superior to the rest; and he, as soon as he grew up, married his own sister, whom they call Juno, in which truly he at once becomes like a beast. Juno bears Vulcan; but, as they relate, Jupiter was not his father. However, by Jupiter himself she became mother of Medea; and Jupiter having received a response that one who should be born of her should be more powerful than himself, and should expel him from his kingdom, took her and devoured her. Again Jupiter produced Minerva from his brain, and Bacchus from his thigh. After this, when he had fallen in love with Thetis, they say that Prometheus informed him that, if he lay with her, he who should be born of her should be more powerful than his father; and for fear of this, he gave her in marriage to one Peleus. Subsequently he had intercourse with Persephone, who was his own daughter by Ceres and by her be begot Dionysius, who was torn in pieces by the Titans. But calling to mind, it is said, that perhaps his own father Saturn might beget another son, who might be more powerful than himself, and might expel him from the kingdom, he went to war with his father, along with his brothers the Titans; and having beaten them, he at last threw his father into prison, and cut off his genitals, and threw them into the sea. But the blood which flowed from the wound, being mixed with the waves, and turned into foam by the constant churning, produced her whom they call Aphrodite, and whom with us they call Venus. From his intercourse with her who was thus his own sister, they say that this same Jupiter begot Cypris, who, they say, was the mother of Cupid.

Chapter XXI.-A Black Catalogue.

"Thus much of his incests; I shall now speak of his adulteries. He defiled Europa, the wife of Oceanus, of whom was born Dodonæus; Helen, the wife of Pandion, of whom Musæus; Eurynome, the wife of Asopus, of whom Ogygias; Hermione, the wife of Oceanus, of whom the Graces, Thalia, Euphrosyne, Aglaia; Themis, his own sister, of whom the Hours, Eurynomia, Dice, Irene; Themisto, the daughter of Inachus, of whom Arcas; Idæa, the daughter of Minos, of whom Asterion; Phœnissa, the daughter of Alphion, of whom Endymion; Io, the daughter of Inachus, of whom Epaphus; Hippodamia and Isione, daughters of Danaus, of whom Hippodamia was the wife of Olenus, and Isione of Orchomenus or Chryses; Carme, the daughter of Phœnix, of whom was born Britomartis, who was an attendant of Diana; Callisto, the daughter of Lycaon, of whom Orcas; Lybee, the daughter of Munantius, of whom Belus; Latona, of whom Apollo and Diana; Leandia, the daughter of Eurymedon, of whom Coron; Lysithea, the daughter of Evenus, of whom Helenus; Hippodamia, the daughter of Bellerophon, of whom Sarpedon; Megaclite, the daughter of Macarius, of whom Thebe and Locrus; Niobe, the daughter of Phoroneus, of whom Argus and Pelasgus; Olympias, the daughter of Neoptolemus, of whom Alexander; Pyrrha, the daughter of Prometheus, of whom Helmetheus; Protogenia and Pandora, daughters of Deucalion, of whom he begot Æthelius, and Dorus, and Melera, and Pandorus; Thaicrucia, the daughter of Proteus, of whom was born Nympheus; Salamis, the daughter of Asopus, of whom

Saracon; Taygete, Electra, Maia, Plutide, daughters of Atlas, of whom respectively he begot Lacedæmon, Dardanus, Mercury, and Tantalus; Phthia, the daughter of Phoroneus, of whom he begot Achæus; Chonia, the daughter of Aramnus, of whom he begot Lacon; Chalcea, a nymph, of whom was born Olympus; Charidia, a nymph, of whom Alcanus; Chloris, who was the wife of Ampycus, of whom Mopsus was born; Cotonia, the daughter of Lesbus, of whom Polymedes; Hippodamia, the daughter of Anicetus; Chrysogenia, the daughter of Peneus, of whom was born Thissæus.

Chapter XXII.-Vile Transformation of Jupiter.

"There are also innumerable adulteries of his, of which no offspring was the result, which it were tedious to enumerate. But amongst those whom we have mentioned, he violated some being transformed, like a magician. In short, he seduced Antiope, the daughter of Nycteus, when turned into a satyr, and of her were born Amphion and Zethus; Alemene, when changed into her husband Amphitryon, and of her was born Hercules; Aegina, the daughter of Asopus, when changed into an eagle, of whom Aeacus was born. So also he defiled Ganymede, the son of Dardanus, being changed into an eagle; Manthea, the daughter of Phocus, when changed into a bear, of whom was born Arctos; Danae, the daughter of Acrisius, being changed into gold, of whom Perseus; Europa, the daughter of Phoenix, changed into a bull, of whom were born Minos, Rhadamanthus, and Sarpedon; Eurymedusa, the daughter of Achelaus, being changed into an ant, of whom Myrmidon; Thalia, the nymph, being changed into a vulture, of whom we re born the Palisci, in Sicily; Imandra, the daughter of Geneanus, at Rhodes, being changed into a shower; Cassiopeia, being changed into her husband Phoenix, and of her was born Anchinos; Leda, the daughter of Thestius, being changed into a swan, of whom was born Helen; and again the same, being changed into a star, and of her were born Castor and Pollux; Lamia, being changed into a lapwing; Mnemosyne, being changed into a shepherd, of whom were born the nine Muses; Nemesis, being changed into a goose; the Cadmian Semele, being changed into fire, and of her was born Dionysius. By his own daughter Ceres he begot Persephone, whom also herself he defiled, being changed into a dragon.

Chapter XXIII.-Why a God?

"He also committed adultery with Europa, the wife of his own uncle Oceanus, and with her sister Eurynome, and punished their father; and he committed adultery with Plute, the daughter of his own son Atlas, and condemned Tantalus, whom she bore to him. Of Larisse, the daughter of Orchomenus, he begot Tityon, whom also he consigned to punishment. He carried off Dia, the wife of his own son Ixion, and subjected him to perpetual punishment; and almost all the sons who sprang from his adulteries he put to violent deaths; and indeed the sepulchers of almost all of them are well known. Yea, the sepulcher of this parricide himself, who destroyed his uncles and defiled their wives, who committed whoredom with his sisters, this magician of many transformations, is shown among the Cretans, who, although they know and acknowledge his horrid and incestuous deeds, and tell them to all, yet are not ashamed to confess him to be a god. Whence it seems to me to be wonderful, yea, exceeding wonderful, how he who exceeds all men in wickedness and crimes, has received that holy and good name which is above every name, being called the father of gods and men; unless perhaps he who rejoices in the evils of men has persuaded unhappy souls to confer honor above all others upon him whom he saw to excel all others in crimes, in order that he might allure all to the imitation of his evil deeds.

Chapter XXIV.-Folly of Polytheism.

"But also the sepulchers of his sons, who are regarded amongst these *the Gentiles* as gods, are openly pointed out, one in one place, and another in another: that of Mercury at Hermopolis; that of the Cyprian Venus at Cyprus; that of

Mars in Thrace; that of Bacchus at Thebes, where he is said to have been torn in pieces; that of Hercules at Tyre, where he was burnt with fire; that of Aesculapius in Epidaurus. And all these are spoken of, not only as men who have died, but as wicked men who have been punished for their crimes; and yet they are adored as gods by foolish men.

Chapter XXV.-Dead Men Deified.

"But if they choose to argue, and affirm that these are rather the places of their birth than of their burial or death, the former and ancient doings shall be convicted from those at hand and still recent, since we have shown that they worship those whom they themselves confess to have been men, and to have died, or rather to have been punished; as the Syrians worship Adonis, and the Egyptians Osiris; the Trojans, Hector; Achilles is worshipped at Leuconesus, Patroclus at Pontus, Alexander the Macedonian at Rhodes; and many others are worshipped, one in one place and another in another, whom they do not doubt to have been dead men. Whence it follows that their predecessors also, falling into a like error, conferred divine honor upon dead men, who perhaps had had some power or some skill, and especially if they had stupefied stolid men by magical phantasies.

Chapter XXVI.-Metamorphoses.

"Hence there has now been added, that the poets also adorn the falsehoods of error by elegance of words, and by sweetness of speech persuade that mortals have been made immortal; yea more, they say that men are changed into stars, and trees, and animals, and flowers, and birds, and fountains, and rivers. And but that it might seem to be a waste of words, I could even enumerate almost all the stars, and trees, and fountains, and rivers, which they assert to have been made of men; yet, by way of example, I shall mention at least one of each class. They say that Andromeda, the daughter of Cepheus, was turned into a star; Daphne, the daughter of the river Lado, into a tree;

Hyacinthus, beloved of Apollo, into a flower; Callisto into the constellation which they call Arctos; Progne and Philomela, with Tereus, into birds; that Thysbe in Cilicia was dissolved into a fountain; and Pyramus, at the same place, into a river. And they assert that almost all the stars, trees, fountains, and rivers, flowers, animals, and birds, were at one time human beings."

Chapter XXVII.-Inconsistency of Polytheists.

But Peter, when he heard this, said: "According to them, then, before men were changed into stars, and the other things which you mention, the heaven was without stars, and the earth without trees and animals; and there were neither fountains, nor rivers, nor birds. And without these, how did those men themselves live, who afterwards were changed into them, since it is evident that, without these things, men could not live upon the earth? "Then I answered: "But they are not even able to observe the worship of their own gods consistently; for every one of those whom they worship has something dedicated to himself, from which his worshippers ought to abstain: as they say the olive is dedicated to Minerva, the she-goat to Jupiter, seeds to Ceres, wine to Bacchus, water to Osiris, the ram to Hammon, the stag to Diana, the fish and the dove to the demon of the Syrians, fire to Vulcan; and to each one, as I have said, is there something specially consecrated, from which the worshippers are bound to abstain, for the honor of those to whom they are consecrated. But were one abstaining from one thing, and another from another, by doing honor to one of the gods, they incur the anger of all the rest; and therefore, if they would conciliate them all, they must abstain from all things for the honor of all, so that, being self-condemned by a just sentence before the day of judgment, they should perish by a most wretched death through starvation.

Chapter XXVIII.-Buttresses of Gentilism.

"But let us return to our purpose. What reason is there, yea, rather, what madness possesses the minds of men, that they worship and adore as a god, a man whom they not only know to be impious, wicked, profane-I mean Jupiter-incestuous, a parricide, an adulterer, but even proclaim him publicly as such in their songs in the theatres? Or if by means of these deeds he has deserved to be a god, then also, when they hear of any murderers, adulterers, parricides incestuous persons, they ought to worship them also as gods. But I cannot understand why they venerate in him what they execrate in others." Then Peter answered: "Since you say that you cannot understand it, learn of me why they venerate wickedness in him. In the first place, it is that, when they themselves do like deeds, they may know that they shall be acceptable to him, inasmuch as they have but imitated him in his wickedness. In the second place, because the ancients have left these things skillfully composed in their writings, and elegantly engrafted in their verses. And now, by the aid of youthful education, since the knowledge of these things adheres to their tender and simple minds, it cannot without difficulty be torn from them and cast away."

Chapter XXIX.-Allegories.

When Peter had said this, Niceta answered: "Do not suppose, my lord Peter, but that the learned men of the Gentiles have certain plausible arguments, by which they support those things which seem to be blameworthy and disgraceful. And this I state, not as wishing to confirm their error (for far be it from me that such a thing should ever come into my thought); but yet I know that there are amongst the more intelligent of them certain defenses, by which they are accustomed to support and color over those things which seem to be absurd. And if it please you that I should state some of them-for I am to some extent acquainted with them-I shall do as you order me." And when Peter had given him leave, Niceta proceeded as follows.

Chapter XXX.-Cosmogony of Orpheus.

"All the literature among the Greeks which is written on the subject of the origin of antiquity, is based upon many authorities, but especially two, Orpheus and Hesiod. Now their writings are divided into two parts, in respect of their meaning,-that is the literal and the allegorical; and the vulgar crowd has flocked to the literal, but all the eloquence of the philosophers and learned men is expended in admiration of the allegorical. It is Orpheus, then, who says that at first there was chaos, eternal, unbounded, unproduced, and that from it all things were made. He says that this chaos was neither darkness nor light, neither moist nor dry, neither hot nor cold, but that it was all things mixed together, and was always one unformed mass; yet that at length, as it were after the manner of a huge egg, it brought forth and produced from itself a certain double form, which had been wrought through immense periods of time, and which they call masculo-feminine, a form concrete from the contrary admixture of such diversity; and that this is the principle of all things, which came of pure matter, and which, coming forth, effected a separation of the four elements, and made heaven of the two elements which are first, *fire and air,* and earth of the others, *earth and water;* and of these he says that all things now are born and produced by a mutual participation of them. So far Orpheus.

Chapter XXXI.-Hesiod's Cosmogony.

"But to this Hesiod adds, that after chaos the heaven and the earth were made immediately, from which he says that those eleven were produced (and sometimes also he speaks of them as twelve) of whom he makes six males and five females. And these are the names that he gives to the males: Oceanus, Coeus, Crius, Hyperion, Iapetus, Chronos, who is also called Saturn. Also the names of the females are: Theia, Rhea, Themis, Mnemosyne, Tethys. And these names they thus interpret allegorically. They say that the number is eleven or twelve: that the first is nature itself, which also they would have to be called Rhea, from Flowing; and they say that the other ten are her accidents, which also they call qualities; yet they add a twelfth, namely Chronos, who with us is called Saturn, and him they take to be time. Therefore they assert that Saturn and Rhea are time and matter; and these, when they are mixed with moisture and dryness, heat and cold, produce all things.

Chapter XXXII.-Allegorical Interpretation.

"She therefore (Rhea, or nature), it is said, produced, as it were, a certain bubble which had been collecting for a long time; and it being gradually collected from the spirit which was in the waters, swelled, and being for some time driven over the surface of matter, from which it had come forth as from a womb, and being hardened by the rigor of cold, and always increasing by additions of ice, at length was broken off and sunk into the deep, and drawn by its own weight, went down to the infernal regions; and because it became invisible it was called Aides, and is also named Orcus or Pluto. And since it was sunk from the top to the bottom, it gave place to the moist element to flow together; and the grosser part, which is the earth, was laid bare by the retirement of the waters. They say, therefore, that this freedom of the waters, which was formerly restrained by the presence of the bubble, was called Neptune after the bubble attained the lowest place. After this, when the cold element had been sucked down to the lower regions by the concretion of the icy bubble, and the dry and the moist element had been separated, there being now no hindrance, the warm element rushed by its force and lightness to the upper regions of the air, being borne up by wind and storm. This storm, therefore, which in Greek is called kataigiv, they called AeGis-that is, a she-goat; and the fire which ascended to the upper regions they called Jupiter;

wherefore they say that he ascended to Olympus riding on a she-goat.

Chapter XXXIII.-Allegory of Jupiter, Etc.

"Now this Jupiter the Greeks would have to be called from his living, or giving life, but our people from his giving succor. They say, therefore, that this is the living substance, which, placed in the upper regions, and drawing all things to itself by the influence of heat, as by the convolution of the brain, and arranging them by the moderation of a certain tempering, is said from his head to have produced wisdom, whom they call Minerva, who was called □Aθ□vη by the Greeks on account of her immortality; who, because the father of all created all things by his wisdom, is also said to have been produced from his head, and from the principal place of all, and is represented as having formed and adorned the whole world by the regulated admixture of the elements. Therefore the forms which were impressed upon matter, that the world might be made, because they are constrained by the force of heat, are said to be held together by the energy of Jupiter. And since there are enough of these, and they do not need anything new to be added to them, but each thing is repaired by the produce of its own seed, the hands of Saturn are said to be bound by Jupiter; because, as I have said, time now produces from matter nothing new: but the warmth of seeds restores all things according to their kinds; and no birth of Rhea-that is, no increase of flowing matter-ascends further. And therefore they call that first division of the elements the mutilation of Saturn, because he cannot any more produce a world.

Chapter XXXIV.-Other Allegories.

"And of Venus they give forth an allegory to this effect. When, say they, the sea was put under the air, and when the brightness of the heavens shone more pleasantly, being reflected from the waters, the loveliness of things, which appeared fairer from the waters, was called Venus; and she, *it,* being united with the air as with her, *its,* own brother, so as to produce beauty, which might be the object of desire, is said to have given birth to Cupid. In this way, therefore, as we have said, they teach that Chronos, who is Saturn, is allegorically time; Rhea is matter; Aides-that is, Orcus-is the depth of the infernal regions; Neptune is water; Jupiter is air-that is, the element of heat; Venus is the loveliness of things; Cupid is desire, which is in all things, and by which posterity is propagated, or even the reason of things, which gives delight when wisely looked into. Hera-that is, Juno-is said to be that middle air which descends from heaven to earth. To Diana, whom they call Proserpine, they hand over the air below. They say that Apollo is the Sun himself, which goes round the heaven; that Mercury is speech, by which a reason is rendered for everything; that Mars is unrestrained fire, which consumes all things. But not to delay you by enumerating everything, those who have the more abstruse intelligence concerning such things think that they give fair and just reasons, by applying this sort of allegory to every one of their objects of worship."

Chapter XXXV.-Uselessness of These Allegories.

When Niceta had thus spoken, Aquila answered: "Whoever he was that was the author and inventor of these things, he seems to me to have been very impious, since he covered over those things which seem to be pleasant and seemly, and made the ritual of his superstition to consist in base and shameful observances, since those things which are written according to the letter are manifestly unseemly and base; and the whole observance of their religion consists in these, that by such crimes and impieties they may teach men to imitate their gods whom they worship. For in these allegories what profit can there be to them? For although they are framed so as to be decent, yet no use is derived from them for worship, nor for amendment of morals.

Chapter XXXVI.-The Allegories an Afterthought.

"Whence it is the more evident that prudent men, when they saw that the common superstition was so disgraceful, so base, and yet they had not learned any way of correcting it, or any knowledge, endeavored with what arguments and interpretations they could to veil unseemly things under seemly speech, and not, as they say, to conceal seemly reasons under unseemly fables. For if this were the case, surely their statues and their pictures would never be made with *representations of* their vices and crimes. The swan, which committed adultery with Leda, would not be represented, nor the bull which committed adultery with Europa; nor would they turn into a thousand monstrous shapes, him whom they think better than all. And assuredly, if the great and wise men who are amongst them knew that all this is fiction and not truth, would not they charge with impiety and sacrilege those who should exhibit a picture or carve an image of this sort, to the injury of the gods? In short, let them present a king of their own time in the form of an ox, or a goose, or an ant, or a vulture, and let them write the name of their king upon it, and set up such a statue or figure in a public place, and they will soon be made to feel the wrong of their deed, and the greatness of its punishment.

Chapter XXXVII.-Like Gods, Like Worshippers.

"But since those things rather are true which the public baseness testifies, and concealments have been sought and fabricated by prudent men to excuse them by seemly speeches, therefore are they not only not prohibited, but even in the very mysteries figures are produced of Saturn devouring his sons, and of the boy hidden by the cymbals and drums of the Corybantes; and with respect to the mutilation of Saturn, what better proof of its truth could there be, than that even his worshippers are mutilated, by a like miserable fate, in honor of their god? Since then these things are manifestly seen, who shall be found of so little sense, yea, of such stolidity, that he does not perceive that those things are true concerning the unfortunate gods, which their more unfortunate worshippers attest by the wounding and mutilation of their bodies?

Chapter XXXVIII.-Writings of the Poets.

"But if, as they say, these things, so creditably and piously done, are dispensed by so discreditable and impious a ritual, assuredly he is sacrilegious, whoever either gave forth these things at first, or persists in fulfilling them, now that they have unhappily been given forth. And what shall we say of the books of the poets? Ought not they, if they have debased the honorable and pious deeds of the gods with base fables, to be forthwith cast away and thrown into the fire, that they may not persuade the still tender age of boys that Jupiter himself, the chief of the gods, was a parricide[1] towards his parents, incestuous towards his sisters and his daughters, and even impure towards boys; that Venus and Mars were adulterers, and all those things which have been spoken of above? What do you think of this matter, my lord Peter? "

Chapter XXXIX.-All for the Best.

Then he answered: "Be sure, beloved Aquila, that all things are done by the good providence of God, that the cause which was to be contrary to the truth should not only be infirm and weak, but also base. For if the assertion of error had been stronger and more truth-like, any one who had been deceived by it would not easily return to the path of truth. If even now, when so many wicked and disgraceful things are related concerning the gods of the Gentiles, scarce any one forsakes the base error, how much more if there had been in it anything seemly and truth-like? For the mind is with difficulty transferred from those things with which it has been imbued in early youth; and on this account, as I said, it has been effected by divine

---

[1] The act of killing one's father, mother, or other close relative.
Source: Dictionary.com Unabridged (v 1.1)

providence, that the substance of error should be both weak and base. But all other things also divine providence dispenses fully and advantageously, although the method of the divine dispensation, as good, and the best possible, is not clear to us who are ignorant of the causes of things."

Chapter XL.-Further Information Sought.

When Peter had thus said, I Clement asked Niceta that he would explain to us, for the sake of instruction, some things concerning the allegories of the Gentiles, which he had carefully studied; "for," said I, "it is useful that when we dispute with the Gentiles, we should not be unacquainted with these things." Then said Niceta: "If my lord Peter permits me, I can do as you ask me." Then said Peter: "To-day I have given you leave to speak in opposition to the Gentiles, as you know." And Niceta said: "Tell me then, Clement, what you would have me speak about." And I said to him: "Inform us how the Gentiles represent matters concerning the supper of the gods, which they had at the marriage of Peleus and Thetis. What do they make of the shepherd Paris, and what of less Juno, Minerva, and Venus, between whom he acted as judge? What of Mercury? and what of the apple, and the other things which follow in order? "

Chapter XLI.-Explanation of Mythology.

Then Niceta: "The affair of the supper of the gods stands in this wise. They say that the banquet is the world, that the order of the gods sitting at table is the position of the heavenly bodies. Those whom Hesiod calls the first children of heaven and earth, of whom six were males and six females, they refer to the number of the twelve signs, which go round all the world. They say that the dishes of the banquet are the reasons and causes of things, sweet and desirable, which in the shape of inferences from the positions of the signs and the courses of the stars, explain how the world is ruled and governed. Yet they say these things exist after the free manner of a banquet, inasmuch as the mind of every one has the option whether he shall taste aught of this sort of knowledge, or whether he shall refrain; and as in a banquet no one is compelled, but every one is at liberty to eat, so also the manner of philosophizing depends upon the choice of the will. They say that discord is the lust of the flesh, which rises up against the purpose of the mind, and hinders the desire of philosophizing; and therefore they say that the time was that in which the marriage was celebrated. Thus they make Peleus and the nymph Thetis to be the dry and the moist element, by the admixture of which the substance of bodies is composed. They hold that Mercury is speech, by which instruction is conveyed to the mind; that Juno is chastity, Minerva courage, Venus lust, Paris the understanding. If therefore, say they, it happens that there is in a man a barbarous and uncultivated understanding, and ignorant of right judgment, he will despise chastity and courage, and will give the prize, which is the apple, to lust; and thereby, ruin and destruction will come not only upon himself, but also upon his countrymen and the whole race. These things, therefore, it is in their power to compose from whatever matter they please; yet they can be adapted to every man; because if any one has a pastoral and rustic and uncultivated understanding, and does not wish to be instructed, when the heat of his body shall make suggestions concerning the pleasure of lust, straightway he despises the virtues of studies and the blessings of knowledge, and turns his mind to bodily pleasures. And hence it is that implacable wars arise, cities are destroyed, countries fall, even as Paris, by the abduction of Helen, armed the Greeks and the barbarians to their mutual destruction."

Chapter XLII.-Interpretation of Scripture.

Then Peter, commending his statement, said: "Ingenious men, as I perceive, take many verisimilitudes[1] from the things which they read; and therefore great care is to be

---

[1] Something that has the appearance of being true or real.
Reference: The American Heritage® Dictionary of the English Language, Fourth Edition.

taken, that when the law of God is read, it be not read according to the understanding of our own mind. For there are many sayings in the divine Scriptures which can be drawn to that sense which every one has preconceived for himself; and this ought not to be done. For you ought not to seek a foreign and extraneous sense, which you have brought from without, which you may confirm from the authority of the Scriptures, but to take the sense of truth from the Scriptures themselves; and therefore it behooves you to learn the meaning of the Scriptures from him who keeps it according to the truth handed down to him from his fathers, so that he can authoritatively declare what he has rightly received. But when one has received an entire and firm rule of truth from the Scriptures, it will not be improper if he contribute to the establishment of true doctrine anything from common education and from liboral studies, which, it may be, he has attached himself to in his boyhood; yet so that, when he has learned the truth, he renounce falsehood and pretence."

Chapter XLIII.-A Word of Exhortation.

And when he had said this, he looked to our father, and said: "You therefore, old man, if indeed you care for your soul's safety, that when you desire to be separated from the body, it may, in consequence of this short conversion, find eternal rest, ask about whatever you please, and seek counsel, that you may be able to cast off any doubt that remains in you. For even to young men the time of life is uncertain; but to old men it is not even uncertain, for there is no doubt that there is but little time remaining to them. And therefore both young and old ought to be very earnest about their conversion and repentance, and to be taken up with the adornment of their souls for the future with the worthiest ornaments, such as the doctrines of truth, the grace of chastity, the splendor of righteousness, the fairness of piety, and all other things with which it becomes a reasonable mind to be adorned. Then, besides, they should break off from unseemly and unbelieving companions, and keep company with the faithful, and frequent those assemblies in which subjects are handled relating to chastity, righteousness and piety; to pray to God always heartily, and to ask of Him those things which ought to be asked of God; to give thanks to Him; to repent truly of their past doings; in some measure also, if possible, by deeds of mercy towards the poor, to help their penitence: for by these means pardon will be more easily bestowed, and mercy will be sooner shown to the merciful.

Chapter XLIV.-Earnestness.

"But if he who comes to repentance is of more advanced age, he ought the more to give thanks to God, because, having received the knowledge of the truth, after all the violence of carnal lust has been broken, there awaits him no fight of contest, by which to repress the pleasures of the body rising against the mind. It remains, therefore, that he be exercised in the learning of the truth, and in works of mercy, that he may bring forth fruits worthy of repentance; and that he do not suppose that the proof of conversion is shown by length of time, but by strength of devotion and of purpose. For minds are manifest to God; and He does not take account of times, but of hearts. For He approves if any one, on hearing the preaching of the truth, does not delay, nor spend time in negligence, but immediately, and if I may say so, in the same moment, abhorring the past, begins to desire things to come, and burns with love of the heavenly kingdom.

Chapter XLV.-All Ought to Repent.

"Wherefore, let no one of you longer dissemble nor look backwards, but willingly approach to the Gospel of the kingdom of God. Let not the poor man say, When I shall become rich, then I shall be converted. God does not ask money of you, but a merciful heart and a pious mind. Nor let the rich man delay his conversion by reason of worldly care, while he thinks how he may dispose the abundance of his fruits; nor say within himself, `What shall I do? where shall I bestow my fruits?' Nor say to his soul, `Thou hast much goods laid up for many years; feast and rejoice.' For it shall be said to him, 'Thou fool, this night thy soul shall be taken from thee, and whose shall those things be which thou hast provided?' Therefore let every age, every sex, every condition, haste to repentance, that they may obtain eternal life. Let the young be thankful that they put their necks under the yoke of discipline in the very violence of their desires. The old also are themselves praise-worthy, because they change for the fear of God, the custom of a long time in which they have been unhappily occupied.

Chapter XLVI.-The Sure Word of Prophecy.

"Let no one therefore put off. Let no one delay. For what occasion is there for delaying to do well? Or are you afraid, lest, when you have done well, you do not find the reward as you supposed? And what loss will you sustain if you do well without reward? Would not conscience alone be sufficient in this? But if you find as you anticipate, shall you not receive great things for small, and eternal for temporal? But I say this for the sake of the unbelieving. For the things which we preach are as we preach them; because they cannot be otherwise, since they have been promised by the prophetic word.

Chapter XLVII.-"A Faithful Saying, and Worthy of All Acceptation."

"But if any one desires to learn exactly the truth of our preaching, let him come to hear, and let him ascertain what the true Prophet is; and then at length all doubtfulness will cease to him, unless with obstinate mind he resist those things which he finds to be true. For there are some whose only object it is to gain the victory in any way whatever, and who seek praise for this rather than their salvation. These ought not to have a single word addressed to them, lest both the noble word suffer injury, and condemn to eternal death him who is guilty of the wrong done to it. For what is there in respect of which any one ought to oppose our preaching? or in respect of which the word of our preaching is found to be contrary to the belief of what is true and honorable? It says that the God the Father, the Creator of all, is to be honored, as also His Son, who alone knows Him and His will, and who alone is to be believed concerning all things which He has enjoined. For He alone is the law and the Lawgiver, and the righteous Judge, whose law decrees that God, the Lord of all, is to be honored by a sober, chaste, just, and merciful life, and that all hope is to be placed in Him alone.

Chapter XLVIII.-Errors of the Philosophers.

"But some one will say that precepts of this sort are given by the philosophers also. Nothing of the kind: for they do indeed give commandments concerning justice and sobriety, but they are ignorant that God is the recompenser of good and evil deeds; and therefore their laws and precepts only shun a public accuser, but cannot purify the conscience. For why should one fear to sin in secret, who does not know that there is a witness and a judge of secret things? Besides, the philosophers in their precepts add that even the gods, who are demons, are to be honored; and this alone, even if in other respects they seemed worthy of approbation, is sufficient to convict them of the most dreadful impiety, and condemn them by their own sentence, since they declare indeed that there is one God, yet command that many be worshipped, by way of humoring human error. But also the philosophers say that God is not angry, not knowing what they say. For anger is evil, when it disturbs the mind, so that it loses right counsel. But that anger which punishes the wicked does not bring disturbance to the mind; but it is one and the same affection, so to speak, which assigned rewards to the good and punishment to the evil; for if He should bestow blessings upon the good and the evil, and confer equal rewards upon the pious and the impious, He would appear to be unjust rather than good.

Chapter XLIX.-God's Long-Suffering.

"But you say, Neither ought God to do evil. You say truly; nor does He. But those who have been created by Him, while they do not believe that they are to be judged, indulging their pleasures, have fallen away from piety and righteousness. But you will say, If it is right to punish the wicked, they ought to be punished immediately when they do wickedly. You indeed do well to make haste; but He who is eternal, and from whom nothing is secret, inasmuch as He is without end, in the same proportion is His patience extended, and He regards not the swiftness of vengeance, but the causes of salvation. For He is not so much pleased with the death as with the conversion of a sinner. Therefore, in short, He has bestowed upon men holy baptism, to which, if any one makes haste to come, and for the future remains without stain, all his sins are thenceforth blotted out, which were committed in the time of his ignorance.

Chapter L.-Philosophers Not Benefactors of Men.

"For what have the philosophers contributed to the life of man, by saying that God is not angry with men? Only to teach them to have no fear of any punishment or judgment, and thereby to take away all restraint from sinners. Or what have they benefited the human race, who have said that there is no God, but that all things happen by chance and accident? What but that men, hearing this, and thinking that there is no judge, no guardian of things, are driven headlong, without fear of any one, to every deed which either rage, or avarice, or lust may dictate. For they truly have much benefited the life of man who have said that nothing can be done apart from *genesis*; that is, that every one, ascribing the cause of his sin to *genesis*, might in the midst of his crimes declare himself innocent, while he does not wash out his guilt by repentance, but doubles it by laying the blame upon fate. And what shall I say of those philosophers who have maintained that the gods are to be worshipped, and such gods as were described to you a little while ago? What else was this but to decree that vices, crimes, and base deeds should be worshipped? I am ashamed of you, and I pity you, if you have not yet discovered that these things were unworthy of belief, and impious, and execrable, or if, having discovered and ascertained them to be evil, ye have nevertheless worshipped them as if they were good, yea, even the best.

Chapter LI.-Christ the True Prophet.

"Then, besides, of what sort is that which some of the philosophers have presumed to speak even concerning God, though they are mortal, and can only speak by opinion concerning invisible things, or concerning the origin of the world, since they were not present when it was made, or concerning the end of it, or concerning the treatment and judgment of souls in the infernal regions, forgetting that it belongs indeed to a reasonable man to know things present and visible, but that it is the part of prophetic prescience alone to know things past, and things future, and things invisible? These things, therefore, are not to be gathered from conjectures and opinions, in which men are greatly deceived, but from faith in prophetic truth, as this doctrine of ours is. For we speak nothing of ourselves, nor announce things gathered by human judgment; for this were to deceive our hearers. But we preach the things which have been committed and revealed to us by the true Prophet. And concerning His prophetic prescience and power, if any one, as I have said, wishes to receive clear proofs, let him come instantly and be alert to hear, and we shall give evident proofs by which he shall seem not only to hear the power of prophetic prescience with his ears, but even to see it with his eyes and handle it with his hand; and when he has entertained a sure faith concerning Him, he will without any labor take upon him the yoke of righteousness and piety; and so great sweetness will he perceive in it, that not only will be not find fault with any labor being in it, but will even desire something further to be added and imposed upon him."

Chapter LII.-Appion and Anubion.

And when he had said this, and more to the same purpose, and had cured some who were present who were infirm and possessed of demons, he dismissed the crowds, while they gave thanks and praised God, charging them to come to the same place on the following days also for the sake of hearing. And when we were together at home, and were preparing to eat, one entering told us that Appion Pleistonices, with Anubion, were lately come from Antioch, and were lodging with Simon. Then my father, when he heard this, rejoiced, and said to Peter: "If you permit me, I should like to go and salute Appion and Anubion, for they are great friends of mine; and perhaps I shall be able to persuade Anubion to dispute with Clement on the subject of *genesis*." Then Peter said: "I consent; and I commend you, because you respect your friends. But consider how all things occur to you according to your wish by God's providence; for, behold, not only have *the objects* of proper affection been restored to you by the appointment of God, but also the presence of your friends is arranged for you." Then said my father: "Truly I consider that it is so as you say." And when he had said this, he went away to Anubion.

Chapter LIII.-A Transformation.

But we, sitting with Peter the whole night, asking questions, and learning of him on many subjects, remained awake through very delight in his teaching and the sweetness of his words; and when it was daybreak, Peter, looking at me and my brothers, said: "I wonder what has befallen your father." And while he was speaking my father came in, and found Peter speaking to us about him. And when he had saluted he began to apologize, and to explain the reason why he had remained abroad. But we, looking at him, were horrified; for we saw on him the face of Simon, yet we heard the voice of our father. And when we shrank from him, and cursed him, my father was astonished at our treating him so harshly and barbarously. Yet Peter was the only one who saw his natural countenance; and he said to us: "Why do you curse your father?" And we, along with our mother, answered him: "He appears to us to be Simon, though he has our father's voice." Then Peter: "You indeed know only his voice, which has not been changed by the sorceries; but to me also his face, which to others appears changed by Simon's art, is known to be that of your father Faustinianus." And looking at my father, he said: "The cause of the dismay of your wife and your sons is this,-the appearance of your countenance does not seem to be as it was, but the face of the detestable Simon appears in you."

Chapter LIV.-Excitement in Antioch.

And while he was thus speaking, one of those returned who had gone before to Antioch, and said to Peter: "I wish you to know, my lord Peter, that Simon at Antioch, doing many signs and prodigies in public, has inculcated upon the people nothing but what tends to excite hatred against you, calling you a magician, a sorcerer, a murderer; and to such an extent has he stirred up hatred against you, that they greatly desire, if they can find you anywhere, even to devour your flesh. And therefore we who were sent before, seeing the city greatly moved against you, met together in secret, and considered what ought to be done.

Chapter LV.-A Stratagem.

"And when we saw no way of getting out of the difficulty, there came Cornelius the centurion, being sent by Caesar to the president of Caesarea on public business. Him we sent for alone, and told him the reason why we were sorrowful, and entreated him that, if he could do anything, he should help us. Then he most readily promised that he would straightway put him to flight, if only we would aid his plans. And when we promised that we would be active in doing everything, he said, `Caesar has ordered sorcerers to be sought out and destroyed in the city of Rome and through the provinces, and a great number of them have been already destroyed. I shall therefore give out, through my friends, that I am come to apprehend that magician, and that I am sent by Caesar for this purpose, that he may be punished with the rest of his fraternity. Let your people, therefore, who are with him in disguise, intimate to him, as if they had heard it from some quarter, that I am sent to apprehend him; and when he hears this, he is sure to take to flight. Or if you think of anything better, tell me. Why need I say more? 'It was so done by those of ours who were with him, disguised for the purpose of acting as spies on him. And when Simon learned that this was come upon him, he received the information as a great kindness conferred upon him by them, and took to flight. He therefore departed from Antioch, and, as we have heard, came hither with Athenodorus.

Chapter LVI.-Simon's Design in the Transformation.

"All we, therefore, who went before you, considered that in the meantime you should not go up to Antioch, till we see if the hatred of you which he has sown among the people be in any degree lessened by his departure." When he who had come from Antioch had imparted this information, Peter, looking to our father, said, "Faustinianus, your countenance has been transformed by Simon Magus, as is evident; for he, thinking that he was being sought for by Caesar for punishment, has fled in terror, and has placed his own countenance upon you, if haply you might be apprehended instead of him, and put to death, that so he might cause sorrow to your sons." But my father, when he heard this, crying out, said with tears: "You have judged rightly, O Peter: for Anubion also, who is very friendly with me, began to inform me in a certain mysterious way of his plots; but unhappily I did not believe him, because I had done him no harm."

Chapter LVII.-Great Grief.

And when all of us, along with my father, were agitated with sorrow and weeping, meantime Anubion came to us, intimating to us that Simon had fled during the night, making for Judaea. But seeing our father lamenting and bewailing himself, and saying, "Wretch that I am, not to believe when I heard that he is a magician! What has befallen wretched me, that on one day, being recognized by my wife and my sons, I have not been able to rejoice with them, but have been rolled back to the former miseries which I endured in my wandering!"-but my mother, tearing her disheveled hair, bewailed much more bitterly,-we also, confounded at the change of our father's countenance, were, as it were, thunderstruck and beside ourselves, and could not understand what was the matter. But Anubion, seeing us all thus afflicted, stood like one dumb. Then Peter, looking at us his sons, said: "Believe me that this is your very father; wherefore also I charge you that you respect him as your father. For God will afford some opportunity on which he shall be able to put off the countenance of Simon, and to recover the manifest figure of your father-that is, his own."

Chapter LVIII.-How It All Happened.

Then, turning to my father, he said: "I gave you leave to salute Appion and Anubion, who, you said, were your friends from boyhood, but not that you should speak with Simon." Then my father said: "I confess I have sinned." Then said Anubion: "I also with him beg and entreat of you to pardon the old man-good and noble man as he is. He was unhappily seduced and imposed upon by the magician in question; for I will tell you how the thing was done. When he came to salute us, it happened that at that very time we were standing around him, hearing him tell that he intended to flee away that night, for that he had heard that some persons had come even to this city of Laodicea to apprehend him by command of the emperor, but that he wished to turn all their rage against this Faustinianus, who has lately come hither. And he said to us: `Only you make him sup with us, and I shall compound a certain ointment, with which, when he has supped, he shall anoint his face, and from that time he shall seem to all to have my countenance. But you first anoint your faces with the juice of a certain herb, that you may not be deceived as to the change of his countenance, so that to all except you he shall seem to be Simon.'

Chapter LIX.-A Scene of Mourning.

"And when he said this, I said to him, `And what advantage will you gain from this deed?' Then Simon said: `In the first place, that those who are seeking me may lay hold on him, and so give over the search for me. But if he be punished by Caesar, that his sons may have much sorrow, who forsook me, and fled to Peter, and are now his assistants.' Now I confess to you, Peter, what is true. I did not dare then tell Faustinianus; but neither did Simon give us opportunity of speaking with him in private, and disclosing to him fully Simon's design. Meantime, about the middle of the night, Simon has fled away, making for Judaea. And Athenodorus and Appion have gone to accompany[1] him; but I pretended bodily indisposition, that I might remain at home, and make him return quickly to you, if haply he may in any way be concealed with you, lest, being seized by those who are inquest of Simon, he be brought before Caesar, and perish without cause. And now, in my anxiety about him, I have come to see him, and to return before those who have gone to convoy Simon come back." And turning to us, Anubion said: "I, Anubion, indeed see the true countenance of your father, because I was previously anointed by Simon himself, as I have told you, that the real face of Faustinianus might appear to my eyes; whence I am astonished and wonder at the art of Simon Magus, because you standing here do not recognize your father." And while my father and mother, and all of us, wept for the things which had befallen, Anubion, moved with compassion, also wept.

---

[1] The original word used in the text was: **convoy**

Chapter LX.-A Counterplot.

Then Peter, moved with compassion, promised that he would restore the face of our father, saying to him: "Listen, Faustinianus: As soon as the error of your transformed countenance shall have conferred some advantage on us, and shall have served[1] the designs which we have in view, then I shall restore to you the true form of your countenance; on condition, however, that you first dispatch what I shall command you." And when my father promised that he would with all his might fulfill everything that he might charge him with, provided only that he might recover his own countenance, Peter thus began: "You have heard with your own ears, that one of those who had been sent before has returned from Antioch, and told us how Simon, while he was there, stirred up the multitudes against me, and inflamed the whole city into hatred of me, declaring that I am a magician, and a murderer, and a deceiver, so that they are eager, if they see me, even to eat my flesh. Do therefore what I tell you: leave Clement with me, and go before us to Antioch, with your wife, and your sons Faust's and Faustinus. And I shall also send others with you, whom I think fit, who shall observe whatsoever I command them.

Chapter LXI.-A Mine Dug.

"When therefore you come with them to Antioch, as you will be thought to be Simon, stand in a public place, and proclaim your repentance, and say: `I Simon declare to you, and confess that all that I said concerning Peter was false: for he is neither a seducer, nor a magician, nor a murderer, nor any of the things that I spoke against him; but I said all these things under the instigation of madness. I therefore entreat you, even I myself, who erewhile gave you causes of hatred against him, that you think no such thing concerning him. But lay aside your hatred cease from your indignation; because he is truly sent by God for the salvation of the world-a disciple and apostle of the true

---

[1] The original word used in the text was: **subserved**

Prophet. Wherefore I advise, exhort, and charge you that you hear him, and believe him when he preaches to you the truth, lest perhaps, if you despise him, your very city suddenly perish. But I will tell you why I now make this confession to you. This night an angel of God rebuked me for my wickedness, and scourged me terribly, because I was an enemy to the herald of the truth. Therefore I entreat you, that even if I myself should ever again come to you, and attempt to say anything against Peter, you will not receive nor believe me. For I confess to you, I was a magician, a seducer, a deceiver; but I repent, for it is possible by repentance to blot out former evil deeds.'"

Chapter LXII.-A Case of Conscience.

When Peter made this intimation to my father, he answered: "I know what you wish; do not trouble yourself further: for I understand and know what I am to undertake when I come to the place." And Peter gave him further instruction, saying: "When therefore you come to the place, and see the people turned by your discourse, and laying aside their hatred, and returning to their longing for me, send and tell me, and I shall come immediately; and when I come, I shall without delay set you free from this strange countenance, and restore to you your own, which is known to all your friends." And having said this, he ordered my brothers to go with him, and at the same time our mother Matthidia, and some of our friends. But my mother refused to go along with him, and said: "It seems as if I should be an adulteress if I were to associate with the countenance of Simon; but if I be compelled to go along with him, it is at all events impossible that I can lie in the same bed with him; but I do not know if I can consent even to go with him." And when she stoutly refused, Anubion began to exhort her, saying: "Believe me and Peter. But does not even his voice persuade you that he is your husband Faustinianus, whom truly I love not less than you do? And, in short, I also myself shall come with you." And when Anubion had said this, my mother promised that she would go with him.

Chapter LXIII.-A Pious Fraud.

Then said I: "God arranges our affairs to our liking; for we have with us Anubion an astrologer, with whom, if we come to Antioch, we shall dispute with all earnestness on the subject of *genesis*." And when our father had set out, after the middle of the night, with those whom Peter had ordered to accompany him, and with Anubion; in the morning, before Peter went to the discussion, those men returned who had accompanied[1] Simon, namely Appion and Athenodorus, and came to us inquiring after my father. But Peter, when he was informed of their coming, ordered them to enter. And when they were seated, they asked, "Where is Faustinianus?" Peter answered: "We do not know; for since the evening that he went to you, no one of his friends has seen him. But yesterday morning Simon came inquiring for him; and because we gave him no answer, I know not what he meant, but he said that he was Faustinianus. But when nobody believed him, he went and lamented, and threatened that he would destroy him self; and afterwards he went away towards the sea."

Chapter LXIV.-A Competition in Lying.

When Appion heard this, and those who were with him, they raised a great howling, saying: "Why have you done this? Why did you not receive him? "And when Athenodorus was going to tell me that it was my father Faustinianus himself, Appion prevented him, and said: "We have learned from some one that he has gone with Simon and that at the entreaty of Faustinianus himself, being unwilling to see his sons, because they are Jews. When therefore we heard this, we came to inquire after him here; but since he is not here, it appears that he must have spoken truly who told us that he has gone with Simon. This, therefore, we tell you." But I Clement, when I understood the designs of Peter, that he wished to make them suppose that the old man would be required at their hands, so that

---

[1] The original word used in the text was: **convoyed**

they might be afraid and flee away, I began to aid his design, and said to Appion: "Listen, dear Appion: what we believe to be good, we wish to deliver to our father also; but if he will not receive it, but rather, as you say, flees away through abhorrence of us-it may perhaps be harsh to say so-we care nothing about him." And when I had said this, they departed, cursing my cruelty, and followed the track of Simon, as we learned on the following day.

Chapter LXV.-Success of the Plot.

Meantime, while Peter was daily, according to his custom, teaching the people, and working many miracles and cures, after ten days came one of our people from Antioch, sent by my father, informing us how my father stood in public, accusing Simon, whose face indeed he seemed to wear, and extolling Peter with unmeasured praises, and commending him to all the people, and making them long for him, so that all were changed by his speech, and longed to see him; and that many had come to love Peter so much, that they raged against my father in his character of Simon, and thought of laying hands on him, because he had done such wrong to Peter! "Wherefore," said he, "make haste, lest by chance he be murdered; for he sent me with speed to you, being in great fear, to ask you to come without delay, that you may find him alive, and also that you may appear at the favorable moment, when the city is growing in affection towards you." He also told us how, as soon as my father entered the city of Antioch, the whole people were gathered to him, supposing him to be Simon; and he began to make public confession to them all, according to what the restoration of the people demanded: for all, as many as came, both noble and common, both rich and poor, hoping that some prodigies would be wrought by him in his usual way, he addressed thus:-

Chapter LXVI.-Truth Told by Lying Lips.

"It is long that the divine patience bears with me, Simon the most unhappy of men; for whatever you have wondered at in me was done, not by means of truth, but by the lies and tricks of demons, that I might subvert your faith and condemn my own soul. I confess that all things that I said about Peter were lies; for he never was either a magician or a murderer, but has been sent by God for the salvation of you all; and if from this hour you think that he is to be despised, be assured that your very city may suddenly be destroyed. *But, you will ask,* what is the reason that I make this confession to you of my own accord? I was vehemently rebuked by an angel of God this night, and most severely scourged, because I was his enemy. I therefore entreat you, that if from this hour even I myself shall ever open my mouth against him, you will drive me from your sight; for that foul demon, who is an enemy to the salvation of men, speaks against him through my mouth, that you may not attain to life by his means. For what miracle could the magic art show you through me? I made brazen dogs bark, and statues move, men change their appearances, and suddenly vanish from men's sight; and for these things you ought to have cursed the magic art, which bound your souls with devilish fetters, that I might show you a vain miracle, that you might not believe Peter, who cures the sick in the name of Him by whom he is sent, and expels demons, and gives sight to the blind, and restores health to the palsied, and raises the dead."

Chapter LXVII.-Faustinianus is Himself Again.

Whilst he made these and similar statements, the people began to curse him, and to weep and lament because they had sinned against Peter, believing him to be a magician or wicked man. But the same day, at evening, Faustinianus had his own face restored to him, and the appearance of Simon Magus left him. Now Simon, hearing that his face on Faustinianus had contributed to the glory of Peter, came in haste to anticipate Peter, and intending to cause by his art that his likeness should be taken from Faustinianus, when Christ had already accomplished this according to the word of His apostle. But Niceta and Aquila, seeing their father's face restored after the necessary proclamation, gave thanks to God, and would not suffer him to address the people any more.

Chapter LXVIII.-Peter's Entry into Antioch.

But Simon began, though secretly, to go amongst his friends and acquaintances, and to malign Peter more than before. Then all spat in his face, and drove him from the city, saying: "You will be chargeable with your own death, if you think of coming hither again, speaking against Peter." These things being known *at Laodicea*, Peter ordered the people to meet on the following day; and having ordained one of those who followed him as bishop over them, and others as presbyters, and having baptized multitudes, and restored to health all who were troubled with sicknesses or demons, he stayed there three days longer; and all things being properly arranged, he bade them farewell, and set out from Laodicea, being much longed for by the people of Antioch. And the whole city began to hear, through Niceta and Aquila, that Peter was coming. Then all the people of the city of Antioch, hearing of Peter's arrival, went to meet him, and almost all the old men and the nobles came with ashes sprinkled on their heads, in this way testifying their repentance, because they had listened to the magician Simon, in opposition to his preaching.

Chapter LXIX.-Peter's Thanksgiving.

Stating these and such like things, they bring to him those distressed with sicknesses, and tormented with demons, paralytics also, and those suffering diverse perils; and there was an infinite number of sick people collected. And when Peter saw that they not only repented of the evil thoughts they had entertained of him through means of Simon, but also that they showed so entire faith in God, that they believed that all who suffered from every sort of ailment could be healed by him, he spread out his hands towards heaven, pouring out prayers with tears, and gave thanks to God, saying: "I bless thee, O Father, worthy of all praise, who hast deigned to fulfill every word and promise of Thy Son, that every creature may know that Thou alone art God in heaven and in earth."

Chapter LXX.-Miracles.

With such sayings, he went up on a height, and ordered all the multitude of sick people to be ranged[1] before him, and addressed them all in these words: "As you see me to be a man like to yourselves, do not suppose that you can recover your health from me, but through Him who, coming down from heaven, has shown to those who believe in Him a perfect medicine for body and soul. Hence let all this people be witnesses to your declaration, that with your whole heart you believe in the Lord Jesus Christ, that they may know that themselves also may be saved by Him." And when all the multitude of the sick with one voice cried out that He is the true God whom Peter preaches, suddenly an overpowering light of the grace of God appeared in the midst of the people; and the paralytics being cured, began to run to Peter's feet, the blind to shout on the recovery of their sight, the lame to give thanks on regaining the power of walking, the sick to rejoice in restored health; some even who were barely alive, being already without consciousness or the power of speech, were raised up; and all the lunatics, and those possessed of demons, were set free.

Chapter LXXI.-Success.

So great grace of His power did the Holy Spirit show on that day, that all, from the least to the greatest, with one voice confessed the Lord; and not to delay you with many words, within seven days, more than ten thousand men, believing in God, were baptized and consecrated by sanctification: so that Theophilus, who was more exalted than all the men of power in that city, with all eagerness of desire consecrated the great palace of his house under the name of a church, and a chair was placed in it for the

---

[1] To take up a position in a line or in order.
Reference: Dictionary.com Unabridged (v 1.1).

Apostle Peter by all the people; and the whole multitude assembling daily to hear the word, believed in the healthful doctrine which was avouched by the efficacy of cures.

Chapter LXXII.-Happy Ending.

Then I Clement, with my brothers and our mother, spoke to our father, asking him whether any remnants of unbelief remained in him. And he said: "Come, and you shall see, in the presence of Peter, what an increase of faith has grown in me." Then Faustinianus approached, and fell down at Peter's feet, saying: "The seeds of your word, which the field of my mind has received, are now sprung up, and have so advanced to fruitful maturity, that nothing is wanting but that you separate me from the chaff by that spiritual reaping-hook of yours, and place me in the garner[1] of the Lord, making me partaker of the divine table." Then Peter, with all *cheerful readiness*[2] grasping his hand, presented him to me Clement, and my brothers, saying: "As God has restored your sons to you, their father, so also your sons restore their father to God." And he proclaimed a fast to all the people, and on the next Lord's day he baptized him; and in the midst of the people, taking occasion from his conversion, he related all his fortunes, so that the whole city received him as an angel, and paid him no less honor than they did to the apostle.

And these things being known, Peter ordered the people to meet on the following day; and having ordained one of his followers as bishop, and others as presbyters, he baptized also a great number of people, and restored to health all who had been distressed with sicknesses.

---

[1] To gather or deposit in or as if in a granary or other storage place. *Reference: Dictionary.com Unabridged (v 1.1).*
[2] The original word used in the text was: **alacrity**

www.ingramcontent.com/pod-product-compliance
Lightning Source LLC
Chambersburg PA
CBHW020736160426
43192CB00006B/217